BEYOND BUSINESS

HOW YOUR COMPANY CAN
BUILD A BETTER WORLD

LONNIE GIENGER

Beyond Business: How Your Company Can Build a Better World

Copyright © 2018 by Lonnie Gienger. All rights reserved.

Published by Business Advantage, LLC.

All Scripture quotations, unless otherwise indicated, are taken from the Holy Bible, New International Version®, NIV®. Copyright ©1973, 1978, 1984, 2011 by Biblica, Inc.™ Used by permission of Zondervan. All rights reserved worldwide. www.zondervan.com The "NIV" and "New International Version" are trademarks registered in the United States Patent and Trademark Office by Biblica, Inc.™

Cover & Interior Design: Useful Group

ISBN: 978-1-7328-5281-5

Printed in the United States of America

TABLE OF CONTENTS

Part 5: Implementing the Master System to Transform the World

Part 6: Finding the Fuel You Need to Build a Better World

INTRODUCTION

If you ever wished your everyday life in business could contribute to building a better world in a more meaningful way, this book is for you. If you are a business leader who has wondered how you could have the most impact on transforming society, this book is for you. If you have been around charities, churches or religions that caused you to believe what you do in the business world is not as transformational or "spiritual" as what people do in those non-profit organizations, this book is for you. If you wish there was more synergy between what you do in the business world and what you'd like to do to make the world a better place, this book is for you.

Playwright Tennessee Williams said we live in two different worlds: the real and the fantastic, the practical and the spiritual. I've straddled those two different worlds most of my professional life.

I've spent the past thirty years with one foot in the world of building businesses and the other in the world of building churches. On the practical level, I have been involved in starting businesses that serve many people well. On the spiritual level, I have been involved in starting churches that serve many people well.

My prevailing paradigm over the years was that the world of building a business to create happy customers and the world of building a church to create happy followers of Jesus were very separate and distinct. Of course, I tried to take my faith into the work world, and I tried to take some basic business savvy into the church world. In reality, though, it seemed quite normal for church and business to be very different spheres.

As I entered the second half of my life and started focusing more on meaning, I began to experience a gnawing angst. When I was in the business world, I felt that I should be focusing more on the church world to do things that "really counted" for my life mission and legacy. When I was in the church world, though, I had a similar gnawing angst–that I needed to do something in the business world that could effectively change society in ways the church world could not.

A few years ago, I felt convicted to write a book on this subject. It was not because I had any ambition to be a published author. It simply felt like I needed the discipline of slowing down to ponder what, if any, connection there was supposed to be between these two worlds that could potentially make me and others more effective at building a better world.

This book is written from my perspective as a business leader who has started and built a number of businesses over the years, including one business that grew from ten employees to over two thousand employees in eighteen states over four years. It is written from the perspective of one who has coached hundreds of business owners and C-suite executives around the country.

This book is also written from the perspective of one who has been very involved in developing leaders in churches over many years. I was a pastor in the early part of my career. I have been on leadership teams of some great churches. I have been involved in providing leadership coaching to hundreds of senior pastors of some of the most significant, high-impact churches around the world.

This is not theory to me. I am writing from the perspective of a leadership practitioner in business and in church who is always seeking to understand how to be more effective at creating value in this world.

You've Got to Wonder "Why"?

On my journey to understand what, if any, intersection there was supposed to be between the business and church worlds, I first questioned my paradigms and assumptions. I did this by asking a lot of "why" questions like:

- Why is it that it seems more noble or spiritual to build a church than it does to build a business?

- Why is it that more parents (especially religious parents) aren't telling their kids that one of the best things they can do to build a better world is to build a highly effective business?

- Why is it that the pursuit of profit is seen by many religious people as somehow being an "unholy" or second class pursuit compared to being a missionary or working in the ministry of a church?

- Why is it that business leaders don't often add to their scoreboard of success the value they create for society just by doing business well and providing quality products, services, and jobs, and thereby helping to build healthy communities?

- Why is it that churches don't celebrate the transformative effect that the business leaders in their church have on their city through the meaningful value they provide to society through their product, service, and/or culture?

- Why is it that when pastors are celebrating the food, clothing, shelter or education their church provides to needy people in the community through charity, they don't at the same time celebrate the business leaders who also provide food, clothing, shelter and education to thousands of people in their community through the income they provide employees, taxes paid, and the goods and services they produce?

- Why is it that being Christian has often come to mean being religious people who isolate themselves from the evil influence of the world rather than being world-changing culture creators, as was the founder of Christianity?

- Why is it that the church is not more effective at accomplishing its original mandate of transforming cities and nations?

- Why is it that the church has become more known for what happens in the programs it holds on the weekend than for the influence it has on society throughout the week?

- Why is it so rare for the effects of the church to show up in improving economies and providing for people's tangible needs?

- Why is it that churches, businesses, and governments have not been able to agree on an ideal system for improving society so they could cooperate more effectively to build a better world?

- Why doesn't everyone understand the role businesses have in building a better world, and why isn't there a defined model for doing this?

- Why is it that faith has been either largely ignored by successful business leaders or relegated to a religious notion that is perceived to have little bearing on success?

What Are We Missing?

As I pondered these questions, I began to wonder: what are we missing here? What if the way I was defining the role of church in this world falls short of the originally intended paradigm? What if the way I was defining the role of business in this world falls short of the ideal value proposition?

What do you do with the fact that the leaders Jesus chose to start the original church were not religious leaders but were actually successful business people and strong leaders in the secular community? The four books of the Bible that Christians call "the Gospels" (Mathew, Mark, Luke, and John) were all written by marketplace leaders, not religious leaders. Matthew had a tax collection business. Mark was the manager of a family business/trust. Luke had a medical practice, and John owned a commercial fishing company. The key women, highlighted in the Bible as influential in the early church, were business leaders. Dorcas was a clothes designer. One of the most famous women in the early church, Priscilla, was a partner in a commercial tent manufacturing business. Another influential woman in the early church, Lydia, owned a textile brokerage company. Men and women who built the early church were actually building businesses.

The founder of the Christian faith was a successful business leader in his community. Jesus wasn't viewed as anything close to a religious leader for at least thirty of his thirty-three years on this earth. He was known as a business leader. He was known as a businessman who ran a profitable business by serving people well as he ran his family construction business.

Jesus didn't go to religious seminaries, temples or synagogues to find the key leaders whom he intentionally chose to launch a world-changing movement. None of the twelve core leaders that Jesus chose were religious leaders, priests or rabbis. Not one of them. They were all leaders in the marketplace.

As I began to ponder these basic facts of history, I had to wonder why for much of my life as a business leader, I'd had this nagging feeling that when I was doing business I was not really doing all I could be doing for God—that if I was really devoted to God and his church, I would just be a pastor or a missionary and forget all this business stuff. If I was really spiritual, I would just build the church and not worry so much about building businesses. At the same time, I had to wonder why for much of my life as a church leader, I had this nagging feeling that when I was doing church stuff, I was not really having the depth of impact on building a better society and transforming the world for God that I could be having–that if I was sold out to seeing the church be as strategic and as well led as a highly successful business, that somehow it would transform cities and nations like it was supposed to.

Could it be that my perspective on the power of business to build a better world was much too limited? Could it be that the effect our business can have on improving society is way beyond what we imagine? What if there could be significantly more synergy between our inner spiritual life and our business life than what we now know? What would it look like if what we do in business truly embodied our highest expression of purpose and our deepest experience of meaning?

I invite you to join me on this journey to answer these questions and explore the powerful role your business and your life can play in building a better world.

PART 1
BUILDING THE BEST PLATFORM TO REBUILD THE WORLD

THE CONSISTENT KEY TO BUILDING SOCIETY

More and more these days as I do business around the world, I see that building successful businesses is the most consistent element to building successful societies across all nations. Recently I was in Ireland with my family. In the period of one day, we toured ruins of a village from 1000 B.C. and a market from 1000 A.D. Then we walked through a modern, vibrant shopping area.

Toward the end of the day I asked my eighteen-year-old son, Sky, "From what you've seen today, what are the top two or three most common elements that build society in all cultures, in all times, in all places?" This led to quite an insightful discussion. We concluded that all societies, at all times, are built on two fundamental foundations: family and commerce.

Societies throughout all times and in all places have been built on families. The famous anthropologist Margaret Mead got it right when she said:

> As far back as our knowledge takes us, human beings have lived in families. We know of no period where this was not so. We know of no people who have succeeded for long in dissolving the family or displacing it . . . Again and again, in spite of proposals for change and actual experiments, human societies have reaffirmed their dependence on the family as the basic unit of human living–the family of father, mother and children.[1]

Yet families have always been economic units too. Throughout history, they engaged in commerce. What they could not hunt or farm for themselves, they traded for by offering something of value to others. They formed cottage industries and engaged in money-making activities. Niall Ferguson, a senior fellow at the Hoover Institution at Stanford University, and a professor and fellow at Harvard, said in his book *The Ascent of Money:* "From ancient Mesopotamia to present-day China . . . the ascent of money has been one of the driving forces behind human progress." He went on to say that money is "as vital as the advance of science or the spread of law" in humankind's exit from drudgery and misery.[2]

As I do business in many countries these days, it has become glaringly clear to me that building better businesses is a vital key to building a better world. The heart of building our world is constructing businesses that make families, communities, societies, and nations flourish.

Yet much of society believes the church and non-profits are the real key to building a better world. There is this huge perceived chasm between building businesses and building churches. No correlation is seen between pursuing commerce

CHAPTER 1

and pursuing cultural change through non-profit ministries. There is this giant perceived gap between going after commerce and going after God.

I am now beginning to see that this perceived gap continually perpetuates a cultural paradigm that denies the church the tangible power to make the world a better place. It also deceives business leaders into missing the real value they bring to building a better world and accomplishing God's purposes on this earth.

This book is the result of journaling my journey in recent years. I have been learning to crystallize new paradigms and processes that give fresh insight and inspiration regarding how my life as a business leader impacts building a better world. I hope you will see how your life as a business leader also impacts society in many good ways, because . . .

God Loves Business!

One of my initial core conclusions is that God loves business and God really loves business leaders! God doesn't hate money, and he doesn't hate people who make a ton of it by serving their fellow human beings well. In fact, I'm not sure there is anything that makes God smile more than seeing business leaders create so much value and serve people so well that those people are willing to give up this thing called money in exchange. At the risk of this statement being a bit of a spoiler, I will say that I am increasingly convinced that God might have even *chosen* business as his preferred method to manifest his presence and perpetuate his values in this world.

What if what you are doing in business right now is the most powerful platform you could possibly have to make this world a better place? What if what you are doing right now as a business leader is really God's ideal strategy for doing his best work to transform society on this earth to be more like his original intention?

Lack of Resources Is an Obstacle to Changing the World

Some business leaders think that it is primarily the responsibility of social institutions, non-profits, faith-based organizations, and churches to address the problems of society. Certainly churches and other non-profits invest an enormous amount of energy, time, and money trying to solve the problems of the world. They work hard to:

- Address world hunger
- Heal the sick
- End poverty and illiteracy
- Shelter the homeless
- End human trafficking
- Protect the environment
- Provide a host of other services addressing the world's endless difficulties

I have spent my life being very involved in many wonderful churches and other non-profits which are valiantly attempting to meet the desperate needs of society. Churches are full of wonderful people, including wonderful business leaders, who believe that the people and programs of the church are the best way to solve the massive societal problems facing our world.

Many churches certainly play a valuable role in attempting to address these problems. Churches mobilize tremendous talent and pour out significant resources to address these needs. Churches have invested two thousand years of hard efforts trying to meet these needs through what we have considered the directly sponsored ministries of the church. The results are mixed, though. In fact, the brutal reality is that churches are not making the progress that they want nor the progress the world needs in overcoming these global societal needs.

Dare I say that the church is not winning the war on poverty, illiteracy, hunger, etc.? For sure, the church can show that it is making some progress. The church can show many benefits it is providing that help meet the social needs of the world. But its contributions are small in comparison with the scope of what really needs to happen in this world. The reality is that there are very few churches or non-profits that make a truly significant dent in these global problems.

Why is that? There are many reasons. Let me just address a couple of practical reasons which cause obvious limitations: money and manpower. Most churches and non-profit agencies believe they could do more if they had more resources. If they just had more people and time committed to the cause, if they just had more money to pour into the mission, they believe they could make a bigger dent in the problems.

This is no doubt true. But the practical reality is that most churches and non-profits operate on a small percentage of the income of their constituents. Because of this there will never be enough resources to meet a large percentage of the world's needs. Even if everyone donated 10% of their income, there would never be enough money to meet 100% of the world's needs. There will simply never be enough donor money to deal with the realities of the societal challenges of the world on a large scale.

So one of the practical challenges the church has is a basic resource problem. I grew up singing an old gospel song that starts with "He owns the cattle on a thousand hills." But as an adult, I have often wondered if God owns the cattle on a thousand hills, then where are the cattle when it comes to meeting all the needs of the world? They don't all seem to be in the church. (Or are they?) Where are the resources to meet the practical and tangible needs of our world?

Only Business Can Create Resources

Resources are created in business! In fact, all money is created by business. Business creates resources when it meets a need at a profit. Business receives revenue when it serves the needs of people in a way that makes those people happy. That revenue produces incomes for employees and results in taxes that fund the building of society and also results in personal charitable donations that fund the building of the direct ministries of the church and other non-profits. Business earns profit when the dollars that are received from the customer exceed the business's cost to serve the needs of those customers. That profit is what pays the business owner for the skill, risk, and time he or she invested to serve that need. Profit does much more than that too.

Some Christians and certain other religious groups see profit as evil, as if business only makes a profit by taking advantage of or doing harm to people. Yet it is profit that empowers the business to create more value to benefit the world. It is profit that allows a business to invest in meeting whatever need the business finds, and profit that allows it to meet that need in ever-increasing magnitude. It is profit that allows the business to increase the scope of the value it provides to more and more people. For example, if you can make a profit by serving ten people, then you have a pathway to make a profit by serving one hundred people, and then a thousand, and then a million. It becomes a self-perpetuating, ever-increasing vehicle to meet more needs in society.

Historically, many pastors believe that the primary value business or business leaders bring to the church is that they will give more donations to the church if they make more money. But after two thousand years, that paradigm has not yet successfully fully resourced the direct ministries of the church or the direct outreach and social service programs of other non-profits. It has not yet enabled non-profit institutions to meet the ever-increasing societal needs of the world.

Of course, business should continue providing resources to the valuable programs of churches and other non-profits. However, what I am proposing here is that business not only has the power to create resources for the mission of the church, it also has the power to build great value in the world *just by doing business well.*

In fact, I believe **business can be the most effective platform for building a better world.**

My hope is that, at minimum, this book will expand your vision and passion for the key role that business can play in transforming society. My hope is that you will more fully embrace the role you and your business play in building a better world. You, as a business leader, have an opportunity to change the world for the better. In fact, you are already doing it!

Businesses build a better world on three levels. In the next chapter, let me unpack for you how you are already making society better and how you can take your positive impact on the world to the next level.

CHAPTER 2

BUILDING A BUSINESS THAT BUILDS A BETTER WORLD

Business leaders build a better world on three levels. The first level is simply building a good business that provides value to people. On the second level, they go beyond basic business expectations to do things in and through their business that provide extra benefit for people and communities. On the third level, business leaders intentionally use their businesses as a platform to make a transformational impact on society, to literally rebuild the world.

If you are in business, you are already on Level 1. You are already building a better world just by doing good business!

Level 1: Building Your Business. At the most basic level, when you build a business you play a vital role in meeting people's needs and thereby building a better world. If you do nothing but build a business that meets needs well and makes a profit doing so, you not only provide a product or service that society needs, you create the resources that put food on tables, roofs over heads, and kids in school. Even better, if you create a healthy culture in and around your business based on enduring values, you can create a little slice of a healthier society.

If you've ever said, "I'm just a business owner . . . " you are not giving yourself enough credit. You're not just a business owner! You're building a better world! Your suppliers are blessed because you're buying from them. You make their world better! Your customers or clients are better off because of what you do. You make their world better! The employees you pay have income to live their lives and support their families. You make their world better! The taxes your business generates make society work. Your business helps fund the roads, the schools, and other public facilities and services. When you build your business, you are building a better world right in your own community! Just a business owner? Just a world builder is all!

The Ministry is in the Margins

As I have coached business leaders over the years, I often come across those who want to make a more significant impact on their community or industry. I find many business owners who want to do more than build a business that adds value to the world by doing good business. Their dream is to take their impact to the next level by doing extra things for their employees or for society. That's a valuable vision for every business even in the startup phase. But I know it's hard to go the extra mile to serve your employees or community if you have a business that controls all your time and money or runs you ragged. It's hard to think about building great value into society if you have a business that leaves you so tired when you get home from work that you can barely drag yourself into bed every night. It's hard to dream about what you could do to make society work right if, while you are trying to sleep, you are stressed out and worried about whether things are going to work right in the business the next day. If you are always focused on survival, it is hard to have the margin necessary to focus on using your business as a platform to change the world.

I know what that feels like. I spent many years in my early business career in that situation. I have experienced that even in more recent years at times during start-up or exceptionally challenging phases of aggressive business initiatives.

If you don't have a business that allows you some margin in your finances, time, and emotional capital, it's hard to use your business to do effective ministry that goes beyond the goodness of simply doing business well. Going the extra mile works best if you've got gas in your tank at the end of the last mile. What I have learned is that ministry happens in the margins.

The Secret is in the Systems

So what's the pathway to create more margin to be able to do more ministry for the world through business? I have found that the pathway is through implementing the right processes. The secret is in the systems that cause success. Implementing the right systems in your business is one of the most valuable means to be more effective at Level 1 and ultimately to allow you to enjoy more time and energy to function at Levels 2 and 3. Because this is so vital to your success in creating a transformational business, I'll take some additional time to share my experience in learning how to do this and examples of what it looks like when businesses make this transition to systems thinking.

I spent a lot of years in my earlier life frustrated by what seemed like elusive dreams of success in business. I didn't have a vision problem. I didn't have an ambition problem. I didn't have a laziness problem. But I did have a success problem.

I thought there must be something inherently wrong with me. Maybe I was one of those who just wasn't born to be successful at a business. I worked harder than just about anyone I knew, but I wasn't getting the outcomes I dreamed of. The quest to understand why ultimately caused me to have a deep conviction that anyone can build a successful business and have the life of their dreams IF they understand and implement the systems needed to produce that kind of success.

Now I'm not here to tell you that I have all the secret systems; I am here to tell you that systems are the secret. If you don't know the systems needed to produce success in any area of your business (or your life), I'm here to tell you that you can find someone who knows those systems, and you can learn. You can apply the principles and processes you learn from that person to create the success you want. The secret to success is only a secret if you don't know where to find it. I have found that the secret to success is successful systems.

The great news is that anyone who is hungry enough can seek out, understand, and implement the systems they need to generate success. Yet it is not just another how to that is needed. If the possession of checklists of systems to follow was the key to success, every capable Googler in the world would be enormously successful. The key to success is not just learning about some systems. It is gaining a deep, real-life understanding of the right systems you need at the right time AND creating a doable pathway to implement those systems in your unique situation.

As I have coached business owners around the country, I have seen, over and over again, the dramatic impact this approach can make. The president of an electronics company that we coached said this: "Our business was good, but our internal mechanisms and systems were terrible. This had set us up for ownership battles that almost led to our demise. With the large workload and limited manpower, we found that we were working ourselves to an early grave with nothing much to show for it. Our personal lives and families were paying a major price since most of our time was going to the business. We knew having better systems in place would free up more time for us to work on the future of the business and for our family lives.

"For example, we were hiring new employees, so we created a basic personnel system including a hiring resource manual, forms for interviews and job offers all the way through employee folders and all the appropriate forms and information in place. This sped up the hiring and training of our employees and they come on board and become productive much faster than expected. We have been going through our business and putting simple systems in place one at a time. This has saved many man-hours and allowed us to be much more productive. I was even able to take three vacation days to get projects done at home and ease tension there without worrying that the business would fall apart. I've become much more confident that we can once again handle growth without self-destructing. My personal life has also been impacted since I have actually been able to get home and eat dinner with my family and spend time with my kids. There is much less stress there, which makes me much less stressed at work."

I'm not trying to come across as someone who knows everything about success in business, because I certainly don't. If anything, I've made more mistakes than the average guy. I am continually learning about the processes that produce success in business and in life.

Yet I've tried doing business without systems and have a list of failures and great visions that never became realities to prove that systems are the secret to success. When I started observing successful business leaders who just had overall life success—you know, those rare people that seem to have it all, with great relationships, peace of mind, joy, loads of positive influence and financial freedom–over time I started to see a pattern. I started to see that they all had one thing in common. Oh, these successful people had all types of personalities, came from different types of businesses or careers, had different religious or non-religious beliefs, possessed different skills, strengths, and weaknesses. The one thing they all had in common, though, was that they all had figured out the systems that cause success in the areas that were important to them. They continually develop, refine, and implement the processes that produce the results they want. They know the secret is in the systems.

Do You Own Your Business or Does Your Business Own You?

I started my first businesses with a hard-working, German work ethic. I grew up as the consummate doer, thinking I could be successful in life and in business if for no other reason than I could outwork them all! That's what I set out to do from a pretty young age in multiple businesses.

After sacrificing a lot of personal and family time to make business happen, though, I began to realize hard work in business can produce more results, but my results were still limited by the number of hours I could put in, and also my results were not very consistent.

I ended up starting multiple businesses so I could have multiple streams of income. Yet ultimately, I became a driven slave to my businesses. That mindset almost destroyed my marriage and my health. It took a major train wreck in my marriage to wake me up and help me fully realize I needed to learn a different approach to business. I needed to get a different perspective on how to create success.

I looked around for better models of success. I would occasionally hear stories about or meet business owners who seemed to have the results they wanted in their business and financial lives and ALSO have discretionary time to do what they wanted. I wondered how that was possible. How could it be that some successful business owners also seemed to have time to really enjoy life? How was it that leaders could run a successful business AND have successful personal lives? I figured they just had some magic formula or some innate skill or talent only the chosen few possessed.

The more I suffered the consequences of my workaholic lifestyle, the more I developed a burning quest to discover what caused some business owners to have a business that worked for them so effectively that they didn't have to work so hard yet still got the results they wanted.

That quest led me to devour a ton of leadership training content from some of the best leaders around the country. I spent tons of time and money on seminars and audio training and books, and I began to get some idea that there was a method (a set of systems) behind certain successful outcomes. That quest led me to purchase a franchise that had a very effective training system for the presidents and CEOs of Fortune 500 companies. I partnered with my good friend and mentor, Paul Monson, to start our own training process for entrepreneurs. Our goal was to find the non-negotiable commonalities among all highly successful, self-running businesses that create great value for society and achieve the vision of the owner AND give the owner/president/CEO great personal and financial freedom.

We invested over two million dollars in research and development in the mid '90s. We hired the best researchers, writers, and developers we could find on this subject. In 1997 we launched Business Advantage with the vision to help business owners learn how to make their business work for them so they didn't have to work so hard for their business and still get the results they want. We worked with hundreds of business owners around the country in a long-term coaching and mentoring system, and we received stacks and stacks of raving-fan testimonial letters and videos like this one from the owners of a landscaping business:

> Before starting the *Systems for Success* program, we were both feeling quite discouraged to be working so hard and still having overwhelming problems. Even though we were making more money than ever and doing great work, we were so discouraged. We didn't know how to effectively go about delegating responsibility. Now we are seeing increased control over how our company runs and have a stronger belief that there really are positive, attainable solutions to our problems. We've always loved landscaping and horticulture; but now we can see our potential for real success. We've also been able to get away from the business to spend more time with family and friends and doing volunteer landscape work—and this is our busy season!

Here is another from the president of a relay panel design, construction, and installation company:

> I strongly recommend your program to any business that feels the frustrations of lack of focus and dilution of effort. The changes you have helped us make have truly improved our approaches and our processes and improved our satisfaction with the success of our company. Our efficiency has easily increased by over 20% in the areas of product development and marketing efficiency. The sales systems alone have increased our client contact success ratio by over 30%. Our thanks to all of you for an exciting approach to the future.

The president of an equipment rental and sales company had this to say:

I have found that since starting the Systems for Success program I feel I am much more in control. I have also seen our store organization and image improve greatly, and now my employees are responsible for much of the quality control that I always weighed myself down with in the past. I feel this is an invaluable program to me and feel that now I will be able to develop my business into an extremely successful business to pass on to my sons.

The president of an industrial electronic repair company talked about their experience implementing systems like this:

I now have an expanded sales system in place and it's yielding three times the sales leads that I normally have at this time of year. I have learned to accomplish more in less time with better results. I'm in control of every aspect of my company's business. The first few projects that we will be doing in the next year, we will be paid about 30% more for the work than we would have been last year. This will increase my profit margin as well as increase my total sales.

The owner of an insurance agency said:

I was not failing in my businesses, I was doing well. I just learned how to do better. When I was in the thick of this, working 12 – 14 – 16 hours a day, if you would have come to me and told me I could implement a program that would give me my time back, I would have said you were crazy and kicked you out of the office. Now I'm working less than 8 hours a day. I have my time back. We're only open 5 days a week. Our production is up. Our costs are down. This has been a tool that has helped me work on my business that has been probably the most valuable thing I have ever done for my business. Also, because of the program, I've been able to duplicate my business in an entirely different industry and product creating over two million dollars in new business last year.

Hundreds of business owners, from doctors to restaurateurs to mechanics, gave similar testimonials. It seemed we had cracked the secret to having success in business and personal life. The secret was in the systems for success that our team coached each business owner to develop and implement.

During this process, we began to experiment with using these same concepts and approaches in the non-profit context. We saw huge successes! Ultimately, we found a unique niche in the non-profit world focusing on helping senior pastors of large and growing churches develop this same systems-based leadership approach. We developed our own 501C3 non-profit called Ministry Advantage. Ministry Advantage provides a unique, systems-based approach to leadership and organizational development to hundreds of leaders of some of the most society-shaping organizations in the world.

The reason I took the time to recount that bit of history is to highlight that what I'm discussing here grows deeply out of the last thirty years of my life experience, over twenty years of which have been focused specifically on this one question: What systems create the greatest success for the greatest leaders in the world?

Most business owners start a business because they're good at a certain trade, craft or profession. No one has ever taught them how to be an effective business owner, though. Many business leaders got into what they do in business because they were good at a certain skill. Yet they are lacking the understanding of how to design a business. Then they get stuck in the trap of being the specialist, doing all the work in the business, and they never learn how to work on their business so that their business creates the results they want independent of their personal efforts. That type of business often ends up controlling the business leader instead of the business leader controlling the business to produce the value they want it to produce.

If you are always in survival mode, if you are always run ragged by the demands of your business, it's hard to think beyond yourself. It's hard to act beyond your immediate business needs. It's hard to focus on building beyond your business. You may have a strong desire to be a business owner who blesses the community in extraordinary ways, but if you're struggling to survive, struggling to barely keep your head above water, or you're swimming so fast you can't take a breath and look at those swimming around you, then how can you get beyond Level 1?

The first step to enable you to use business as a platform to build a better world is just to become more effective in building a better business. Many people start businesses and go into business leadership positions like I did, with primarily the doer mentality. They do the work of the business themselves. They never learn to design a business that produces good work to bless others beyond what the business owner or leader personally does. They never develop the systems that will help the business act as a strong platform to build a better world.

To move beyond this, to do more on Level 2, you must learn to build a business that accomplishes the mission of your business through implementing effective business operating systems in nine critical areas. If you're interested in learning more about these nine categories of business operating systems you can check out the additional information in the Appendix at the end of this book. As you continue to implement processes that produce better outcomes and create greater margins of time and money, it will help launch your business into more Level 2 activity and impact.

Level 2: Building Beyond Business. Once you have a business that is generating some consistent value for others and creating some consistent profit, you have the greater ability to move to the next level where you are building beyond business. At this level you are going the extra mile to intentionally create value for others beyond the fundamental value of doing good business.

When a company begins to succeed at Level 1, the leaders get to decide what to do with that success. They can increase salaries and distributions, or they can increase the positive impact that they have on company culture or on customers. They can decide to invest extra profits in customer service or lower costs to customers, even if that doesn't further increase profit margins. Obviously, you need to be profitable enough to sustain a viable, growing business. But if you are a purpose-driven company, you can strategically invest in things that better accomplish the mission of your company. The highest purpose of the company can't be to build profits. It needs to build beyond business. Your company exists to make the world better for people. People don't exist to make your company better. The sooner you get straight on these priorities, the better.

In every business I have led in the last twenty-five years, we have embedded the following core value, even at the startup phase when we were primarily only able to focus on the process of building the business:

WE VALUE BUILDING BEYOND BUSINESS. WE BELIEVE THAT OUR BUSINESS EXISTS FOR PURPOSES BEYOND FINANCIAL OR BUSINESS INTERESTS. ALL OUR DECISIONS AND ACTIONS ARE BASED ON MOTIVES AND GOALS WHICH WILL ULTIMATELY MAKE A SIGNIFICANT DIFFERENCE IN LIVES AND IN COMMUNITIES. WHAT WE DO TODAY MUST ALWAYS BE MEASURED AGAINST WHAT WILL MATTER MOST BEYOND THIS LIFE.

Your business is not your purpose. Your business is a platform to build a better world. If you think that your business is your purpose, you're underestimating its power and short-selling your potential. To optimize the real world-changing potential of your business, you need to recognize it exists for something beyond just the doing of good business. Yes, a good business can provide good value to the world just by doing good business. But a good business has so much more potential to provide great value to society beyond what it does in doing good commerce.

For example, a good business can go beyond basic business expectations to add value to its employees' lives. This could be something as simple as helping employees feel extra special on their birthdays. If an employee mentions he or she is having an anniversary, you could tell the person to take half a day off and give a gift card to a restaurant so the person can have a nice date with his or her spouse.

It could be something more systemic, like reinvesting a bit of profits into providing extra training or resources for a healthier or safer work environment. A business can invest some of its profits in providing personal financial management training to employees to help them get out of debt and reduce the financial stress that is the number-one killer of marriages these days. Or your business can provide time and money for its employees to do service projects for the community, serving together in a homeless shelter, adopting an orphanage, or building wells for people who need water in developing countries.

A Sure Way to Shape Society

You can do business in a way where you are a true steward of your city. Find out what your city needs and find a way your business can help meet that need. Your business can do things to help sustain our planet that are beyond just basic "green" best practices. Your business can provide a quality or quantity of products and services that create value for society beyond what customers pay for or expect.

It can become a sure way to shape society for the better.

As your business begins to do things that build beyond business, you'll begin to notice a virtuous upward success cycle. Being socially responsible is a pathway to greater profit, which is a pathway to even greater social responsibility. You do well by doing good. When you do these types of things to build beyond business, you are building a better world! And you'll likely see an increase in customer satisfaction, employee engagement, business outcomes, and personal fulfillment.

In the company I've been leading for the last dozen years, we recently paid nearly a thousand of our employees to go through a process of establishing personal goals for five spheres of their lives (physical, intellectual, spiritual, relational and financial). We paid them to take time to define their personal life values: the non-negotiable principles that will guide their entire lives. Since we have many locations around the country, I did some basic training on video and then sent all managers the process to facilitate this with their teams.

The impact of this was much more profound than what we thought it would be. I did a debriefing call with the managers from around the country who facilitated this. Several managers said that this was the highest impact thing we had ever done as a company. It built more morale and produced more enthusiasm for our business goals than anything we had done in years—and it wasn't even about business! It was beyond business.

Nan, one of our long-time managers, said, "I've been doing these meetings for years every month; this is the first time any employee came up to me to ask when the next month's meeting is! And after this meeting I had three different people who told me they couldn't wait for the next meeting and asked me when it would be!"

Employees said things like, "I can't believe a company would care about my personal life and helping me to be the person I want to be." Michael came to me after the training and said, "Is it okay if I take all this training material and show the video to my extended family and grandkids?" This man has ten kids (the majority of whom are married) so he had a pretty good size "team" of his own! In the following weeks he would periodically pop into my office and enthusiastically talk about the impact it was having on his family as some of his kids or grandkids were establishing their personal goals and values.

What did all that have to do with business? Nothing directly but everything indirectly. And how much did it cost? It cost very little. The time the company paid employees to work on their personal values and goals would have been spent in some other meeting. Payroll didn't go up. Did it help them? Absolutely!

In the following weeks we heard stories of employees sharing personal goals with each other. They were now supporting each other in losing weight, starting new educational paths, saving money, paying off debts, mending broken relationships, etc. Did it help the business? Sure! Employees were more eager to go to work and more engaged in the mission of the company than ever.

What was the impact on the bottom line? I don't know, because that's not why we did it. We did it because it was one way to express our commitment to build beyond business.

Here's another example of building beyond business without spending more resources but engaging employees in making a significant positive impact in the community. A few years ago our company built a large assisted living and memory care community on the river in Rochester, Minnesota. We ended up selling the building to a local business owner and entered into a twenty-five-year lease to continue owning and operating the business at that location. As I developed a relationship with our new landlord, we quickly realized we shared a passion to use our businesses to bless our communities. Dan owns a regional construction excavation company. Like many businesses, he spent some money each year on a holiday party for his staff. They would rent out a big banquet hall, serve fancy food, and give gifts to all the kids. One year, Dan had a brainstorm to try something a little different. He talked to the employees and told them that next year they were going to downscale their Christmas party a bit and provide the employees the opportunity to give the savings to people in their community. Instead of spending quite so much on a Christmas party, he would give them some of that money so they could then turn around and give it to causes that were important to them in the city of Rochester.

His management team thought it was a good idea, so they put all the employees into cross-functional groups of eight people all from different departments. They let these giving teams be completely self-directed. They chose the leader of the team and the project(s) they would support. The only guideline Dan gave was that they had to do it together and that it had to be something that did not in any direct way benefit their business. It had to be something that was beyond business.

The first year the company gave each team a relatively small amount, and most of them simply donated the money to causes they were passionate about. That next Christmas party was in their big warehouse instead of a beautiful banquet hall. The company provided the main course and everyone else brought salads, drinks, and desserts, potluck style. I still remember getting chills as Dan told me that everyone without exception said that it was the best holiday party ever. People got up and shared stories of what happened with the money their team had donated. Some people shared pictures of the causes they were passionate about. People cheered and yelled and laughed and cried.

Dan told me they have done this now for several years, and each year they set aside more and more of the company's profits for these giving teams to work with. It went from the teams simply donating money to teams actually working on projects together to see which team can make the biggest impact on their city with the money they have. At the Christmas party, many of the teams have people who are beneficiaries of their service come and tell the story of what was done for them. The whole Christmas party is full of tears and cheers!

Last year, someone on one of the giving teams knew a family that had just experienced a major accident that caused a serious disability in the family. Their home was not friendly for disability access, and this family didn't have the money to do anything about it. So this team used some of the money to buy supplies and volunteered their time to completely retrofit that house! They built ramps and even an elevator-type mechanism to take the disabled family member up and down the stairs. The family came to the Christmas party, and with tears in their eyes, they shared what it meant to them that someone in their community cared enough to meet this huge need.

Now that family was never going to give this heavy machinery construction company any money, right? But what did that do for the city? The company met a need that other social institutions and churches in the city were not able to meet.

Of course, the impact on the morale of the company and the engagement of employees is huge. The employees are saying,

"Look what our company did this year for our community!" That makes them proud of where they work, and it makes them want to invest their very best effort. Obviously, it provides one more incentive to help the company make more money so they can continue to do these impactful things in their community. Dan has now tied the amount that each giving team receives to the profit the company makes, so they know that the more money they make, the more they get to give away. They are now more excited about this than anything else in business, and they plan all year around who is going to be on what team and who will do what.

This is just one way that Dan's company is building beyond business to be a benefit to the community. His employees find meaning and inspiration in their work as they use their business to build value into their community.

Even if your business isn't focused on changing the world, when your business goes the extra mile to create out of the ordinary value for employees, customers or their community, you are applying best practices that some of the greatest companies in this world follow. Larry Fink is the CEO of BlackRock, which is currently the world's largest asset manager with over six trillion dollars in assets under management, clients in over 100 countries and investments in thousands of companies. Larry says it this way: "To prosper over time, every company must not only deliver financial performance, but also show how it makes a positive contribution to society. Companies must benefit all of their stakeholders, including shareholders, employees, customers and the communities in which they operate."

So it just makes good sense to lead your company to build beyond business. And these Level 2 initiatives are a good warm up for playing in the "big league" of Level 3 where you intentionally use your business as a platform to shape society and rebuild our world.

For more information and inspiring stories about Building Beyond Business, go to www.buildingbeyondbusiness.com.

Level 3: Rebuilding the World. After you have basic success in building your business and some wins at building beyond business, at some point you begin to embrace the paradigm that your business is actually a powerful platform (some might even say an elaborate front) to transform society. You begin to see that the real power of business is more than creating valuable products, services, and environments. It's even more than going the extra mile to benefit humanity. It is a powerful tool to transform the world. For those who are followers of Jesus, their business can become a powerful platform to perpetuate the values of Jesus on this earth. For those who are church-going Christians, their business could even become an extension of the ministry of their church to intentionally infuse God's good purposes into the world.

Think of the impact that TOMS has had. The name stands for Shoes of Tomorrow, or Tomorrow's Shoes, because the company's whole reason for being is to provide a better tomorrow for those in need. The company's owner is not named Tom. His name is Blake Mycoskie, and his company is a perfect example of the virtuous upward success cycle I mentioned earlier.

Blake Mycoskie founded TOMS in 2006. Mycoskie liked the Argentinian canvas-bodied and rope-soled shoes he came across when he was there. Then, as he did volunteer work near Buenos Aires, he met a woman who distributed shoes to poor families. When he saw a mother weep when they handed her shoes, he went back to California and started his company out of his apartment.

He made shoes similar to the ones he had seen and worn in Argentina. In a 2016 article in the *Harvard Business Review*, he explained laughingly that the first pairs had visible glue stains, but retailers soon noticed that these shoes were different. Blake's concept was "one for one". In other words, for each pair of canvas shoes that he sold, one pair would be donated to a child who didn't have shoes.

By 2014, the company had created so much value for society that it was valued almost $700 million, and Blake's portion was valued at over $300 million.

But Blake's mission is not about the money. It is beyond business. Here's what he said in an article entitled, "The Founder of TOMS on Reimagining the Company's Mission":

> The 'why' of TOMS—using business to improve lives—is bigger than myself, the shoes we sell, or any future products we might launch.

Blake could have stayed at Level 1, providing valuable foot protection for people around the world, and that would have been a noble thing to do! He could have stayed at Level 2, going the extra mile doing things beyond the dollars and cents of business, like giving away extra shoes to those in need. That too would have been a noble thing to do! But Blake moved to Level 3, using his business as a platform to improve lives by rebuilding societies. This didn't happen overnight. It took time and many trials as it does for most businesses to effectively engage in Level 3 focus.

At one point, TOMS realized that some of what they were doing at Level 2 could be counterproductive to improving societies. The Level 2 noble action of going beyond business to donate something to someone who might never buy from their business was good, but it didn't transform communities that needed more of a systemic approach to economic development, health, sanitation, and education solutions. Blake realized that giving away shoes could even hurt local cobblers and have a negative impact on the local economy. Although it was better for kids to be running around with shoes than without, TOMS began to realize that they could do more. They could take more of a Level 3 approach to use their business as a platform to rebuild the world.

TOMs started developing more effective ways to make what was wrong in societies right. Their product line expanded to include coffee, and each sale generates a donation of a week's worth of clean water to people who live in unsanitary conditions around the world. TOMS has already created more than 175,000 weeks of clean water for people who otherwise wouldn't have this life-giving substance most of us take for granted. Rather than simply donating the money to build a well or cistern, TOMs has partnered with an international organization that has years of experience bringing together local entrepreneurs, community members, and local governments to build and deliver water and sanitation services that are sustainable. The company also sells bags and uses those profits to attack the societal challenges of bullying in schools and unsafe birthing conditions. For example, with the sale of every bag they donate a birth kit which includes a clean pad, gloves, and sterile equipment to cut the baby's umbilical cord. And while TOMS still donates shoes, it now tries to source them from local producers to help strengthen struggling economies.

TOMS evolved to see their business as a tool to make what's wrong in this world right: to eliminate bullying, to eradicate unnecessary prenatal and infant deaths, to bring clean water and sanitary living conditions to entire communities. That is a Level 3, world-changing business vision!

At this level you embrace your business as a tool not just to meet the needs of the world but to actually make what's wrong with the world, right. You see your business as a platform to rebuild the world. You may even see your business as an elaborate front to build the culture and values of a good God into the world.

My motivation for writing this book was really all about my

own journey of trying to understand this third level: how does the purpose of business intersect with the purposes of God in transforming this world? So the rest of this book is focused on what I am learning about the role that business can play in transforming this world to be more like what God intended it to be. It is dedicated to understanding the powerful impact that business leaders can have on building a better society.

If you are a church-going person, hearing how business can do things that you thought only the church was supposed to do might be a bit disturbing to you. If you are a business leader, this might stretch your vision for the role you have in transforming society, and it might even scare you to think that you could have an impact similar to what you thought church leaders should have.

But what if the ultimate purpose of church and the ultimate purpose of business are not all that different?

What if?

What if the church and the business leaders in the church all shared the common vision that business is to be an extension of the church to meet the needs of the world and even to bring a God-honoring transformation to society? What if instead of the church believing that it must accomplish its ministry to the world on 10% of people's incomes, the church saw itself as designed to meet the needs of the world and bring the leadership and values of God into the world through 100% of the work of its business leaders? What if pastors, instead of praying for business leaders to succeed so that their tithes and offerings increase, prayed for business leaders to see their business as a missional extension of the church—as God-ordained vehicles to build a better world? What if churches would lead the way in partnering with business to facilitate a cooperation that helps both more effectively meet the needs of society?

What if pastors and other Christians changed how they view the potential of business leaders to transform the world? What if business leaders changed how they view themselves, and see themselves not just as doing business, but as having the most effective platform on the planet to make this world a better place?

President Calvin Coolidge once said, "The business of America is business." But what is the business of business?

What if it is to build the world as God originally intended it to be?

CHAPTER 3

THE FORCE THAT SHAPES SOCIETY

Let me expand a bit more about the way business builds the world and shapes society. My good friend Greg Gunn told me a story of a time when he was trying to help one of his kids understand this concept. Greg's passion and life purpose is helping families develop an intentional direction that lasts for multiple generations. Check out his website at www.family-id.com. Greg built a successful business and a successful family, and I have learned more from him than probably any man on how to live life with a multigenerational intention. Greg is also a master teacher, especially to his own family. One day as I was telling Greg how I wanted to teach this concept to my kids, he told me the following story to illustrate how he was doing that.

"I was driving down the highway one day discussing with my children the tenets of our Gunn family mission statement. The second part of our family mission statement is 'to help each family member to discover their individual bent that makes money and serves mankind.' I was talking to my son Jacob, who was nine at the time, and I said, 'Jacob, this highway we are driving on–where do you think it came from?' We passed the hospital and I said, 'Where do you think that hospital came from?' And as we drove on, I realized there were also highway patrolmen, so I asked, 'Where do police and fire departments come from, and where does clean water come from?' And as I looked around the highway I noticed there were fences and buildings and homes, and I said, 'Where did all of this stuff as far as the eye can see, that is not plant or human or animal–in other words, anything that is not natural–where did all of this come from?' Jacob said, 'Dad, I have no idea. I guess somebody made it.'

Jacob is really conscious of people who are homeless and every time we drive he asks if we can stop and give these people something. I said, 'Jacob, what if we stopped and gave a guy twenty dollars? How long could he live on $20? How many nights could he stay in a hotel, how many meals could he have? In fact, he could not spend even one night in a hotel, and he would be able to eat for maybe one to three days on $20. But what if we could get him a job and he could make $50 a day? Who, besides him, would get blessed if he bought food regularly? Yes, the grocery store, and how about the farmer who grew the corn? How about the company that built the tractor that the farmer was able to buy, and how about the guy who stocks the shelves or the lady who checked him out at the store or the person who provided the sacks? Think of all the people who would be blessed if this guy had a job and could spend his money on food. Also, he would pay sales tax and that tax would go to pay for various things in the city. The grocery store pays a property tax that goes to the city to the school system so kids get to go to school for free. And there's a medical center that the county has for those kids to get medical care. All that comes from the man who got a job. If you and I Jacob could create jobs, we could bless everybody. In fact, everything we can see that is man-made was made by someone who had a vision to start a business, and that business provided income so that people would have jobs, and those jobs created incredible blessing. When you make money you serve everybody, you bless everybody. Everything that is not in its natural state is there because somebody had a vision they turned into something that would bless somebody, something that would give value to someone.'"

There's nothing like the impact of a business that provides jobs. All the employees then contribute to society. Those jobs create incredible blessing to society. Even a plumber with two employees can change the world! The process of making money is a way to make the world better. It's a powerful process to serve and bless people.

As the late, great Steven Jobs said, "Everything around you that you call life was made up by people that were no smarter than you; and you can change it, you can influence it, you can build your own things that other people can use."

Where do cities come from? How do cities originate and grow? If you read or watch stories about how early American cities started, there is a bit of a predictable pattern. The city probably started with a farmer, and then more farming businesses started with more crops. Then merchants came to open businesses in town so the farmers could buy shovels and plows and groceries that they couldn't grow on their farm. Then a doctor came because there were now all of these people. Because there was commerce, people had money to pay a doctor. When the people wanted a spiritual leader in the town, they would hire a pastor and start a church. Then they got the railway in their area to help them transport their products to other cities.

Where does a city get water? It wasn't until someone developed the municipal bond business that water and electricity could be brought to every small city and town. Municipal bonds exploded the ability to get electricity to everyone. Cities borrowed the money from individual bondholder investors to fund the installation of electrical generation and clean water systems, and city residents paid for those services so the city could pay the interest to the bond holders. The people in this now thriving town or city wouldn't have had the money to pay for clean water and electricity unless someone started a business!

What Transforms Societies?

Some may argue that business isn't the only thing that influences the world. They're right! It's not. There are seven primary forces that shape society in any city, nation, and country. They are: Government, Arts and Entertainment, Family, Religion, Media, Education, and Business.

Of these seven forces, there is one that has the most pervasive effect on shaping or driving the other six. You guessed it. That one force that influences all the others is business. Business is the primary driver or influencer of all the other six.

Government

Government certainly has a significant impact on society. But where does government get tax money so it can operate? From the income created by business. People who make money in a business pay taxes that support the government.

Arts and Entertainment

There is no question that arts and entertainment shape cultural norms. What drives the growth of arts and entertainment in society? Who have been the primary patrons of the arts?

Who is on the board of directors of the arts councils, the cultural centers or museums? Is it a homeless, jobless guy? Generally, it is the wealthy, who have become so through business. It is mostly business leaders who are the influencers of the makers of art. Robust businesses drive the arts and entertainment, which are influencers of society. If there was never any money exchanged or given to the artist or the one who created, what would happen to art and entertainment? If art has changed society or culture over time, it's because somebody was offering it as a business. If someone sets up an art studio or a theater, they do marketing, sell tickets, provide customer service, and maybe have employees, etc. Of course, there's a lot of good art that never results in money or has anything to do with money. But generally, art that transforms culture has a business element attached to it. Sitting in your room and painting or making music just for your own pleasure is good, but it is not going to transform culture. That work has to be marketed, as a business.

Family

I firmly believe that healthy families are the foundation of any healthy society. Yet the family requires money to function, and that money is generated by some type of business. Even if your family has inherited wealth, someone at some point made that money through business. The Bible indicates that if you don't work and provide for your family you are "worse than an infidel." Unless you are stealing to provide for your family, you will probably be providing for them as a result of some type of commerce. What has given me the opportunity to focus on raising our family and for my wife to homeschool our kids has been businesses that produced income that allowed my wife to be home to give the best efforts of some of the best years of her life training our children.

Religion

Religion has certainly had a significant influence on shaping society throughout the ages. Every dollar that every church has ever used to do the good work it does, though, was created by a business. You can't give offerings if you don't have money to give. Where does that money come from? Business! Who is on the boards of churches? Who is on the financial committee? Who are the volunteers? None of these important roles are employees of the church. They are all employed by some business. Every volunteer in the church, by definition, is not paid by the church. It is those volunteers who do most of the important work that is done for communities by any church.

Media

Media doesn't just report on what's happening in the world; it influences what people know and believe about the world. How does business influence media? Every media company is ultimately a business. Furthermore, many types of media are strongly influenced by the businesses that become their customers. When a company says, "Our business will not pay for this million-dollar advertisement on your media because we don't agree with your agenda," they have real influential power over that media. Business influences media by voting for or against any media outlet with their dollars.

Education

Education shapes the future of society in many ways, and educational institutions are ultimately run as businesses if they are going to survive. Who is on the boards of universities? Where did money come from to build and run those educational institutions? Even educational systems that are completely free to the student ultimately receive some type of funding (with money created by business) and/or have leaders who volunteer their time on boards who make money to support their lives and their ability to give to causes through business.

I'm not saying that business is the entirety of what shapes this world. All seven of these forces shape the world along with some less dominate factors that I have not mentioned. And certainly, there are other integrated or overlapping influences between these seven forces. For example, one could argue that government or religion could influence all the other forces. But you can see that business has an inordinate influence! Business and business leaders don't control the other forces that shape society. They simply have a significant impact, both through the influence of being an economic driver as well as through the systems and processes of business within each of those other six areas.

If you took business out of a community, the other six forces would suffer greatly and eventually disappear. Of course, government could try to control all the other six forces. It might have the power to take control of resources and even to eliminate businesses. The Soviet Union tried that and demonstrated that this doesn't create sustainable success in society. Of these seven forces that shape society, business has proven over many generations and in many cultures to have the most profound and consistent impact on all the others.

One has to at least ask the question: "Since all the primary forces that shape society are all influenced by and fueled by business, what is the best way to influence the world? What is the highest potential platform to transform society?"

My bet is on business!

CHAPTER 4

THE ROOT OF EVIL OR A REASON FOR INFLUENCE

If business and the money it generates has such an inordinate impact on shaping society, why is it that money seems to get such a bad rap, especially from many well-meaning religious folks? Some people think that the Bible says that money is the root of all evil. In reality it says: "The <u>love</u> of money is a root of all kinds of evil."[3]

Far from being evil, money is meant to be the result of loving people well. It is only when we love money more than we love people that it causes all kinds of problems. Whenever my company begins loving the money more than we love the process of serving our customers and our team, we ultimately end up with all kinds of challenges. That's why a couple of the core values in every business I've led for the last twenty-five years have been to always act in the best interest of our customers, and to always do the right thing regardless of the personal or corporate cost. These are non-negotiable guiding principles that keep money in proper perspective as the measure of how well we are serving people. Sustainable success and positive influence comes from putting the needs of other people first.

Not every company or business leader thinks that way. Because some people love money more than they love people, the wealth that commerce can create has sometimes been seen as something that is bad. But there is a long tradition of cultures that see business success as the epitome of service to society.

Jewish tradition has no problem with wealth because it is seen as resulting from and producing great benefit to the community. Rabbi Daniel Lapin, in his book *Thou Shalt Prosper*, recounts how money and wealth were viewed throughout the history of the Jews. It's insightful to understand how historic Jewish people understood money and wealth.

Money as a Medal

Jewish people believed that the wealthiest person in the community was the greatest servant in the community. Wealth was simply a measure of how well and how much you served humanity. Every dollar bill represented a certificate, or medal, proving that you had served someone, just like a military medal received for service to your country. Money was viewed as a medal for giving your life in service to humanity. Thus, in the traditional Jewish paradigm, if you had no money, you were not serving society. In historic Jewish communities, they gave the best seat in the house, the best seat in the synagogue to the wealthiest man. This was not because they were trying to suck up to him. No! It was because they truly saw the wealthiest person as the greatest servant of society, deserving the best seat.

Today people often view making a lot of money as a sign of greed and spending money as a curse to avoid. We view spending as a curse because we feel we lose something by doing so, or we feel an aversion to materialism. Yet in the Jewish mindset, spending is a blessing to the world because we are paying for a product or service that adds value in some way to the world.

The Tale of Two Tactics for Influence

Let's go back in history to some time in the Middle Ages to a little Jewish community somewhere in Europe. Let's make it a village in Germany, where my grandparents were born. In that little community, they would take their Jewish boys and find the most aggressive, self-motivated young boys and send them to school for a rabbinical education. Then they would bring these boys back to their community. They were now highly educated, self-motivated young boys. As the boys came of marriageable age, the community would arrange a marriage, possibly to the daughter of the wealthiest man in the community.

Then this highly educated young man would say to his young growing family, "Kids, let me tell you, the money that you're going to end up inheriting from your grandfather isn't yours and it isn't mine. Let me tell you a story. If it weren't for Mordecai, Esther, Daniel, Shadrach, and Joseph, most administrations in every city our people have lived in would have killed us. We exist today because of the platform that previous generations have built for us. This wealth that we have is for us to manage and protect because it is designed to give us the ability to add value in and therefore influence every one of the cities and cultures where our people live. This is so our lineage can survive and thrive in future generations. So I want you to know, grandkids, you are not to spend this inheritance, wasting it on yourselves. Use it to build a business that builds a platform to add value to society. Your ancestor Mordecai, who saved our people from certain death, wasn't working a job somewhere in a field. He was a leader with influence where he could hear about the plot of King Artaxerxes to kill our entire people. Thus he was able to save his life and save Esther and thus keep our people from being killed. So we've got to continue stewarding our wealth by using it as a platform to create value and build influence in society. This wealth that we have and the wealth that we can create is designed to give us influence in every city. It isn't yours to be wasted on yourself."

With this ethic, the Jewish people became influential in many of the countries and cities where they lived. In Germany, for example, by 1923, 150 of the 161 privately-owned banks in Berlin were Jewish. About 75% of the attorneys, and nearly as many doctors, were Jewish. Although only 1% of the German population, representing a negligible electoral power, by the early twentieth century the Jews' economic, social, and political impact was considerable. By the 1930s, who in Germany owned and controlled most of the companies and industries? Who controlled the steel industry, the fur trade, the newspaper industry, etc.? It was the Jews.

Now, in a normal society, this would simply be an example of how business and the wealth it generates can allow a minority population to exert significant influence on society. Unfortunately, as we all know, the Germany of the 1930s was taken down an abnormal path by an evil madman named Hitler. The evil forces of this world wanted to exterminate this group of people who were leading influencers of building a better world through doing commerce well. Hitler absurdly made the Jews' influence in society into a scapegoat for society's ills instead of honoring them for serving society, and we all know the atrocities that followed. However, this story and the Jew's resurgence of influence illustrates how much impact a healthy view of the value of wealth generated by business can have on a society, even when exercised by a small and even unpopular part of the population.

For contrast, let's go back to that same place in Germany, only let's go to a Catholic community instead of a Jewish one. Now the Catholic community takes their aggressive and self-motivated young boys and sends them off to the Jesuits and they come back as highly educated, self-motivated, and aggressive young boys, many of whom become priests. These educated young boys begin influencing all of Central and South America and parts of the United States for Catholicism. These young priests are like pioneers. They gain vast amounts of wealth for the church and influence society quite a bit. Fifty-four cities in the United States are named after Catholic saints (Santa Fe, Santa Barbara, San Francisco, and Los Angeles are just a few of the more famous examples). Yet because these celibate priests didn't have families, the wealth they collected over their lifetimes was passed on to institutions.

Institutions are not wealth creators. Individuals and families doing business are wealth creators. Wealth was never designed to be managed, protected, and built upon inside of an institution. Attempts to build wealth within an institution inevitably cause the influence of the institution to be viewed as paramount over the influence created by serving people well.

I have come to believe wealth was designed to be managed and built upon inside the family and used as a platform for people to serve society in increasingly effective ways across the generations. This is a new paradigm in recent years for me. It has caused me to cast a new vision for my family and even revise my estate and trust structures to accommodate this new paradigm, where the wealth I create in this generation is passed on to the next generation, not for them to spend on themselves, but as a platform in trust for them to use as a basis for adding more value to society and rebuilding the world. This is, in many ways, the Jewish model throughout the centuries. Although there have certainly been abuses and mistakes made in this model, it has resulted in inordinate influence on societies.

Today, the Jewish people are relatively few in number (there are less than 15 million Jews in the world). Yet in relationship to their numbers, they have huge business and financial influence. Though more persecuted than almost any group in the world, Jews control more wealth per person than any other group. Arguably, they have more influence per person on society than any other group in the world. There are undoubtedly multiple causes for this inordinate influence. However, one significant cause is clearly their deeply embedded belief that money is a medal of honor for doing business that blesses society.

Today, the Catholics are huge in number with more than 1.2 billion in the world. There are many highly successful and influential Catholic leaders around the globe. Some are my dearest and most respected friends. Yet in relationship to their numbers overall, this people group doesn't have nearly the economic strength or influence the Jewish people group has on society. In fact, many of the poorest countries in the world are primarily dominated by the Catholic Church. There are undoubtedly multiple causes for this. However, one significant cause is the historic religious belief that money and materialism are evil, and that commerce is a necessary evil to make a living and create donations to the church.

This also illustrates that churches existing on donations cannot exercise the same influence that businesses can. The Catholic Church primarily created wealth through donations, not by providing a product or service for a profit. On the other hand, the Jews primarily created wealth by providing a product or service for profit. Thus, their influence is both wide and deep, especially in proportion to their numbers.

A company is in some ways like an extension of the family concept, where people work together to create value that has a positive influence on society. Those companies and families who understand how money and business can redeem culture are world changers and history makers.

An Ancient Teaching on Influence

Jesus was one of those history-making leaders who really got this. A couple thousand years ago when Jesus was teaching how God's ideal society would develop in cities, he told a story that illustrates how business leaders who are able to turn one gold coin into ten gold coins are the ones who would end up having influence over ten cities. Society is built by business leaders who multiply their money and increase their net worth by providing a product or service or creating value so that it multiplies. This is what Jesus taught about how God's ideal society (what he called God's kingdom) is designed to grow. Yet it is interesting that the Catholic Church, which is supposed to be one of the primary vehicles for bringing God's kingdom to earth, ended up following a system that was not at all based on the system Jesus taught was to be used for building God's ideal society on this earth. Instead the Catholic Church fostered what is in reality more like a socialistic system that takes from the producers to give to the non-producers. And for the most part, the institutional church around the world continues to perpetuate this basic paradigm of taking from the producers to give to non-producers more than it perpetuates the paradigm of people producing tangible value to build a better society.

Don't get me wrong. I do believe there is great value in producers giving to help people who can't produce. I do believe there is great value in generously giving to the church or charity you believe can use those resources to do really good and important work that wouldn't otherwise get done in this world. For the last forty some years, my wife and I have regularly donated a pretty good percentage of our income to churches and charities like this. And I think many of our donations do make a positive impact on the world. I am simply making a statement about the systems that I believe will ultimately have the greatest impact on transforming our world. I would put transformational commerce at the top of the list.

God's ideal society is not built best on a paradigm that takes from the one who produces and gives to the one who doesn't. I believe "the church" as Jesus envisioned it, as you will see in subsequent chapters, was actually designed to be people providing value to society through the marketplace.

One Last Lesson on Leadership Influence

This notion first started to dawn on me one day when I was reading the apostle Paul's last speech to the leaders he had been mentoring for years. Paul is known as the leader who did more to build the early church than perhaps any other person after Jesus. He developed leaders (none of whom were paid professional religious leaders) to oversee the church in various cities. He was about to make a long trip to Jerusalem, where he knew he would very likely be killed for going against the religious norms of that time. Just before he left, he gathered these church leaders, what we would call "pastors" today, and gave his farewell speech. With tears, Paul gave these pastors his final leadership advice for building the church.

He didn't tell them to preach better sermons, build better buildings, start more programs to feed the poor, or raise more money to fund the ministry. What he said was that he had not coveted silver or gold or clothing.[4] In fact, he said he had always produced the money for these himself: "You yourselves know that these hands of mine have supplied my own needs and the needs of my companions."[5] Paul had worked for his own money, and he had been able to help others with that money too. He suggested that they do the same: "In everything I did, I showed you that by this kind of hard work we must help the weak, remembering the words the Lord Jesus himself said: 'It is more blessed to give than to receive.'"[6]

In his last speech to the pastors he is mentoring in the early church, Paul is essentially saying, "I want you to be like me. I want you to produce so much profit from the work you do in business that you have plenty of money to give to those in need."

Now that's a switch. He's not telling pastors that the secret to success is to get their congregations to give more. He was telling pastors to make more so they could give more to their congregations! I want you to make enough money so you can give! Make profit so you can give to those who have need in your congregation!

I don't know about you, but I have never heard a sermon on how pastors are supposed to do so well in business that they can give to people in the congregation. That, though, is the essence of Paul's last speech. Clearly Paul did not see money or business as the root of all evil but instead as the basis for blessing society. When this dawned on me, it became clear that business and the church are supposed to have a more significant influence in building a good society than what most of us understand today.

Much of the potency of business to permeate every aspect of society for good flows from the genius of the free enterprise system in promoting good human relations and creating value in society.

Let's take a closer look at this.

CHAPTER 5

THE SOCIAL GENIUS OF FREE ENTERPRISE

One of the things I love about a free-market economy is that it is a system where money is earned by serving someone well enough to make them happy with what you provided. If I paint your house, fix your car, make a certain tool that you need, you give me money. That money is in essence a certificate proving that I served you. With these certificates of service that you have given me, I can then go online and order some new tool I need from Amazon that some other business leader made well enough that others traded their certificates of service for it and were served well enough that they gave it a five star rating.

Essentially, Amazon says, "When you place your order, you're making a claim on something that some other business leader created. You're asking this other business leader to provide value to you. But first can you prove that you provided value to someone else?" And I say, "Of course I can!" Amazon essentially says, "Prove it." So I enter my PayPal account linked to my reservoir of certificates of service and prove that I have provided enough value to others to receive the value of this new tool I am buying for myself.

Commerce is really an exchange of value. Money is just the symbol of value exchanged.

Obviously, some people are more effective at creating value for society than others. Is it magic that they receive more certificates of service (make more money) than others who provide less value? Think about Bill Gates, for example. Why is his income so much more than mine? It's because millions of people use the software his business created. I'm using the software he created right now as I type this manuscript, because it makes me more productive than just writing it all by hand. The mission of Microsoft is to empower every person on the planet to achieve more. Their mission is not to make money. Their mission is to serve people by helping them achieve more. I pay hundreds of dollars a year to the company Bill Gates started because it empowers me to be more productive. People pay me less than they pay Bill Gates because I haven't provided as much value to as many people as he has.

There are some who would say it is not fair that Bill Gates makes so much, especially compared to others. They would even cheer the government on in trying to take more money from him (and other wealthy people like him) and give it to others. In doing this they are basically announcing to the world that they don't agree with the deliberate decisions of millions of people to give Gates's company their hard-earned certificates of service. They are negating the decisions of millions of people who felt they were getting more value than they were giving up when they bought the products and services of his company. Instead, they are suggesting that we should use the arbitrary control of government to nullify all of those deliberate, independent decisions and redistribute those certificates of service without regard for the value created.

Just as an aside, when you think through this lens, it almost appears that income redistribution is just a government-authorized version of what a robber does. They take what rightfully belongs to one person for the benefit of someone who didn't actually earn it.

Free Enterprise Is a Gift to Humanity

Think about the self-perpetuating system of positive regard for humanity that is built in to this free enterprise system of business. There is a built-in incentive to provide value to others before I receive value myself. There is a built-in system to reinforce the positive principle that the greatest servant will become the greatest success. There is a catalytic mechanism to encourage the Golden Rule of doing for others as we would want done for ourselves.

Harvard Professor Steven Pinker says, "Commerce, trade and exchange. . . mean that people try to anticipate what the other guy needs and wants. It engages the mechanisms of reciprocal altruism."[7]

That, in a nutshell, means that business makes people want to serve others' needs. That sounds to me like a real gift to humanity!

Now think of the alternative. For the sake of contrast, let's talk about socialism. A socialist economy can essentially say, "Lonnie, you don't have to provide value to other people in order to deserve the value that someone else produces. As long as you're a member of our party, we will take what your fellow man produces and give it to you based on equality or need rather than based on what you produce." This system has been well proven throughout history not to create sustainable success in relationships or true abundance in society. When it comes to relationships, Alexander Solzhenitsyn, a Soviet dissident who won the Nobel Prize, said that the Union of the Soviet Socialist Republic was a government at war with its own people. The very nature of the socialist system diminishes the dynamics that cause sustainable success in relationships. Peace and prosperity for societies have not resulted from such systems—quite the opposite.

Socialism has demonstrated fairly well that if you take away the free enterprise business system of profit for productivity, it is likely that the real wants and needs of people won't be met as effectively. In our generation, some countries that have historically been most deeply entrenched in socialistic and communistic systems are now becoming more capitalistic in their approach to commerce. They simply realize that this creates healthier relationships and stronger societies. China is a great example of this transformation.

When I started making regular trips to China a few years ago, I would have never even put "communism" and "capitalism" in the same sentence. Yet now that I have done a lot of business in China over the last three years, I can honestly say that China, while still clearly communistic in government, is one of the most effectively capitalistic in business. I vividly remember getting off a bullet train in Guangzhou, and my Chinese business partner mentioned that this was considered one of the wealthiest cities in all of China.

I asked, "How does the Chinese government measure wealth in cities?" I was thinking he would respond with measures like we use in America: per capita income or average household income, but no. He said with great clarity, "In China we measure the wealth of a city based on the number of new businesses that are being started and the success of those businesses in providing value to people in the city based on how much profit they make."

Wow! The Chinese government measures the wealth of a city

based on these leading indicators of success rather than lagging indicators like household income. They clearly understand capitalism, maybe even better than some governmental systems in America. The rapid social and economic transformation of China over the last three decades has once again demonstrated the power of capitalism to improve societies.

In general, in a free market society, people who are wealthy have become so by providing substantial value to other people. I'll provide a few well-recognized and somewhat extreme examples to illustrate this point. Think about the extraordinary value these business leaders have provided to people that has enabled them to earn billions of dollars.

- Jeff Bezos, through Amazon's efficient shopping and data systems
- Steve Jobs, through Apple's revolutionary products
- Mark Zuckerberg, through making people more connected than ever before with Facebook
- Elon Musk, through developing Paypal to enable simple and secure online money transfers for people around the world and then creating Tesla's most energy efficient yet powerful luxury cars on the market
- The Mayo Brothers through developing Mayo Clinic as the number-one medical clinic in the world solving health challenges no one else can solve
- Richard Branson, through his four hundred plus companies that provide products and services that improve the lives of people around the world

Branson says, "I've always seen business as a group of people trying to improve other people's lives." Zuckerberg started simply with a clear passion to help people be more connected. The Mayo brothers didn't intend to build the number one medical center in the world. They began with a simple radical vision to eliminate disease in humanity. Often, these titans of business begin with an altruistic vision to provide value to society, and society rewards them handsomely when they do.

Do we really mind that these iconic business leaders became very wealthy or that their companies made a lot of money? Do we really wish they had kept their ideas to themselves and not offered to sell them to us for an amount of money that would allow them to continue to make better products and services that we value? Do we begrudge them for making a lot of money? No, because they gave us so much "bang for our buck"! We're grateful to them!

When Steven Jobs died, a cartoonist showed him entering heaven as he was welcomed by Benjamin Franklin and Thomas Edison. Is there any doubt that these three people contributed more value to society than they received? Ben Franklin contributed too many inventions and discoveries to name. How could we ever repay Thomas Edison for lighting up the world? How could we ever repay Steven Jobs for putting the world of information in our hands in the form of smartphones?

These people gave more value than they received by far. Isn't that a beautiful and virtuous cycle that we would want to see continue, whether on a large scale or happening at your favorite small local restaurant that continually makes better tasting, healthier food served in a great environment that fosters relationships? What these business leaders do with the free enterprise system is truly a blessing to humanity!

Profit Perpetuates Customer Satisfaction

Whenever the profit incentive is missing, the probability that people's wants can be safely ignored is the greatest. This is because the ability of a business to make a profit depends on two simple factors. The first is whether the business is producing a product or service that society values enough to pay what they are asking for it. The second is whether that business is well led enough to use limited resources in a way that is efficient and effective enough to consume less resources than the resources others are willing to give in exchange for it. That's how profit is earned, and it makes profit dependent upon meeting people's wants and needs.

As I have mentioned, I have spent a lot of time in both the non-profit and the for-profit worlds. I have led boards in both worlds, and I can tell you that in general there is a higher degree of consistency in customer satisfaction in the for-profit world than in the non-profit world. Why is that? I believe it is because in a free market economic system, profit is a built-in catalytic mechanism to constantly encourage service and value creation as of primary importance. Capitalism is compelled by the profit motive to look for and respond to people's needs and wants.

I'm not saying that capitalism or the free market economic system always produces other-centered people or companies. Certainly, greed and corruption can and do enter in to this system just as they do in many other good systems. At the same time, this does seem to be the system that is most closely aligned with the principles of an ideal society where the one who serves others best becomes the greatest success. In a healthy free enterprise system, the pursuit of profit by serving people and the building of what some might call "God's kingdom on earth" are one and the same.

No one argues that the free enterprise system is perfect or free from abuses, but I believe it is the system that most effectively promotes the principles of God's ideal society where the greatest servant becomes the greatest leader.

To take this a step further, let me give you a case study illustration of one of the greatest examples of a business leader who modeled this system of ideals to transform society through everyday life in the marketplace.

PART 2
FOLLOWING THE HIGHEST
IMPACT LEADER IN THE WORLD

CHAPTER 6

THE MOST TRANSFORMATIONAL BUSINESS LEADER EVER

Let me share with you a story about the founder of one of the most extraordinary companies in the world. When I was a kid, my parents used to read me stories about this guy that seemed almost too amazing to be true. His is the classic rags-to-riches story; he was born into a poor family from a tiny town in the middle of nowhere. His dad started a small family business, and he learned from an early age the advantage of building a business that creates great value for people. He eventually became CEO of a highly successful regional construction company where he learned to build beyond business using his business platform and credibility to bring out-of-the-ordinary benefit to people in his community. Ultimately, this business owner transitioned to Level

3 where he used his influence in the marketplace to rebuild the world. For example, he did more to eliminate systemic poverty than any other leader I know. His organization, JC International, raised the bar of effectiveness in rebuilding society on a global scale. In fact, some might say that he is the most transformational business leader in the world.

You might not have heard of JC International because it is more like a holding company and its subsidiaries go by various brands. However, JC International is currently the largest provider of health care in the world. It is also the largest provider of education in the world, having started more private schools than any other entity on earth. What's more impressive is that it has over two billion customers world-wide. Yes, two billion! Nearly one third of the entire world's population are customers of JC International or one of its subsidiaries.

So let me ask you this: if the founder of JC International sent you an invitation on social media, would you click "follow"? I've been a follower for a while, and it's been amazing to see what's happened in this organization over time. Even many years after the founder turned over the day-to-day operations to his leadership team, they are still as passionate about the mission as the day the founder gave it.

In one of his last meetings with his leadership team before he retired from his active in-person involvement in the organization, he articulated a clear and compelling mission statement. Although JC International is now one of the oldest enterprises around, it still uses that original mission statement to guide the direction, decisions, and actions of the organization and all its subsidiaries. What's even more impressive is that over 50% of the two billion customers know the mission statement. Notice I didn't say employees. I said 50% of the customers! You know it had to have had some good leadership to create that kind of result over all these years!! Imagine if over half of your customers could recite your mission statement to someone else? Let me show you the original mission statement that was developed by the founder of JC International two thousand years ago:

"Therefore go and make disciples of all nations, baptizing them in the name of the Father and of the Son and of the Holy Spirit, and teaching them to obey everything I have commanded you. And surely I am with you always, to the very end of the age."[8]

You might have guessed that the founder of JC International is Jesus. He built a construction business for the first thirty years of his short, thirty-three-year life. In the last three years of his life, he focused primarily on training up leaders who would continue his mission to transform the world. He fully empowered his leadership team to run the day-to-day operations and expansion of the enterprise he started. Unlike most charismatic leaders, after Jesus died, the enterprise continued to grow in size and effectiveness. In fact, over two thousand years later, it is the longest running continual enterprise in the world.

I'm not trying to get religious on you. As you'll see a bit later, I'm actually not into religion at all. The reality is that great leaders learn from great leaders. Great mentors have great mentors. So what would it be worth to you if you could understand and emulate that kind of profound, world-changing leadership success? The good news is that, like all great leaders, Jesus made sure that his key leaders created good documentation of his systems for success. In fact, we have the benefit of an entire operating manual full of case studies, training, and processes to build transformational enterprises from families, to businesses, to nations. This book is the #1 best-selling book in the world. It is translated into more than 2,500 different languages. The next most translated book (Pinocchio) is translated into a whopping 260 languages–just 10%!

Jesus' systems for life success are documented by his original management team in the last twenty seven of the sixty-six books in the Bible starting in Matthew and ending in Revelation. It is what followers of Jesus for more than two millennia have come to rely on as the guidebook on his systems to rebuild the world.

Even if you don't call yourself a Christian, there is no denying the incredible transformational impact Jesus has had on civilization over the last two thousand years. When someone is as successful as that, it is important to take a closer look.

Jesus' NewsFeed

Just in case you aren't yet convinced that you should follow this transformational leader named Jesus, check out these highlights from his newsfeed over the last two thousand years. For ease of reference, I'll categorize these reposts by type of impact.

Jesus Christ
@realJesusChrist

Followers: 2 billion **Following:** 7.6 billion

Impact on History

 Human history is formally divided into before and after the birth date of Jesus. Everything before is B.C. (Before Christ) and everything after is A.D. (Annus Domini, which is Latin for "The Year of Our Lord"). 2018 is 2,018 years after the birth of Jesus.

 Yale historian Jaroslav Pelikan: "Regardless of what anyone may personally think or believe about him, Jesus of Nazareth has been the dominant figure in the history of Western culture for almost twenty centuries."

Jesus is the major focal point of two main holidays celebrated en masse worldwide. Christmas and Easter are based on the birth, life, death, and resurrection of Jesus.

The lives of two Christian saints inspire two holidays celebrated by Christians and non-Christians alike: St Patrick's Day and St. Valentine's day.

Writer H.G. Wells: "I am a historian, I am not a believer, but I must confess as a historian that this penniless preacher from Nazareth is irrevocably the very center of history. Jesus Christ is easily the most dominant figure in all history."

Historian Bruce Metzger: "Today no competent scholar denies the historicity of Jesus."

There are hundreds of times more evidence that the historical facts of Jesus life are true than there is for the lives of Caesar Augustus, Emperor of Rome, or Plato and Socrates.

Anyone would say that Plato and Socrates were brilliant and revolutionary Greek philosophers, yet we have no historical documents that Plato and Socrates wrote or even documents that were written about them in their generation.

The earliest documents we have about any of these three were written one thousand years after they died by people who didn't actually know them or their descendants. There are less than a dozen copies of any of those manuscripts about these great men. Yet no one questions that they lived, or that they did or taught or what is said of them.

The manuscripts about Jesus that form the basis for what we now call the New Testament of the Bible date to less than one hundred years after Jesus' death and all perfectly corroborate his life, teachings, and actions.

 There are 5,600 manuscript copies of the New Testament, making it one of the most copied documents of ancient history with 99% accuracy between copies.

 The writings we have about Jesus in the Bible were recorded by people who either personally knew him or knew people who knew him in his lifetime. Since that time, Jesus has been the topic of more books than any other person in history.

Impact on Education

 Many leading colleges and universities in America are started by Jesus' followers so that people could truly learn to love God.[9] Of the 123 colleges in colonial America, 122 were Christian institutions.

 The motto of Oxford University is Dominus illuminatio mea referring to Jesus and meaning "The Lord is my light."

 Harvard is founded on this statement: "Let every student be plainly instructed, and earnestly pressed to consider well; the main end of his life and studies is to know God and Jesus Christ which is eternal life" (John 17:3).

 Martin Luther argues the idea from the New Testament that referred to a priesthood of believers.[10] He points out that people need to be able to read and write so they could study the Scriptures for themselves.

 This results in the goal of universal literacy. Luther proposes that monasteries be turned into schools. Some theorize that the emphasis on literacy and education was as important to the economic success of Protestant countries as was the Protestant work ethic.

Impact on Health Care

Because of missionaries and people who do things for society in the name of Jesus, health education and healthcare facilities and practices are founded around the world.

According to Encyclopedia Brittanica, after his conversion to Christianity, Roman emperor Constantine began hospitals with the idea that it was important for communities to care for their sick.

St. Basil also founded a hospital, and monks had infirmaries in monasteries supplied with medicinal herbs from the monastics' gardens.

Throughout the Middle Ages, Christianity shouldered the burden of caring for the sick through the establishment of hospitals.

Even though many hospitals came under public control, their benevolent missions began with the Jesus-inspired ethic of healing and caring for the sick.

The founder of modern nursing, the great Florence Nightingale, does all her work because of the teachings of Jesus Christ.

According to Dr. Lynn MacDonald, posting about his speech at University of Guelph in Canada, Nightingale's lifelong devotion to reading the Bible led her to believe that active service to make the world better was the calling of God.

Impact on the Value of a Person

David Bentley Hart: "The autistic or Down Syndrome or otherwise disabled child; the derelict or wretched or broken man or woman who has wasted his or her life away; the homeless, the utterly impoverished, the diseased, the mentally ill, the physically disabled; exiles, refugees, fugitives; even criminals and reprobates . . . We used to view people like this as mere problems to be discarded. Jesus saw them instead as 'bearers of divine glory who can touch our conscience and still our selfishness.'"

Nicholas Wolterstorff: "Jesus' understanding of who are the downtrodden has been expanded well beyond the Old Testament understanding, to include not just the victims of social structures and practices –widows, orphans, aliens, the poor, the imprisoned –but also those excluded from full participation in society because they are defective, malformed, or seen as inferior. The coming of God's just reign requires that these too be lifted up."

John Ortberg (Who Is This Man) says that the heroic figure in Conan the Barbarian was paraphrasing from Genghis Khan when he gave his famous answer to the question: "What is best in life?" and said it was "To crush your enemies, see them driven before you, and hear the lamentations of their women." Yet, as Ortberg says, "an alternative idea came from Galilee: What is best in life is to love your enemies and see them reconciled to you."[11]

This underscores the value of each human person, even the "enemy."

Jesus' teaching on the value of every human life leads to the abolition of slavery in Britain and America. William Wilberforce ends the slave trade because he brings the message of Jesus into politics, and many abolitionists in the United States were motivated by religious feeling.

International benevolent organizations such as YMCA, YWCA, Samaritan's Purse, Compassion International, and World Vision are all founded based on following Jesus.

Millions of people around the world who once led lives of prostitution, drug and alcohol dependence, theft, and murder claim Jesus as the explanation for their life transformation.

More advancements in human rights have been accomplished by followers of Jesus than any other cause in the world.

David Livingstone helps end the slave trade. William Carey brings the first printing press to India and also ends the ritual murder of women on their husbands' funeral pyres. William Booth founds the Salvation Army to help those in poverty.

To this day, the Salvation Army still rings its bells in shopping malls across the nation.

George Meuller and Dr. Barnardo open children's homes to save children from the street.

In Britain, Lord Shaftesbury takes Jesus' teachings and values into parliament and helps end the terrible abuse of men, women, and children in work environments.

In the U.S., Martin Luther King Jr., a pastor, and Rosa Parks, a Christian believer, are inspired by the message of Jesus to fight for equality.

In South Africa, Archbishop Desmond Tutu partners with Nelson Mandela to end Apartheid and to encourage reconciliation.

Impact on Government

One of the earliest followers of Jesus, Paul, says this about radical human equality at a time when Gentiles, slaves, and women were unequivocally devalued: "There is neither Jew nor Gentile, neither slave nor free, nor is there male and female, for you are all one in Christ Jesus."

U.S. President John Quincy Adams: "The highest glory of the American Revolution was this: It connected in one dissolvable bond the principles of civil government with the principles of Christianity."

The United States of America is founded on Jesus' values. Our Declaration of Independence proclaims, "We hold these truths to be self-evident: That all men are created equal; that they are endowed by their Creator with certain inalienable rights; that among these rights are life, liberty, and the pursuit of happiness."

Larry Schweikart, Professor of History at University of Dayton: "Half the signers of the Declaration of Independence have divinity school training."

U.S. President Andrew Jackson says of the Bible, "That book, sir, is the rock on which our republic rests."

Civil War Union general and U.S. President Ulysses S. Grant: "The Bible is the sure anchor of our liberties."

The 31st President of the United States, Herbert C. Hoover says, "The whole inspiration of our civilization springs from the teachings of Christ and the lessons of the prophets. To read the Bible for these fundamentals is a necessity of American life."

President Abraham Lincoln says, "In regard to this Great Book, I have but to say, I believe the Bible is the best gift God has given to man. All the good the Savior gave to the world was communicated through this Book. But for this Book we could not know right from wrong. All things most desirable for man's welfare, here and hereafter, are to be found portrayed in it."

George Washington says, "It is impossible to rightly govern the world without God and the Bible."

While ruling the world's largest empire, Queen Victoria of Great Britain, is asked the secret of England's greatness. The Queen's answer is found in the famous painting The Secret of England's Greatness, which shows Queen Victoria presenting a Bible to an African chieftain at Windsor Castle.

Impact on Music, Art, and Literature

Had people not followed Jesus throughout history, we would likely be missing much of the world's great music. For example, the symphony, the cantata, and the concerto may have never been created.

Handel, Vivaldi, and Bach create music as an expression of their values from following Jesus and honoring God.

Bach signs all his works with Soli Deo Gloria ("Solely to the glory of God").

The life of Jesus is the inspiration for many great musical works such as Handel's "Messiah" with its magnificent "Hallelujah Chorus" as well as Mozart's "Requiem."

St. Pope Gregory the Great encourages music to be used to point people toward God, and the Gregorian chant becomes the bedrock for music in Middle Ages.

 Shortly thereafter, what is now known as modern music notation was invented by monks who wanted a method to spread music.

 Technically, no one knows what Jesus looked like, yet he is the subject of more paintings than any other figure in history.

 Jesus and his followers continue to be key subjects in myriads of artistic creations for two thousand years of art.

 Jesus' values and vision fuel the imagination of artists throughout history. Jesus is the inspiration for such great works of art as Michelangelo's Sistine Chapel and La Pieta, Leonardo Di Vinci's The Last Supper, and Raphael's The Marriage of the Virgin, among others.

 The influence of Christianity is called the single greatest factor in the development of architecture over the last two millennia.

 Just think of the myriad of stunning churches, missions, chapels and other buildings around the world that have been erected in the name of Jesus, like the Cathedral at Notre Dame, to name just one.

 Jesus didn't write a single book, but he is the most written about person ever and the greatest inspiration for the development of language around the world.

 Jesus is the inspiration for many grand literary works and classics by Chaucer and Shakespeare, John Donne, Milton, Charles

Dickens, and the great Russian writers Fyodor Dostoevsky and Leo Tolstoy, among others.

 In modern times, Christian writers C.S. Lewis and J.R. Tolkien are inspired by Jesus, and these twentieth-century writers' works are made into blockbuster movies in the new millennium.

Impact on Business

 The teachings of Jesus buttress a new brand of capitalism based on servant leadership.

 Our purest and most sustainably successful form of capitalism in the world is modeled after Jesus' revolutionary teaching that the greatest leader is the one who serves the most people with the best quality service.

 Private property rights can be traced to the Judeo-Christian ethic: "Thou shalt not steal; Thou shalt not covet your neighbor's goods."

 Sixteen of the thirty-eight teaching stories Jesus tells were concerned with how to handle money and possessions.

 In the four books of the Bible about Jesus (called the Gospels), an amazing one out of ten verses (288 in all) deal directly with the subject of money.

 The Bible that followers of Jesus use as their guidebook offers five hundred verses on prayer, less than five hundred verses on faith, but more than two thousand verses on money, business and possessions.

 Jesus himself teaches about parents supporting their children, people paying taxes, estimating costs, helping the poor and less fortunate, husbanding resources wisely, et cetera.

 Vishal Mangalwadi argues that while the technology for many inventions was created around the world across the centuries, it was most often developed and harnessed by Christian monks.

 Mangalwaldi shares that the theological factor that pushed technology was that the Bible distinguished "work" (to do work is to be like God) from "toil" (which is the curse of sin). Therefore, using creative reasoning, Jesus wanted to liberate people from toil and graduate them into well-rewarded and honorable work. Part of this was achieved through the invention of technologies, which, as we all know, generate businesses.

The first recorded use of a windmill to grind grain is invented by Abbot Gregory of Tours in the sixth century, to free his monks to pray to Jesus. Mechanical clocks are invented by monks who follow Jesus because they needed to know when to pray.

 Communal prayer after dark meant everyone needed to share the same time, and the clock became a religious as well as a practical necessity. For centuries it was the church from which villages learned the time.

 Ortberg says that eyeglasses are first mentioned in a sermon around 1300 A.D. It was monks who required them as they strained their eyes to pore over texts.[12]

Impact on Women, Children, and Family

 Jesus changes the world's perspective on women at a time in the ancient Greco-Roman world where women are often left to die when they are born.

Jesus teaches and models respect and honor for women of all classes at a time when women are seen as second-class citizens of society with no rights.

Far from believing a woman's only place was in the kitchen, Jesus encourages his women followers, like Mary and Martha, to take their places among the men and listen to his teachings.[13]

The life of Jesus shifts society's thinking about children. In Jesus' day, many babies did not grow up at all. Children were considered disposable, and some unwanted ones were left to die through exposure.

Ortberg posts that followers of Jesus outlawed the practice of exposure completely by the fourth century, and monasteries and churches became places where unwanted children were abandoned for care. This was the beginning of orphanages.[14]

Jesus changes the prevailing paradigm about children's worth when he says that the kingdom of heaven was made up of those who were like children and that he loves it when the children come to him.[15]

Followers of Jesus found the first agencies to protect children. In July 1884, Christian leaders Lord Shaftesbury, Rev. Benjamin Waugh, and Rev. Edward Rudolf found what would become the National Society for the Prevention of Cruelty to Children (NSPCC).

Jesus changes society's perspective of marriage. More people have been united in marriage, more wedding vows have been spoken, and more nuptial blessings have been asked in Jesus' name than any other.

Jesus explains that God wants a parent-child type of relationship with human beings,[16] one that was loving, compassionate, and full of good communication.[17] This new model of parenthood inspires countless acts of compassion, solicitude, and loving kindness in parenting alongside healthy discipline.[18]

As you can see from these newsfeed highlights, this one leader, Jesus, has had more impact on the world than any person in history. And note that his platform for influence was building a business until he was thirty. By the age of thirty he developed the freedom to spend the last three years of his life focused primarily on teaching his philosophy for rebuilding the world.

Think about this. Socrates taught for forty years, Plato for fifty, Aristotle for forty, and Jesus only for three. Yet the influence of Jesus' three years of teaching infinitely exceeds the impact left by the combined 130 years of teaching from these men who were among the greatest philosophers of all time.

Based on what you just read—why wouldn't we be followers of Jesus? Who wouldn't want to follow him?

These highlights from Jesus' newsfeed are historically verifiable facts. There is clearly no way a myth or a delusion could so dramatically alter history and transform so much of the world. Even if you don't believe in God, you can't deny the transformational impact this leader has made on history, and that it just makes sense to consider continuing the revolution toward building a better world that he and his followers have caused throughout history.

If you are not really interested in exploring Christianity, you may be wondering why you should even read on. Well, actually, if you don't like to be labeled as a Christian or if you don't consider yourself a Christian, the next chapter is specifically for you. But it's not for the reason you might think!

CHAPTER 7

RECONSTRUCTING CHRISTIANITY

If you don't consider yourself to be a Christian, this chapter is for you . . . not because I'm trying to convince you to be into Christianity, but because I'm trying to convince you NOT to be into the religion of Christianity! So, if you don't consider yourself to be religious, that's good. I'm not trying to make you religious. I'm actually trying NOT to make you religious.

If on the other hand, you are someone who considers yourself to be a Christian, you may have started looking for the nearest fire to burn this book when you read that I am trying to convince you not to be into Christianity! If that's you, please bear with me. I'd like to propose what might be a revolutionary paradigm shift that you might find liberating and empowering.

Those who consider themselves to be good Christians or are the very religious types, typically have a harder time digesting the concept that business is the best way to rebuild the world. Or–to use an idea more familiar to Christians–it might be hard to wrap your mind around the concept that business is the best way to build God's kingdom. If you are not a Christian or don't consider yourself to be religious, you may actually be in the better position to embrace the power of using your business to build society. The person who has been a lifelong Christian may be too used to the paradigm that the conventional church is the best way or even the only way to build a better society.

A Christian friend was telling me the other day how he was frustrated with a co-worker he's been repeatedly inviting to church. He said his co-worker doesn't see church as relevant to his life and refuses to be called a Christian. My friend was looking for advice from me on how to make his co-worker want to come to church and want to be a Christian.

I think my response surprised him: "That's great that he doesn't want to be a Christian!"

After he picked his jaw up off the floor, I went on to explain that the goal is not to get the guy to come to church or to make him a Christian. The goal is to help him become a follower of Jesus. I've never met anyone who said they didn't want to be a Christian because of the destructive principles Jesus taught, or the terrible things Jesus did, or the people Jesus hurt. (Chances are the person was resisting church, not God, because of some negative experience related to church or Christianity.) What I was proposing to my friend, and what I am proposing to you is to rebuild your definition of Christian to simply mean one who follows Jesus, who, as we saw in the last chapter, is the greatest leader EVER!

If it has seemed unattractive or unfulfilling to be a Christian, by the end of this chapter, I hope you will become fully convinced that the best thing you can do to build your business and to better the world is to become a follower of Jesus. I hope you will be convinced that the best way to change the world is to follow the lead of Jesus, if for no other reason than that Jesus has had the single greatest impact on shaping the history of the world than any other leaders.

On the other hand, if you are someone who views yourself as a Christian, by the end of this chapter I hope you will consider reconstructing your spiritual journey to be oriented 100% around following Jesus rather than following a certain set of religious beliefs, doctrines, rules or traditions.

I was fortunate to be raised in a wonderfully religious, Christian home. My father was a pastor in a conservative Christian denomination that I still have much respect for today. I grew up in a culture where life centered around following a certain set of mostly helpful religious beliefs, doctrines, and traditions. These defined for me what it meant to be Christian. Following the "rules" of the religion I was raised with provided guidance for daily life and a sense of security about my eternity.

I found a lot of good in that, for sure. But there was something missing. It wasn't until much later in life that I began to realize what Jesus came to establish was not the ability to follow rules, but the ability to foster relationships. Jesus didn't come to establish a new kind of religion; he came to help us establish a new kind of relationship—an authentic, unconditionally loving and empowering relationship with God and with each other. Human systems and institutions over time have created multiple sets of rule books that have defined the religion that has become known as Christianity. Different denominations (or groups) within Christianity have different rule books and nuances of doctrine. It is often those differences that tend to become the flag they wave to attract people to join their particular religious expression within Christianity. And now there are over forty thousand different Christian denominations in the world! So the word Christian or Christianity has come to mean a lot of different things to a lot of different people.

The Pink Elephant in the Room—Jesus Wasn't a "Christian"!

If I say "pink elephant," a screen comes up in the visual portion of your brain that shows a pink elephant, right? The size of your elephant and the shade of pink is different on your screen versus my screen based on what kind of pink elephants we have seen.

So it is with the words Christian or Christianity. When I say the word "Christian", the screen that comes up in your mind depends on which flavor of the Christian religion has populated the pixels of your mind.

We all have different pictures, paradigms, and concepts that are attached to those words based on the version of the Christian religion we have seen or experienced. Christianity has meant anything from the horrible atrocities that happened under the Crusades in the Middle Ages, when people were killed for not being a "Christian", to the Bible thumper on the street, to a church that is doing wacky things, or one that is doing wonderful work in a community, from a reformed prison inmate to Mother Teresa.

Clearly, the word Christian can mean a lot of different things. However, if you say, "I am a follower of something or somebody," there is much more clarity and consistency of meaning. If the person you are talking to knows who that person is, they know who you are following. If they know what that person teaches; what that person did, or is currently doing, then the only question becomes "How devoted are you to following that something or somebody?" Are you just a casual follower checking in once in a while out of curiosity? Or do you connect all day, every day trying to emulate everything they do? Or are you somewhere in between?

Although there may be a question about how devoted you are in following someone, there is no question about the principles you are referencing. If I say "I am following Rush Limbaugh," not one person will think "Oh, he's into that liberal stuff!" Everyone pretty much knows what Rush Limbaugh stands for, and it's not liberalism! There may be gradations of how much I am devoted to what he stands for, but there is no question about what he stands for.

So while I recognize that the entire world is not likely to drop the use of the word "Christian" after it has been used for over two thousand years, I personally prefer to identify myself simply as a follower of Jesus.

Now if you have been around Christianity awhile you might be thinking "Isn't this a bit of a dichotomy? How can you try to bifurcate Jesus from Christianity?"

You would think Christianity would be pretty important to Jesus, right? So let's see what Jesus taught about Christianity. Oh, wait. Actually, the terms Christian or Christianity were never used by Jesus. Jesus never called himself a Christian. Jesus never called his followers Christians, nor did his early followers call themselves or each other Christians. It was the anti-Jesus people, then called "pagans", who first called them "Christians". In fact, the first reference comes from the pagans in the city of Antioch.[19] Then a bit later the pagan King Agrippa used it to refer to this sect in a derogatory fashion.[20]

That's right, the name "Christian" originally appears to be a derisive nickname given to followers of Jesus by those who were not into Jesus at all. It seems to have been meant as a derogatory term. The third and only other time the term Christian appears in the Bible is again clearly referencing a pejorative experience: "However, if you suffer as a Christian, do not be ashamed, but praise God that you bear that name."[21] Even sixty three years after the death of Jesus, the ancient historian Tacitus wrote that "The vulgar call them Christians."[22]

If someone says with raised eyebrows, "Oh, so you're one of those politicians!" you probably wouldn't take it as a warm fuzzy compliment any more than the early followers of Christ would take it as a warm fuzzy compliment if someone said to them, "Oh, so you are one of those Christians!"

Most Bible scholars agree that it was highly unlikely that the followers of Jesus themselves thought up the name "Christian." The early church had other terms for themselves, such as "brothers", "disciples", "apostles", "servants", "believers", "followers", "the faithful", "the called" and "the chosen". The name that seemed to gain the most traction for the movement in the book about the acts of the followers of Jesus is "Followers of the Way".[23] Jesus had given himself the title of "The Way", so "Followers of the Way" was code for followers of Jesus.[24]

I'm not saying that the word Christian or the concept of Christian is bad just because of how it started. That's not the point here. What I am saying is that there is nothing inherent in the concept of following Jesus that means you have to call yourself a Christian or adopt any of the negative baggage that you may associate with that label. You can be a follower of Jesus and not buy into negative, destructive or unhelpful concepts you may associate with the religion of Christianity.

Christianity Versus Christ

In dismantling the term Christian or the religion of Christianity, I don't want to be perceived as simultaneously diminishing the value of the word "Christ." Although we use Christian today as a noun, in the original language, the three times it was used in the Bible, it is an adjective. It was a descriptive term that was made up as a put down of followers of Jesus. However, the noun from which it is derived, "Christ," is full of very valuable meaning.

I would like to do a little reconstruction of this word too. You often hear the name "Jesus Christ" as if it is the full and proper name of Jesus. In reality, Christ was not the last name of Jesus. Christ was a title that was given to him during the last three years of his life. The word "Christ" comes from christos, a Greek word meaning "anointed." It is similar to the word mashiach, or Messiah, in the Hebrew language. So, to be the Christ, or Messiah, is to be "the anointed one of God."

But What Does that Mean?

In those days, to be anointed literally meant having a special oil poured on your head, as a ceremonial symbol that God had chosen you for a special role. Kings were anointed by pouring expensive oil on their head during their coronations rather than the more modern practice of putting a crown on their head. Although sometimes prophets and priests were also anointed, the phrase "anointed one" or "the Lord's anointed" was most often used to refer to a king. The primary meaning of the word "Christ" or "Messiah" is that of a king chosen and given authority by God to lead.

For instance, David used "anointed one" or "the Lord's anointed" many times to refer to King Saul, even when Saul was trying to murder David and David was on the verge of killing Saul to defend himself: "Far be it from me because of the Lord that I should do this thing to my lord, the Lord's anointed (mashiach), to stretch out my hand against him, since he is the Lord's anointed (mashiach)."[25] So if you do want to call Jesus "the Christ," you are simply acknowledging Jesus as the King—your King—the one you choose to follow. For the purposes of this chapter in this book, though, I am going to ask you to do what they have done every year for more than sixty years at the White House on the National Day of Prayer. At the beginning of the prayer breakfast that day, they ask everyone to agree that they can simply be followers of Jesus regardless of their religious belief.

One of my friends attended a recent prayer breakfast at the White House where the initial speaker, who was not a Christian, said, "You Christians have hijacked Jesus. He is not yours alone. He is ours too."

Regardless of your religious persuasion or lack thereof, let me share what it might mean for you to consider following Jesus.

Just Click Follow

The most prevalent single word which the early followers of Jesus used to describe themselves is mathetes, which is translated into English as "disciple." A disciple is more than simply a "student" or "learner." A disciple is a "follower," someone who learns because they want to do what the teacher or mentor teaches and does.

You may not be ready to call yourself a devoted disciple of Jesus yet, but I am suggesting that the pathway to transform our world is to at least begin following Jesus. As you become more fully devoted to following him, you engage in a powerful movement that has transformed the world and will continue to transform the world for the better.

So for the purposes of understanding what I am trying to convey in this book, I am going to suggest you let "follow" mean whatever it means to you at this point. It can be as basic as what it means to "follow" someone on social media. How many people are you following on social media (Twitter, Facebook, Instagram,

LinkedIn, etc.) right now? With some, you just click follow because you are just interested in learning from what they do. With others you constantly comment, share, and repost. If you are following a personal trainer on Instagram, do you simply like their posts or are you joining their challenges, reposting their content and spreading the word? I follow Tony Robbins, and I can tell you that I don't fully buy in to or follow everything he says, but I still follow him. Conversely, I have some friends who are on the other end of the spectrum and would say, "I follow Tony Robbins and fully support, follow, and promote all his views." In this case, we are both followers, but it means something different to both of us.

Each of my kids own their own businesses and you better believe that I am a follower of them and their businesses. In that case it means I believe in them, promote their stuff and support them with my time, words, and resources. I follow other businesses I am less committed to and invested in just to learn what I can from them or be inspired by what they do or say.

So being a follower can mean different things to different people. I want you to know that in the context of this chapter and this book, it can mean whatever it means to you at this point in your journey. With that in mind, if you got an invite from Jesus to follow him, would you do it?

I'm suggesting it's worth at least clicking follow. Jesus' impact on this world is more significant than any other great person throughout history, and perhaps greater than the cumulative effect of every other great leader in the world. The famous French emperor Napoleon Bonaparte said, "I know men and I tell you that Jesus Christ is no mere man. Between him and every other person in the world there is no possible term of comparison. Alexander, Caesar, Charlemagne, and I have founded empires. But on what did we rest the creation of our genius? Upon force.

Jesus Christ founded his empire upon love; and at this hour millions of men would die for him."

It's okay if you aren't into Christianity. Or maybe you could reconstruct Christianity to simply mean following the greatest leader ever. If millions would die for Jesus, would you at least consider clicking "Follow"?

CHAPTER 8

DECONSTRUCTING RELIGION TO REBUILD THE WORLD

I believe that Christianity has been largely influenced by what mega-church pastor and popular leadership podcaster, Andy Stanley, calls the Temple Model. I thank Andy for opening my eyes to the stark contrast between what I call the Religion Model and the Jesus Model.

The Religion Model originated from the religious culture that was present when Jesus lived on this earth. The Religion Model is based on a religious culture that Jesus overtly rejected. In fact, the reason Jesus was killed was largely because of the reaction of the religious and political leaders to Jesus' desire to reconstruct the Religion Model to something new.

The Jesus Model Versus the Religion Model

When Jesus showed up, he built something that was absolutely brand new! It wasn't a knock-off or a version of something that had happened previously. It was a complete rebuild. He said, "See, I am doing a new thing!"[26] for all people, for all nations and for all time! He inaugurated a new covenant, a new arrangement between God and man. Instead of telling people to live life guided by long lists of religious rules, he gave the rule of love as the ultimate measure. He gave just one simple rule or value statement as the filter through which all other rules should be viewed. Stated as a question, it is: What is the loving thing to do?

Jesus didn't come to establish a new religion. Jesus came to establish a brand new movement that was for all people, all ethnic groups, all nations and generations forever and ever. This was a movement where love would replace law keeping, where self-sacrifice would replace animal sacrifice, where the vertical relationship with God would be measured by the integrity of the horizontal relationship with others.

For example, at one point Jesus said to his followers, if you are at the temple but you recognize that you have done something wrong to your brother, God can wait! Go make things right with your brother.[27]

The Religion Model and indeed all the religions of the world are based on the idea that there are certain things I must do in order to earn God's love and/or rewards. I must experience him in sacred places where sacred texts are read by sacred men who are followed by a certain group of people who rely on these men to interpret where they stand with God. This template for religion has been in play for thousands of years.

Yet when you think about it, the Religion Model is ME centered. It always asks the question, "God, are you okay with me? What must I do or believe in order to keep things right with you and me?" and "God, how am I doing?" In this way, the Religion Model is always a vertical interaction where I'm checking in with God and trying to do things in order for God to be okay with me.

The new model for building the world that Jesus introduced (the "Jesus Model") is based on the idea that God loves me regardless of what I do or don't do. God offers to give me an abundant life and the ultimate reward of living forever in perfect relationship with him and others, not based on who I am but based on who he is. All I have to do is trust him enough to accept his love and embrace his leadership in my life.

God didn't ask us to come to a certain place to meet him; instead he came to this earth in the form of a human being (Jesus) to meet with us to show us what he is really like. Jesus modeled throughout his life the kind of love he wants us to have for God and others. When the religious leaders tortured and killed him, it became the ultimate demonstration of love— the kind of love that when you understand and experience it, there is an irresistible appeal. People want to follow someone who loves completely and unconditionally.

In fact, when Jesus was suffering and dying on the cross, we see a stark contrast between the religious model and the Jesus model. The religious leaders were brutally abusing this man who did nothing but good for all, and they did it specifically because he wasn't following the expectations of their religion. Here is a man who loved people and built people up better than anyone had ever seen in one lifetime. He did this even to the point of not retaliating against or cursing those who were senselessly and brutally torturing him but blessing them instead. Jesus, as the ultimate representation of what God looks like in human form, was demonstrating from the beginning until the very end of his life that God is really a good God who is always out for our best interests. No matter what we do–or don't do–for him, he is "all in" for us. What Jesus did on the cross was intended to set us free from a life bound up by an external, rule-keeping, religious guidance system. It was meant to set us free from the guilt, shame, condemnation and striving to measure up that accompanies the religious model.

Paul wrote a letter to an early group of Jesus followers who were slipping into the religious model and he says to them, "It is for freedom that Christ has set us free. Stand firm, then, and do not let yourselves be burdened again by a yoke of slavery."[28] If your version of Christianity doesn't make you feel free, then you are doing it wrong! If you are following Jesus, there is nothing but freedom and a loving, empowering, world-class effective leader in sight!

Following Jesus is a perpetual experience of receiving love and favor that we don't deserve, getting benefits we haven't earned. That's just who Jesus demonstrated that God is. Jesus demonstrated in his life and death that God is the kind of person who knows everything about you and loves you anyway. That's grace. The moment we start bargaining with God or trying to earn our way into his good favor, we start slipping away from the grace of the Jesus Model and back into the Religion Model.

What Does Love Require of Me?

The days of fighting for approval or benefits from God are over! We're in! We need to quit worrying about what God thinks about us. If we believe Jesus was God coming into this world to demonstrate his love even for humans who reject and kill him, that he died to help us understand and experience that love, then we're in! If someone will die for you, they are FOR you. You never have to go to bed one night of your life wondering if God is okay with you. So you can stop looking up all the time and start looking around! Because the only thing of any value is how you treat other people. God is fine with you. With that faith that God is okay with you, you can now put your full focus on serving others and building a better world.

The ONLY thing that counts is faith expressing itself through love.[29] Jesus said, "A new command I give you: Love one another. As I have loved you, so you must love one another."[30]

The Jesus Model is OTHER-centered. It asks the question, "What does love require of me?"

Some might ask, "Well isn't there still a need for some rules even without religion? Isn't there a need for a code of conduct?" Sure thing! The reality is, though, in the religious model we tend to dumb down "the law" until it is something we can do and it won't bother our conscience. Jesus showed up and said, "You have heard that it was said, 'You shall not commit adultery.' But I tell you that anyone who looks at a woman lustfully has already committed adultery with her in his heart."[31] He brought it right back to the heart and what love requires. He also said, "You have heard that it was said to the people long ago, 'You shall not murder, and anyone who murders will be subject to judgment.' But I tell you that anyone who is angry with a brother or sister will be subject to judgment."[32] Jesus was saying you can be so focused on the specific laws and miss the point of the law which is to promote love.

Clearly, if I don't have sex with another man's wife, but I am constantly lusting for her body, is that really loving and building up my wife? Is that loving the other couple like God intended? I don't think so! If I don't kill someone but I live in seething anger toward them, is that demonstrating love for them?

Religion that focuses on "keeping the rules" will still result in people being mistreated. Have you ever had someone put a rule or a law over love? It's not pretty. It doesn't build people.

Paul agrees with Jesus that we are to use our freedom to serve and build each other because the entire law is fulfilled in keeping this one command: Love your neighbor as yourself. He said, "You, my brothers and sisters, were called to be free. But do not use your freedom to indulge the flesh; rather, serve one another humbly in love. For the entire law is fulfilled in keeping this one command: Love your neighbor as yourself."[33]

The Jesus Model says love God and love other people –the rest is detail. The Religion Model says, "God, how are we doing?" and is always looking for extra credit. The Jesus Model says, "Look around and then you'll know how you're doing. Get things right with the people around you because when things are right with them, things are right with God! The only thing that counts is faith expressing itself through love.

What would it look like if during every conversation, every interaction, every temptation to do something harmful, you asked the question: "What does love require of me?" Imagine how different our communities and our world would be, if everyone decided there was really only one thing that mattered: faith (or trust) in Jesus manifesting itself in love for other people. What if the rating scale went from giving ourselves points for what we give at church, church attendance, or some holy thing, to rating ourselves on how well we treat others? Would this not build God's ideal society on earth more effectively than all the "churchy" things in the world?

Here are some examples of the Religion Model versus Jesus Model:

STIMULUS	RELIGION MODEL RESPONSE	JESUS MODEL RESPONSE
I make a moral mistake.	"What will God do to me?"	"What will happen to the person I hurt?"
I get in a big fight with my spouse on Sunday morning and miss church.	I feel more guilty about missing church than I do about the hurtful things I said to my spouse.	I am glad I could take the time I had allocated to going to church to resolve the conflict with my spouse, really taking the time to understand his or her concerns and needs and apologize, kiss, and make up.
I do something that hurts or harms someone.	I practice a religious ritual and feel absolved of the responsibility to make restitution. Then I feel forgiven and whole in the eyes of God.	I apologize and make restitution to the person I harmed. I ask: "Will you forgive me, and what can I do to make it right?"
I hear about or observe someone's big failure or mistake.	I feel morally superior. "Thank God I'm not like that. What a weak person. I'm glad I'm strong."	I feel and show compassion. "My poor friend. How much shame and guilt he must feel. I'll say or do something to encourage him."
I receive a huge, unexpected windfall of money or resources.	"Wow, I must have really done something good to impress God for him to bless me like this. "	"I'm thankful I was able to create something of value for others that allowed me to receive this benefit. How can I use this unexpected benefit to create even more value to bless others?"

In all of these instances, the Religion Model response is more concerned with ourselves and our standing with God than we are concerned with the well-being of the people around us.

The entirety of Jesus' message and in fact the entire Bible can be summed up in two laws: Love God and demonstrate your love for God by loving and building other people. These are the two non-negotiable guiding principles of the leader who had the greatest impact on building this world.

Now you see why I said if you don't consider yourself to be religious, that's great! Now you see why I don't want to make you religious. If you're a follower of Jesus, you don't have to be a follower of religion. Jesus himself was killed because he didn't follow the religious system of the time; he was killed by religious leaders. He was all about relationships, not about religion.

Although religion has been a great influencer of culture throughout the centuries, religion has done much damage to relationships and cultures too. Of course, it has also done many good things! It has resulted in both damage and good. Following Jesus, just purely following Jesus has not done any damage. His entire teaching and life modeled, "What does love require?" If you ask that question, how can that focus damage cities, cultures, or relationships?

Some of you intuitively or experientially already get this. You see right through the religious model. You want nothing to do with it. That's why you may have walked away from all religion and all churches. Hopefully, you are beginning to see that the paradigm I'm suggesting is deeply spiritual, but not at all religious. It is not based on any religious creeds, rites or rituals. It's not based on holy places led by holy men. It is spiritual in that it is based on following Jesus as the guide of your inner spirit. It is trusting a good God to empower our efforts from the inside out to transform the world through love.

CHAPTER 9

THE ADVANTAGE OF FOLLOWING A WORLD-CHANGING LEADER

Business leaders who follow Jesus do have a significant advantage in transforming the world. For starters, you are led by the most effective leader who ever set foot on this planet! If you are willing to experiment with his real-time involvement in your life, you will find he is ready, willing, and able to coach and empower you for great success on a day-to-day basis. If you're up for the challenge, try going to the next level of following Jesus where you engage in a practical daily relationship. Invite him into your thoughts, plans, and actions on a real-time basis.

The Bible refers to this phenomenon as God within us. Instead of just following Jesus based on some external rules or based on something you've seen or heard, you proactively pursue a real-time relationship with him. You talk to him. You listen in your mind for thoughts and feelings that may be prompted by him. From him, you get insight, creativity, and solutions for world-changing opportunities.

Just try it! Take this next step as a follower of Jesus. Why not invite him to be an internal guide as well as external one? Follow him from the inside out. Invite him into the day-to-day thoughts, decisions, and actions of your business and your life. You're essentially saying, "I don't want to just click 'follow' and watch your newsfeed from a distance. I want you, your values, and your real-time leadership in my life to be my daily, personal internal guidance system."

When you do that, the Bible says God works in you to will and to do his good pleasure.[34] God, the most powerful, creative entrepreneur in the universe, will actually go to work in your heart and mind to help you do what he wants to do in this world. History proves that what God wants to do, he eventually gets done! He is the most effective and powerful leader EVER! He executes on what he plans, every time. So as business leaders who invite Jesus to be our internal guidance system, we can pursue our dreams with more confidence than anyone else in the world. Why? Because we are confident that our dreams are God's dreams for the world. If our dreams are God's dreams for the world, then why wouldn't he want to empower us and resource us to accomplish them?

If you want to know what God wants to accomplish in the world, just ask a fully devoted follower of Jesus what that person's dream is. As the poet and songwriter David put it, "Take delight in the Lord, and he will give you the desires of your heart."[35]

I grew up thinking this means God will give me everything I want. Life, though, proved I don't always get everything I want. And in hindsight, not everything I've wanted would have been good for me. This does not mean God is going to give you whatever you want. Rather, it means he will give you what to want. God will give you the same desires he has!

How does this happen? By delighting yourself in the Lord. What does that mean? Think of "Lord" as another way of referring to Jesus as your leader. What does it mean to delight myself in Jesus as my leader? Think of other things that you consider a delight: your favorite desert; a beautiful sunset, a kiss with your lover. When we have the mindset that our relationship with Jesus is a cherished delight like those things, it is then that we start to take on his desires in our hearts.

Sacred Versus Secular?

A lot of Christians wonder about the validity of their spirituality when they have a passion for what they consider a "secular" vision rather than a vision related to church or ministry. They wonder: "Is it 'holy' or 'godly' if I want to go build a successful business, have a big house or invent a game-changing technology?"

Here's the reality. If you've asked Jesus to be your internal guide, then he is working in you to give you the desires of your heart. Again, I'm not talking about him giving you the things you want but giving you your wants. He'll show you what to want! If Jesus informs your internal guidance system, you can trust that what you want is what he wants.

What could be more spiritual, what would be more "holy" than to pursue with all your might what God wants to happen!

You can live your life as a leader with a higher degree of confidence than the average person. When you have a dream or vision, you know it is from God! When I believe Jesus is God and that same Jesus is my internal guidance system, then I can pursue those dreams even if they sound "secular" (like building a great business, enjoying abundance or inventing a new product). I can know this is God's will on earth to happen through me.

But Is Jesus Really for My Business Success?

If you are a business leader reading this book, you may be wondering if Jesus is really relevant to your business or economic success. Does he even care about stuff? Most churches give the impression that the Jesus of Christianity is really all about "spiritual" stuff and not about economic stuff. I want you to know that despite what many teach, Jesus was not only pro-business, it was his first and last priority during his time on this earth.

Our first and last acts are often markers of priority and importance. We remember the first and last words of a person's life. I remember the first words of my children, and they will remember my last words. We remember the first shot and the last shot of wars. Races are won or lost based on how they start or how they end.

When the God of the universe executed his paramount plan to reveal himself to human society, you would think he was highly intentional about how he began and ended his mission on earth. Let's look at the first and last significant supernatural actions of Jesus' adult life.

The first miracle of Jesus, the first marvelous, supernatural action recorded took place at a wedding in Cana. The wine ran out before the wedding was over. The Bible says that Jesus' mother came to him about this problem. But before that happened, it is almost certain that somebody, whoever the wedding coordinator was, first talked to the bride or the bridegroom or the parents or relatives and asked them to solve the problem of no wine.

At my daughter's wedding we ended up having more guests than we thought and less food than we hoped. When I saw we were possibly getting low, I talked to my wife and she talked to her father and we put him on standby alert to be ready to go to the store to buy more food if we ran too low. Surely something like this must've happened behind the scenes in the story of the wedding in Cana. Surely someone must've gone to the wine supplier store to look for more wine, and the supplier must have been out of wine.

This was a personal and family crisis –but it was a business crisis too. Jesus steps in and demonstrates what God is like. He solves this multi-pronged crisis. His first miracle is a miracle of increasing production. His mother came to him. Now she may not have known that he could do a miracle, but she knew that he had about eighteen years of experience as CEO of a company and had demonstrated the ability to solve production challenges. So she said, "Listen to the boss. Just do what the boss tells you; he's good at solving production and supply chain challenges."

We think she was expecting Jesus to do a miracle, but there is no biblical basis for believing Jesus had ever done a miracle as we think of them. There is, however, good basis for thinking Jesus was CEO of the family construction business and that he had probably solved a lot of production problems over the years. He had probably faced impossible delivery dates that somehow, some way, he resolved. If Mary did expect a miracle, maybe that was the kind of miracle she expected. Maybe she remembered that time where they had a huge order and two brothers on the manufacturing line got sick, and the production equipment broke down. Yet somehow Jesus still met the deadline and met the customer's expectations.

What was the economic value of this first miracle of Jesus?

Jesus Is a Multiplier

Here is what Jesus created during that supply chain crisis at that wedding in Cana. The wine at Cana ran out,[36] leaving the hosts embarrassed. Jesus directed the servants to fill six big stone water jars with water.[37] The servants did that exactly, filling the stone jars to the brim.[38] Each jar held twenty to thirty gallons for a total of 120-180 gallons of water; that's about 680 liters. When the steward tasted the water, it was wine; not just any wine but the best wine.[39] For comparison's sake, the average bottle of wine, which pours about six, four ounce glasses per bottle, is 750 milliliters. So Jesus provided the party with almost 700 liters, which would be about 980 bottles of wine.

We know this wine was not cheap wine because the groom specifically comments that they saved the best for last. The average wine served at a wedding these days is about $30 a bottle. The "best wine", the quality that might be saved for the final bridal toast, would be at least $50-100 per bottle. So, in today's terms, Jesus produced what may have been $100 per bottle wine multiplied by 980 bottles. That would be $98,000 worth of wine in today's economy!

The first recorded public miracle of Jesus, the one that launched his campaign to show what God was like and bring God's rule and reign to this earth, was to manufacture almost $100,000 worth of quality product to solve a business and personal crisis– to meet a need–to provide tangible, practical value to people. His first miracle provided $50,000-100,000 of value.

Now let's look at the last miracle of Jesus.

It happened this way: Simon Peter, Thomas (also known as Didymus), Nathaniel from Cana in Galilee, the sons of Zebedee, and two other disciples were together.

"I'm going out to fish," Simon Peter told them, and they said,

116

"We'll go with you." So they went out and got into the boat, but that night they caught nothing.

Early in the morning, Jesus stood on the shore, but the disciples did not realize that it was Jesus.

He called out to them, "Friends, haven't you any fish?"

"No," they answered.

He said, "Throw your net on the right side of the boat and you will find some."

When they did, they were unable to haul the net in, it was so heavy because of the large number of fish. Then the disciple whom Jesus loved said to Peter, "It is the Lord!" As soon as Simon Peter heard him say, "It is the Lord," he wrapped his outer garment around himself (for he had taken it off) and jumped into the water. The other disciples followed in the boat, towing the net full of fish, for they were not far from shore, about a hundred yards. When they landed, they saw a fire of burning coals there with fish on it, and some bread.

Jesus said to them, "Bring some of the fish you have just caught."

So Simon Peter climbed back into the boat and dragged the net ashore. It was full of large fish, 153, but even with so many, the net was not torn.

Jesus said to them, "Come and have breakfast."

None of the disciples dared ask him, "Who are you?" They knew it was the Lord. Jesus came, took the bread and gave it to them, and did the same with the fish.

When they had finished eating, Jesus said to Simon Peter, "Simon, son of John, do you love me more than these?"

"Yes, Lord," he said, "you know that I love you."

Jesus said, "Feed my lambs."

Again Jesus said, "Simon, son of John, do you love me?"

He answered, "Yes, Lord, you know that I love you."

Jesus said, "Take care of my sheep."

The third time he said to him, "Simon, son of John, do you love me?"

Then Peter was hurt because Jesus had asked him the third time.

He said, "Lord, you know all things; you know that I love you."

Jesus said, "Feed my sheep."[40]

In reading this story through fresh eyes, it is interesting that the disciples go back to fishing, which was their business. Peter was a businessman. He owned a commercial fishing business. Jesus' miracle for him was to cause him to prosper! Jesus provided more fish than he needed. Peter probably had some vision of what it would be like if his production outstripped his capacity to contain the inventory. What they caught this night at Jesus' instruction exceeded Peter's grandest vision for productivity in his business. One of the first things that Jesus does when he appears to these disciples is to show them how to make their business prosper! He helps them get more business product. As a result of that business benefit, Peter falls down and worships Jesus. Peter doesn't fall down at Jesus' feet because Jesus gave him a sermon or a lecture on all the things he was doing wrong. Jesus could have pointed out things that Peter was doing wrong, but he didn't. He just gave Peter and his company more than he needed, more than he deserved, more than he could have accomplished on his own even on a good day in business.

Jesus can work for you and your business beyond your own reach and your own capabilities.

Why does the Bible specifically say there were 153 fish? They had to count them. That many fish is not a haul one would catch to feed a family. That was a net designed for catching fish to make money. That net was clearly a business tool. And Jesus helped them succeed at bringing in more revenue with the business tool they had.

118

Three days after Jesus died on the cross, the Bible reports that the first thing he did after he rose from the dead was not to preach a sermon. It was not even to heal the sick. It was not to gather people for a worship event, though he would have been very worthy of that. The first thing he did was to help someone make money! The first thing he did was to optimize the revenue of a business owner. His first priority was to coach a business owner on how to get the most from his capital (Peter's crew, boat, and net.)

Being out all night in a fishing business and catching nothing was like a manufacturing business having all of its equipment shut down so it couldn't make any new products to sell for a whole day. Disastrous! What did Jesus do? Did he tell them to roll out their scrolls and read holy writings more? Did he tell them to put their oars down, fold their hands, and pray? No. He coached them on how to improve their production machine.

Then, right after that, while he was standing around the fire cooking the fish to feed his disciples, he told these business owners: "Feed my sheep." They would have recalled that in prior teachings, Jesus had referred to sheep as an analogy of people who need care.

Through my old lenses I thought "feed" referred to providing some type of spiritual food. I asked my dad recently what that meant, and he said spiritual food. That is the answer one would expect from a good pastor like my dad because that is what pastors typically see themselves as having available to feed people. Yet, as Paul taught in his last sermon, "feeding" the sheep can be taken literally too. Paul told the church leaders to make enough money, as he did, to be able to provide for people's needs.

Jesus' last miracle was to help a business owner to create more food to feed more people than the business had ever done in one day. Then, while he was handing them food he had cooked himself to feed them, he said, "If you love me, then feed my sheep." Could it be that he was referring to real food? After all, they were there, stuffing their mouths with real food. There is nothing in this context that would indicate Jesus was referring to spiritual food.

Think of it. Jesus had just coached Peter, a business owner, on how to produce enough food to feed a few hundred people. Then he instructed Peter to feed people. Is this really as much of a spiritualization as we have made it out to be? Could it be that Jesus was literally saying, "Build your business; listen to my coaching on how to increase your business results so that you can literally feed hundreds of people every day"?

We have so hyper-spiritualized this that we've missed the obvious point of the story. The point of the interaction was all around the business that produced food. Jesus was feeding his disciples with real food from the business he guided to increased production. He told Peter the evidence of loving him from this point on would be to build the business trusting his guidance as Lord (leader) of his business for increased production so he could literally provide food to hundreds of people.

What was the economic value of the last miracle?

The disciples caught 153 large fish from the Sea of Galilee. The average size of a large fish in that body of water would probably produce about three pounds of fillets. Three times 153 is 459 lbs. If fish cost $5 per pound, that is $2,295. Jesus helped this business create about $2,300 to $2,500 in value. Not bad for one catch of fish!

Jesus' first and last miracles involved multiplication and production at high dollar values. Could it be that the message here is that building a business –production and multiplication of value in terms as real as food and drink–is what Jesus intended for you to do to bless the world? That he was saying, "I will show you where the money is hidden so you can use that money to feed hundreds of people. I will help you provide economic benefit to thousands of people. I will help you build a business that blesses the world?"

If Jesus was saying that to you right now, how would you answer?

Now, wait a minute, you might say. Didn't Jesus tell his disciples early on that they should leave their nets, come follow him, and he would make them "fishers of men"? Didn't he tell them to leave their fishing businesses and instead do ministry things like preaching and evangelizing to help mankind?

First of all, Jesus didn't tell them to leave their nets, even though that is often what is quoted. Jesus just said, "Come, follow me, and I will send you out to fish for people."[41] Then it says they left their nets.

The word for "left" literally means to drop or to let go of or go to a different place. When Jesus said to come and follow him, of course they had to let go of their nets and drop what they were working on right then. Of course, they had to leave their nets where they were. They couldn't wrap them up and put them in their pockets! There is nothing in this story that indicates they quit or shut down their fishing businesses.

If you look at the stories of what happened over the next three years, there is more evidence that they kept their fishing business and equipment. For example, there are times when Jesus needs a boat and his disciples seem to magically show up with a boat. Where did they come up with a boat? In that culture, there weren't pleasure boats setting around ready for someone to use whenever they wanted. If you had access to a boat it was because you owned a boat for commercial purposes. It seems more plausible that the disciples kept their fishing businesses with others doing the majority of the work during those three years they were on the road with Jesus so they still had access to their equipment and boats.

As I just described, when Jesus died, the disciples immediately show up in the next scene back with their fishing boats and nets. In that culture, those boats and nets wouldn't have likely been unused in storage for three years. Nor is it likely they could have just built or bought new boats and nets so quickly after Jesus died so they could immediately go back to fishing. If doing their fishing business was some kind of a bad thing, you'd think Jesus would have corrected them when their commercial fishing operation was one of the first sights he saw after his resurrection. But no, his first miracle after he rose from the dead was to help them increase the productivity and profit of their fishing business.

Could it be that the "religion" Jesus came to establish was not at all what we think of when we think of religion? Maybe it was not about rules, regulations, rites, and rituals. Could it be that it was about doing real good, providing real, tangible or economic benefit for the real needs of people? Could it be that is why James, who was the brother of Jesus, said, "Religion that God our Father accepts as pure and faultless is this: to look after orphans and widows in their distress."[42]

Take a minute right now to make sure you have dismantled any paradigms about Christ or Christianity that have prevented you from following Jesus. I want to challenge you to make a decision to simply follow Jesus, period. Drop all the religious baggage you have associated with Christianity or religion. Just follow Jesus. His way is the best, the most exciting, the most success-producing and society-changing way to live. Just let Jesus help you and your business meet the real needs of real people in this world. Let Jesus help you and your business rebuild this world to become more like the place of abundant resources and fulfilling relationships he intends it to be.

Since following Jesus is a progressive journey, take a minute to think about what that means to you now and what your next step might be to follow this world-changer more fully. If you are one that just clicked "Follow," that is great! Welcome to the journey! Or maybe you're someone who "liked that page" eight years ago and have been ignoring all his posts and all the newsfeed for some time. If that's you, I invite you to at least start paying attention and maybe even letting him impact your thoughts and actions. Or if you are a devoted follower of Jesus, I challenge you to take it up a notch and invite him into your every thought, plan, and action. See what happens as his dreams become your dreams and those dreams become realities that rebuild this world!

Wherever you are, take the next step in following Jesus, because that is your best step to gain the greatest advantage possible in your efforts to build a better world!

PART 3
FULFILLING YOUR ULTIMATE
MISSION TO THE WORLD

CHAPTER 10

REDEFINING MINISTRY

If you have decided to follow Jesus, it won't be long until someone asks if you participate in a ministry in some way. By "ministry" they mean: Are you serving some cause that Jesus cares about? Certainly, it is a logical assumption to think that if you follow Jesus, you will care about what he cares about and serve his purposes in some way. However, what most people asking this question really want to know is whether you are involved in some type of ministry in or through your local church. Since many churches pursue causes that Jesus cares about, ministry in and through the local church can be a very valid and valuable expression of following Jesus for many people.

It's not the only valid expression of ministry, though. For many business leaders, it's probably not the most valuable expression of ministry. In fact, the highest and best expression of ministry for many business leaders is to serve the purposes of Jesus in and through your business.

If you haven't hung around church much, this may seem like a logical conclusion to you. If you've hung around church or church people much, this may seem almost a bit heretical! Yet, at the same time, some of you have already been asking some penetrating questions in your own mind as I have. Like, why is it that we think something is only a legitimate ministry if it is part of what flows out of the place or programs of the church that meets on the weekends? Why is it that when one is focused on business success, church leaders think it is to the exclusion of ministry success or doing things for God? Why is it, as a business owner, I sometimes feel less spiritual because the "ministry" or "service" I provide is not a part of the ministry of a local church?

What if it was, though? What if we embraced the service business leaders provide as a part of the service/ministry the conventional church provides to its community? What if the definition of ministry we have come to know in churches is too small to encompass what Jesus originally had in mind as his primary method to serve his cause and his people?

I'd like to challenge you to rebuild your understanding of business and ministry. Let me start by sharing a bit of my journey on this topic in the hope that you may find yourself somewhere in my story and join me in the discovery of what Jesus really intends for business.

My Business Ministry Story

I grew up as a preacher's kid and felt the "call to ministry" at a very early age. It seemed that the zenith of spirituality, the highest expression of commitment to the Jesus I had come to know and love, was to devote my life to full-time ministry as a pastor or missionary. This seemed like the top rung of the ladder of the Christian life. I remember sitting in on many altar calls with emotional appeals to serve Jesus by "going into ministry."

Ministry in this context meant ministry in and through the conventional church. Ultimately, if you could possibly attain the highest expression of commitment to ministry, it would mean being in a full-time ministry paid by the church.

There is nothing inherently wrong about this. It is totally logical, as I reflect on it. Most of the people giving those talks about commitment to the cause of Christ were in full-time ministry in and through the conventional church or as a missionary somewhere. They had most likely received "the call to ministry" in some similar emotional altar call themselves. Therefore, it was only logical they would try to replicate for others the experience that had become so central to their journey.

Because of these altar calls and my commitment to the cause of Christ, I took theology in college and became a youth pastor even as I was still working on my theology degree. I got married to my amazing childhood sweetheart and "took a call" to be the pastor of a small congregation in Alaska, eighteen miles from the border of Siberia. It was among the Yupik Eskimos.

Here the majority of the people I was around were not only unchurched, but they were still deeply entrenched in shamanism and the worship of nature. It was during this season that I realized I didn't even know how to relate to someone who was not a Christian.

I had never been around many of those people "in the world." It was like being a fish out of water. Overall, I was probably not very effective in that role, but we did see a handful of people become followers of Jesus. Some experienced such a radical life change that it could only be explained by God's supernatural forgiveness and empowerment.

That experience of seeing people who were far from God come to a personal relationship with Jesus that transformed their lives —that ruined me for life! I was no longer content to be a pastor just to "shepherd the flock." I was no longer content to pastor the people and programs in a church full of the already convinced. I concluded that somehow, some way, I needed to learn to connect with people who were far from God.

That is when God led me into business.

My first interactions in the early years of business were minimally productive because I still had such prejudices about non-Christian "people of the world." It's hard to love people in the world unless you love the world like Jesus loved it. It took me a few years to learn to relate to non-church people. It took me even longer to begin to understand the playbook by which they ran their lives so I could even get on the playing field with them enough to connect and serve them well. Through this, I discovered that I loved the process of building leaders and teams and developing businesses that added value to people's lives.

I Became an "Apostate"–a Black Sheep

I remember vividly when I told my parents that I was going to be a business owner rather than a pastor. I remember the disappointment in their voices. They had genuine concerns about me leaving my "calling." There were tears of concern and prayers from my mom, who thought I was losing my way. I was just as committed to God and reaching people for God as I always had been, mind you. Maybe I was even more committed! Yet because I was not continuing on the path as a full-time conventional church pastor, I was labeled as falling away from my high calling.

I remember getting a call from the head of the theology school I attended. He told me he had had such high hopes for me, and that I had so much potential for God. He was concerned I was throwing that all away and pursuing the world.

He said something like, "Ministry is God's plan A for your

life, and you will never be fully satisfied or effective for God following plan B."

Where do we get this idea that spending forty to fifty hours a week earning a living or building a business to bless people is God's plan B for our lives? My dearly loved and respected theology professor, my mentor, was telling me that I was disobeying God and living in God's plan B.

I experienced well-intentioned criticisms from friends and peers who were with me in theology school. Accusations were made that I had "given up on my call" (i.e., I had turned my back on the ministry and Jesus). People said that I loved money more than Jesus because I decided not to stay in the ministry.

Yet even then, I felt intuitively I was connecting with and serving people in unique and perhaps more effective ways than if I had continued being employed by a church. These were people who would never walk through the doors of a church, but I was connecting them with the God who loved them. Nevertheless, it didn't count as "ministry" because it wasn't being done in or through the church.

This is not an uncommon thought process in the church world. This way of thinking has created tremendous guilt and diminished the value of just shy of 100% of the Christ followers out there—all but those who are paid for doing ministry in the conventional church! It makes them feel like spiritual under-achievers or even failures. It makes them feel like second class citizens in God's eyes because they are not committed enough to be in full-time ministry.

Now don't get me wrong. I'm not in any way diminishing the value or importance of the local church. I have spent most of my life believing and teaching that the local church is the hope of the world. It's just that until recent years, when I said that, I defined the local church as the gathering and the programs of local congregations. I believed, like most good, church-going Christians, that true ministry only happened in and through the local church. It never entered my mind that what happened in business during the week could be ministry, let alone an expression of the local church.

I grew up as PK (pastor's kid). I have given my heart and soul to building conventional churches. In 1997 I launched a company called Ministry Advantage which has now spent more than twenty years coaching pastors to be more effective in building the people and programs of the local church. Never once in all that time did it occur to me that church could be just as much about what happened when people went to work as it was during a worship event or during an outreach event.

I share this bit of my story because I want you to know I empathize with those who have not yet put on the new paradigm about ministry that I am advocating in this book. If you are someone like that, please know that I understand where you are coming from. I want to encourage you to at least be open to expanding your concept of ministry and church. What if there was more to it than what you have seen or experienced?

The way things have been has done much good. So much of what has happened and is happening in and through conventional churches is good. God only knows where many people and many communities would be without the redemptive power of the local church pushing back the tide of evil and giving people regular opportunities for meaningful worship, spiritual teaching, and Christian community. Yet there is more.

There is more to ministry than what happens in and through the conventional church. What God's people do when they are working in business can be considered ministry just as much as leading worship on Sunday, leading Sunday school class, serving in children's ministry on Sunday or preaching a sermon. I'm not saying those conventional church activities are bad. There is so very much good in them! It's just that there's so much more world-changing power when we embrace God's plan for using business as a platform for ministry.

I didn't always think business could be a valuable ministry. Over the years I have gained new insights on God's view of the potential of business to serve his purposes. I started out thinking that business was a necessary evil. I advanced to thinking of business as a means to reach people who are far from God. I went on to learn how to do business God's way and then on to experiencing business as worship. Now I experience business as my highest expression of ministry to serve God's purposes in this world.

I'll unpack each of these stages in a bit more detail in the next chapter to help you identify where you are in your journey and what your next step might be in redefining your business as ministry.

CHAPTER 11

SCORING FOR WORLD-CHANGING WINS

I grew up in a church culture that put business in the same category as "the world," which in religious terms is in opposition to God. It was us against the world. Business was essentially a necessary evil to survive in the world. I believed that a calling of the church was to go into the evil world–as a stranger–for short stints, but not to be a part of the world. The world was not the playing field. The church was the real playing field and the only place I could really score wins for God.

What that meant to me was that it would be okay to spend time in the business world to feed my family and to create tithes and offerings for the church, but the goal was to get back to the safety and security of the church as much as possible and as often as possible. "Come out of her, my people" was the motto I was raised with.[43] "Come out from Babylon" (the world's system) and get into the secure fortress of the church. As a child, I believed the playing field that mattered was the church, and the score that counted was the wins the church had at securing and retaining people in its safety zone. Over my lifetime, my understanding of the role business can play in scoring world-changing wins for God has morphed through several phases.

Business as a Tool of Outreach

In the early '80s when I was just hitting my twenties and starting my first businesses, I began to see the marketplace not as an evil world to be avoided but as an opportunity. From the religious viewpoint I had at that time, business became an opportunity to evangelize–to convert people to Christianity and get them out of the world and into the safety of the church. I remember how excited I was when I realized business could help me score wins for the church by being a vehicle for what churches often call outreach! Groups like the Christian Business Men's Committee (CBMC) helped me understand this concept. CBMC is active in over seventy countries with over fifty thousand members. It continues to help businessmen see their business as a tool for evangelism. It brought a gratifying new dimension to my entrepreneurial endeavors as I began to see the businesses I led as opportunities to lead people to follow Jesus.

Business by the Book

The next phase in my journey of understanding how God could help me score some world-changing wins was when I began to believe that godly, biblical principles should be the basis for how I do business. There were many books written on this in the '80s. Larry Burkett's Business by The Book influenced me a lot regarding the power and value of doing business based on God's principles. I continue to believe the principles in the Bible are the basis for most business philosophy and strategies that produce sustainable success. Yet I still largely disconnected my personal spiritual life and my worship of God from what I did every day in business. What I did in business was business. What I did in church, or while reading my Bible or praying, was spiritual or worship.

Business as Worship

It wasn't until I was in my thirties that I began to realize that what I do in business could be a win in my worship of God. There were many books on this topic written in the '90s. I remember light bulbs coming on when I first learned the Hebrew word for work is the same as the Hebrew word for worship–avodah. This verb conveys the idea that worshiping God and serving God are one and the same.

For a guy who grew up in a conventional church culture where worship primarily meant what happened during a church worship service, or what happened while singing songs about God, this concept rocked my world! It overwhelmed me that the work I did in business could actually be a form of worship! Who would've thought it! But at that point I still believed, the only legitimate service to God–the only real ministry that counted– was what I did in and through the church.

Business as Ministry

If you have the paradigm that worship and ministry are primarily something that happen in and through the conventional church, let me expand your thinking on this a bit more. The Greek word usually translated as ministry, diakonia, is where churches get the word "deacon." This same Greek word is translated into our English Bibles about half the time as "ministry" and about half the time as "service." So, according to the Bible, whenever we are serving someone, we are in ministry. Any time we serve someone in business, we score a win in ministry. When you are serving food at your restaurant, you are ministering to the customers. When you are serving someone by fixing a car at your auto repair shop, you are ministering to your customers. When you are serving your clients, you are ministering to them.

To associate "ministry" only with matters related to religion or the conventional church is inaccurate. A minister is literally a person who serves someone. Since the basis for all effective business is serving the needs of people well, good business leaders are good ministers. They minister to the needs of people well. We are accomplishing a God-directed, "holy calling" when we meet the needs of humanity through our businesses. By doing this we serve (or minister to) God and serve (or minister to) those who receive our services on this earth.

If you are a business leader, I'm asking you to consider embracing the fact that your work is a primary means of ministry. That's why the Bible says, "Whatever you do, work at it with all your heart, as working for the Lord, not for human masters."[44]

The Tale of Two Playbooks

Over the years, I've had a lot of opportunities to experiment with using my business as a basis for helping people find a pathway to God and follow Jesus. For a long time we had more than thirty business associates meeting weekly in our home to study the Bible and learn about Jesus. As they decided to follow Jesus, I told them to find a church. The challenge was, though, that they didn't relate to what happened in conventional churches. For them, it was like walking into a foreign culture where a foreign language was spoken.

It was like trying to understand how to keep score your first time on a rugby field when all you knew was the playbook of football. The playbook the conventional church played by was so different than what they were used to playing by in the business world. For example, the playbook of the business world was that he who serves the most people in the world through business throughout the week wins. The playbook in the church seemed to be about he who serves the most people for an hour or two on Sunday or in the church programs wins.

The playbook of the church didn't say much about how to get wins on the scoreboard of life through business. The playbook of the church was focused on how to get wins on the scoreboard of life based on doing the things that the church saw as important. For most conventional churches, the prevailing paradigm is that ministry is done in and through the local church, and what is done out in business is "just business," not ministry.

This is not the result of ill-intentions by people in the conventional church. This paradigm is established by the playbook and strategy of the conventional church. It's their system for ministry. Business leaders who participate in church understand that conventional church playbook but they also understand the playbook of business. Most church leaders, on the other hand, only understand one playbook and one scoreboard system–that of the church.

Most pastors don't understand the playbook that many of their members operate by throughout the week because they have never experienced it. Many pastors tend to evaluate the lives and spiritual success of their church members all seven days a week based on the church's playbook and scorecard.

I understand the playbook of the conventional church, and I've played by it and kept score by it for years. There's a lot of good in it. I have been a full-time and part-time pastor. I have also been a business leader on the core volunteer leadership team of conventional churches. In all these roles, I tended to evaluate my own success in life based on the playbook and scorecard of the church. I played to the strategy of the ministry of the conventional church. What showed up on my scorecard? Things like how much I was volunteering in various programs of the church showed up, or how many volunteers I was recruiting into the programs of the church. How well I was leading volunteers to serve in the programs of the church showed up; how many people were in my small group, and how well I was discipling them all counted. I got points for how much time I spent serving as a greeter or usher or teaching in children's ministry. These are the things that showed up on my spiritual score card. Nothing I did in business ever was recorded on my spiritual scorecard.

Pastors come by this mindset honestly. Pastors didn't take a class in seminary on the role of business in the ministry of the church. Most pastors have not experienced the playbook and scorecard of the business world. As a rule of thumb, we tend to miss the importance of or overlook what we don't experience.

For example, before I played in an orchestra, I thought the symphony was boring. After playing in an orchestra and working hard to understand and play by the rules of a symphony orchestra, I developed a deep appreciation for listening to symphony music. I valued things I would have never even heard before. Those who have been waiters and waitresses in the past often tip the best, because they know how hard it is to play by the playbook of the restaurant business and score a win on customer expectations.

It all depends on the playbook you know and are used to. That's how you tend to keep score.

I know many business leaders regularly oversee employee teams larger than the largest volunteer team at their church. I know business leaders who regularly manage budgets larger than their entire church budget. Yet when these talented and dedicated leaders show up at church, they often feel either under-appreciated or under-deployed. They may even feel unqualified to serve "in ministry" in any significant way. They doubt their own calling and effectiveness. One reason for this is that the playbook and scorecard the church uses doesn't allow for business leaders to have many wins. It leaves the business leader asking, "What of all that I do can possibly be counted as ministry?"

Of course, if the business leader gives enough money, then at least he or she gets that one tick on their church scorecard! We need to celebrate the kingdom wins on both scoreboards, in both playbooks. Neither is wrong. The playbook for football is different than the playbook for baseball. It doesn't mean either one is wrong.

Business is ministry. The reason it is not perceived as ministry is because those who lead church ministry, mainly pastors, have a different playbook, a different scorecard, and a different agenda.

I'm not asking pastors to change their playbook but to recognize and appreciate the playbook of business leaders and to celebrate their wins at doing God's purposes in the marketplace on their scoreboard as part of the ministry of the church.

Pastors need to say to their business leaders: "Your greatest impact is probably not changing diapers in the church nursery. Your greatest ministry impact is investing your time and resources into your business, which is a vital part of the ministry of the church in this city!"

I am simply asking pastors to recognize the value of the other playbook. Pastors don't have to stop what they are doing, but we need to add an addendum to the conventional church's playbook that is about the ministry of the church through business.

It Takes Everyone All the Time to Win

The apostle Paul was the primary entrepreneur of church startups in the early days of the church. He wrote a letter to the church he founded in the city of Ephesus to give them his thoughts on the playbook for church leaders. I have taught on the core of his instruction to church leaders found in Ephesians 4 to thousands of pastors around the world. This syllabus for church leaders makes it clear that the work of apostles, prophets, evangelists, pastors, and teachers is "to equip the saints for the work of ministry."[45]

I am ashamed to admit that for twenty years of my teaching on this topic, I applied everything to doing the work of the ministry in and through the conventional church. I saw the "apostles, prophets, evangelists, pastors, and teachers" as all conventional church leadership roles. Now I have come to see that those leadership roles existed in the marketplace in Bible times, and they exist in the marketplace today.

For years I saw "the work of the ministry" that all the "saintly" people were doing as ministry in and through the programs of the conventional church. The reality is, though, that most of those saints aren't full-time staff in the church and therefore most of their time is not invested in ministry in the conventional church. Most of their time is in the marketplace.

Paul makes it clear that the work of the ministry is to be done by 100% of the followers of Jesus, not just by church leaders, and not just one day a week or in one or two church ministry programs a week. Ministry is not just discipling those in a church-sponsored small group. What we do in business the rest of the week is real ministry! In fact, Paul doesn't even say pastors should do ministry! It is the saints (the majority of whom aren't employed by the church and don't spend most of their time at church) who do the ministry.

This was the paradigm of the early church. But over time there developed a marked distinction between "the clergy" and "the laity"–between the pastors who did the ministry and the people who received the ministry. Most pastors would say they no longer believe that paradigm. Most would preach and teach about the ministry of all members. Yet even those churches that teach this don't refer to the average Joe and Jackie in the church as a minister. It's the staff of the church who are the ministers. Even churches that are significant proponents of the ministry of all members are ultimately talking about the service that the members provide in and through the programs of the local church. They are not referring to the ministry the members have in and through their local businesses.

Let me emphasize again: what I am saying here is not intended in any way to diminish the high calling or value of the dedicated pastors and staff of local churches. They are hugely important ministers of God. Yet so are those who minister through business.

It drives me crazy when I hear people in a church service on the weekend say, "I am just a layman" or "I'm not a minister." Biblical and historical evidence demonstrates that working in business is a benefit to building God's kingdom. It is not a detriment. "Pulpit ministers" are vital and so are "business ministers." If you are a follower of Jesus, both are equally important missions; they are simply in different jurisdictions. Both roles are just as "spiritual." The skills required and the type of influence exerted for God's kingdom may be different, but the same mission applies. There can and should be strong synergy between the two.

After all, God's playbook supersedes them all, and his end game is pretty big; pretty all-inclusive. It's basically world domination, or world dominion. The game plan Jesus laid out was to "go and make disciples of all nations."[46] We will only score this world changing win when all followers of Jesus embrace their role as ministers on "Team God" all the time, in everyday life–the majority of which takes place in the marketplace.

CHAPTER 12

MARKETPLACE AS A MISSION FIELD

Recently I was in Minneapolis finishing up a couple of days packed with business meetings. In the morning I had coffee with Mary, who is the CEO of the regional chapter of an organization called Impact Hub. Impact Hub supports entrepreneurs who want to use their business as a platform to improve society. She is leading several initiatives to help businesses collaborate in a way that addresses some specific societal problems in the Elliot Park neighborhood where we are building a hotel right now.

This was the first time I had met Mary. It didn't take long to realize that this young lady was passionate and highly effective at fostering businesses that build a better world. She had helped to build a company called Peace Coffee, which became one of the foremost coffee companies to foster the "fair trade" movement in that industry. She has been on leadership teams of several other social entrepreneur and impact investing organizations.

We were brainstorming about how the new hotel we are building could support social entrepreneurism in this city and how to collaborate in the creation of a business incubator for social entrepreneurs in a space adjacent to our hotel that could be shared by our business guests.

We were doing the typical first meeting self-introductions. As I was telling my story to Mary, I got to the point where I mentioned our non-profit leadership coaching organization for leaders of non-profits and churches. Just to understand her context on church, I asked her what her experience was with church. She looked down and quickly said, "Honestly, not very good!" She went on to describe to me how she was raised attending church but left it quite a while ago. It became clear that although Mary still believed in God, she had felt condemned and estranged by the church and church people, apparently for certain lifestyle choices that the church didn't agree with. I listened and then briefly shared with Mary the exciting realization I'd had: that when God decided to implement his ultimate strategy for rebuilding human society, he came as a business leader. He recruited other business leaders to create a non-religious movement to do exactly what she was doing—leverage marketplace influence to eliminate poverty and to build better relationships and stronger community cultures. The surprised look on her face indicated that she clearly had never thought of that before.

I looked her straight in the eye and said, "Mary, I want you to know that you are actually doing more to serve people and build God's values into this community than most churches and many pastors are doing in this city." She looked away for a minute as her eyes started to water up.

Choking back tears, she said, "You'll never know how much that means to me."

At that moment, perhaps for the first time in a long time,

Mary not only felt that maybe God loved her but that maybe God was even very pleased with the cause, the ministry, to which she was devoting her life. Mary went on to tell me that she knew some churches were doing some things to help society, but she just couldn't understand why most of the churches seemed to just talk about improving society. The business leaders she works with, she told me, were in the thick of things. They were rolling up their sleeves every day and working hard in society to make it better in specific, tangible ways.

Could it be that the Marys of the world, who haven't set foot in the doorway of a church building for years, but who are devoting their lives to making this world a better place through business are more effective missionaries for God than many who go into a church building but leave their good intentions to change the world at the door of the church?

How many times have we heard people complain that most people's Christianity goes out the window as soon as they are fighting each other to get out of the parking lot after the service? How many people say they wish the Christmas spirit could be around each and every day instead of for a couple of weeks and one special day per year? It's the mission of permeating society with God's good values that everyone longs for and that Jesus taught about.

As I was catching my Uber ride from that meeting to the next, I wondered at the irony that my new friend Mary was doing more ministry and had a clearer mission than thousands of people who faithfully show up at a church building every Sunday in her city. An even greater irony is that most pastors don't even consider such work to be a valid ministry or mission for God. But what if what Mary was doing in business was impacting the mission field of city transformation as much or more than the missionaries who are paid by local churches to bring transformation to a city in a foreign mission field? What if her form of transformational commerce actually had more impact on rebuilding the world for God?

Bringing the Marketplace into the Embrace of the Church

What if the conventional church pastors embraced the possibility that when a business provides valuable service to their community, it could be a valuable missionary activity–maybe even an expression of the mission of the church? To take it a step further, what if pastors saw it as their job to train business leaders to be more effective in their mission to transform society in and through their businesses? What if pastors saw the business leaders who attend their church as an extension of their church missions team? What if pastors saw businesses represented in their churches as key expressions of their evangelism and discipleship ministry? What if pastors recognized that a business owner's ministry "preaches" every day to probably around 90% non-church goers, most of whom never connect with the conventional church?

Imagine what it would be like if you were a part of a conventional church where your pastor took time to really connect with you as a business leader and sought to understand your playbook. What if they understood how your scoreboard works? What if a pastor could help you see how you could get wins for God on your scoreboard in business? What if you felt empowered to be a minister in the marketplace? What if they spoke up for you, built you up, equipped you, and encouraged you in your business mission? Imagine what it would be like if your pastor was meeting regularly with you saying, "Let me help you pastor your part of this city that you serve through your business. What can I do to help your mission to bring God's purposes into your world? What can I do to help you minister more effectively to the people God has entrusted to you to pastor? How can I help you turn the platform of influence God has given you into something that goes beyond business to rebuild our world? If you have any people in your company who need a spiritual counselor, let me know. I'll be a chaplain for your business. And I'll help you raise up chaplains from within your business as it grows. I'll commit to pray for you and your business that you will have creative insights and all the resources you need to continually serve more people with better and better products and services. I will pray that every customer, client, and supplier will be better off because of their interaction with your business. And I will commit to develop a team of people who will pray for you and your business, just like I have for the missionaries in Africa that we support. Any time you have a business challenge or opportunity that you don't know how to deal with, you can call your personal prayer team and have several prayer warriors call on the supernatural resources of God to come to your aid." Imagine the potential!

There have been hundreds of times over the years where I have had what seemed like insurmountable business challenges, and I have reached out to a close group of faith-filled, praying people for support. In these instances, I have seen God come through with what can only be considered supernatural interventions and solutions! I recount a couple stories like this in a later chapter, but these days I have specific people on my business team that I know are powerful prayer people. I've given one of my team members, Kellee, who is Director of Investor Relations, the unwritten title of Director of Prayer Power! It seems that every time I reach out to her and ask for prayer related to a specific need, she comes through and God comes through! Business challenges are resolved and new pathways open up to make significant new progress on business opportunities that benefit a lot of people.

What if every conventional church had Directors of Prayer Power to support business leaders in their desires to do good in this world through their business endeavors? What if pastors of conventional churches trained up people to provide that type of support?

Imagine for a minute what it might look like if conventional church pastors really believed that what business leaders do in their business is a vital part of the mission of the church. How would this impact church programming, teaching, and financial strategy? What would be celebrated when the church gathers on Sundays? Instead of only celebrating things like the number of kids who attended Vacation Bible School, the church would also celebrate the new jobs a business created that provided food, education, and other benefits for ten new families in their community. What would be taught when the church gathers? Maybe instead of just teaching good doctrine, there would be more practical teaching on how to apply biblical principles to succeed in business. What would the next new hire be on the conventional church payroll? If the church budget reflected the belief that business leaders could be leading some of the highest impact missional endeavors of their church, the next new hire might not be another worship pastor or children's pastor. It might be a chaplain whose entire focus was to help the business leader take care of the people in their business—or to put it in church terms, to shepherd the flock under their care! Or it might be a prayer intercessor team lead whose entire focus was to rally supernatural power to come to the aid of businesses represented in their church to accomplish impossible goals and build society God's way.

What I am talking about here is not starting another mission program of the church and calling it "marketplace ministry" or something. This cannot be another program of the church. This

IS the church! This is not about creating a marketplace ministry. It is about helping marketplace leaders understand that they are the ministry of the church. It is about helping business leaders discover their spiritual gifts and passions and coaching them to use those as a vital expression of the mission of the church in their business world.

Your Mission Is More than Your Money

Let me more fully address another common paradigm that fosters this under-utilization of the value of the business leader to the mission of the church. Have you ever had the feeling that the primary value church leaders hope to get from you as a business leader is the money you donate to help fund the ministries of the church? Or that bigger donations are the primary reason your pastor wants your business to succeed? Granted, many church ministries provide valuable service to the community, and granted, these ministries do require money to function. Granted also is that business is the ONLY way this money is actually generated. So it is logical that one valuable benefit your business can provide is creating resources to fund ministries of churches and other non-profits. This is a good value of business to the local church, but it is not the best value. As is often the case, we can focus so much on the good that we miss out on the best. The highest and best value of your business to the church is what happens when you use your business as a platform for God's mission to this world–when you view your business not just as a means to fund ministry but that what happens in your business IS the ministry of the church.

Not long ago, I had lunch with two pastors of large churches who were also business owners. I was so excited to spend some time with these rare leaders who understood the playbook of the church and the playbook of business. One of these pastors told me it was his goal to make one thousand Christian millionaires in his lifetime. Pumped about such an audacious goal, I asked what his reason was for wanting this. He said, "Can you imagine what kind of ministry a church could do with the tithe (10% of income) from even ten millionaires in their church?"

Just to make sure I understood his primary purpose, I clarified: "So you see the primary benefit a Christian millionaire has to offer the church is the funding of the ministry of the church?" The pastor looked at me with that "no duh" facial expression and said "Absolutely!" Then I asked him to consider something: could it be that although the donations from a millionaire might be a helpful outcome to the church, was there a chance that this might not be the primary benefit to the church or to the mission of God for this world? That perhaps the primary benefit is in the creation of a powerful platform of influence in that business leader's life that will enable him or her to build God's purposes into this world through the ministry of business?

I started to share some of the concepts of this chapter and challenged this pastor to think of the business owners he was helping to become millionaires as pastors of a campus of his church. That resulted in a big debate about whether it could be possible to view these businesses as viable ministries. Both pastors at the lunch table adamantly argued they could not consider the businesses of the business owners in their church as a ministry of the church. They certainly couldn't call those business owners ministers or pastors or missionaries. They couldn't fathom calling their own businesses a campus of their church.

Their primary reason? Business owners don't have Sunday services and therefore couldn't be a campus of their church.

I went home after that lunch with a huge, holy discontent that somehow, we have a paradigm that excludes the majority of people who serve God faithfully in the marketplace from believing their business is part of the mission of God's church in their city! The lie of this paradigm is that when they are building their business, they cannot be building their church or contributing anything to the success of the mission of their local church except for the money they give and maybe the small fraction of time they are able to spend serving in the programs of the conventional church.

Business Leaders as Missionaries

In order for conventional churches to maximize their redemptive potential in society, they must equip and support business leaders in ministry as much as they train and equip and support long-term missionaries. Just imagine what would happen if business leaders were viewed by pastors with as much or more honor and missional potential as a missionary or anyone else who is paid to do church ministry! If every church could look at their business leaders with the same kind of society-building potential, the impact would be exponential.

Why do churches overlook this world-changing resource?

I do wish all pastors would look at business leaders the way they view the missionary their church supports. A missionary has typically gone through specialized training. He or she probably studied the culture where they are going on mission, even studied a foreign language so they can communicate more effectively. They'll be involved in a place where there are few or maybe no followers of Jesus. The culture could be hostile to the message about Jesus and maybe even hostile toward them. Depending on where they are going, they could be discriminated against or even persecuted because they are followers of Jesus. Because of all that, the church supports and celebrates them. The church sends them out into the mission field with blessing as an extension of the mission of the church. They regularly pray for their success. They eagerly await updates on their progress in establishing God's purposes in the mission field. Why, they even send volunteers on short-term mission trips to support their efforts and bring back reports to the rest of the church about the good work that God is doing through the missionaries.

What if every church and every pastor could look at their business leaders with this same kind of honor and respect and say, "I am so glad God has called you into the mission field, where 90% of the people you deal with everyday are non-churchgoers. We bless you and send you out each week as an extension of the mission of this church. We commit ourselves to regularly pray for your success and to support the ministry of your business in any way we can. I know you have even a greater, more powerful opportunity to minister to and attract people to follow Jesus than I do as the vocational minister/pastor here. I have an opportunity to preach to 100% church-goers because the only people that will hear my voice are church-goers. I have the opportunity to teach them an hour or two a week, but you have 80-90% non-church-goers that you 'preach to' through your influence, forty hours a week. So, Mr. or Ms. Business Leader, I am going to start calling you a missionary pastor! You've got a congregation; your congregation is your employees, their spouses, their families, all of your customers, your vendors, and your suppliers."

Imagine what would happen if pulpit ministers equipped, resourced, honored, and celebrated business ministers like that – as missionaries sponsored by their church? Imagine what it would look like if church was a place where pulpit ministers celebrated the kingdom wins that business ministers accomplished during that week. It could be as simple as a pastor having a three-minute video that celebrated the work that a business owner in the church did that week in their community, or it could be as substantial as volunteers from the church going on short-term mission trips to help support the things the business is doing to bless society.

I work with one business in Minnesota that has given away significant amounts of its profits for fifteen years to feed the hungry. This business has two hundred employees but it has two thousand volunteers who serve in the business at various times, helping with community service events and even business events. This business owner told me that last summer there was a city-wide event at the fairgrounds, and the city called her and asked if they could employ her volunteers to serve at the event because her volunteers were better, more effective, more engaged, and more happy than other vendors they could hire.

She looked at me with a chuckle and said, "Can you believe that my company earned $17,000 from the city to pay my volunteers for serving at an event that helped our community, and then I was able to donate that $17,000 to feed the hungry in our community?!"

These two thousand volunteers are not from a specific church but are from the community at large. But what if—what if there were volunteers from the church that offered to show up and support "business missionaries" in their cause of rebuilding society for God? If the business was viewed as a ministry of the church and the business leader as a missionary, why wouldn't they?

Why is it that the most exalted role model of spirituality and ministry is the person behind the pulpit in the church once a week, when in reality, what you are doing in business can be the most powerful pulpit to model eternal values and serve/minister to people?

A Stocked Pond!

Pulpit pastors have a pond that fish swim into for an hour or two a week. Most fish who don't follow Jesus don't swim into this pond at all! As a business leader, you have some of the greatest bait of all time to get fish who don't follow Jesus into your pond—paychecks, benefits, meaningful work, and relationships. There are people who will drive an hour each way every day to get to your pond. And many of them can't wait to show up every day, not just because of the paycheck but because you have given your employees a place to learn and grow and contribute to a valuable cause that benefits society.

If you were a pulpit minister you'd have to at least ask yourself the question whether there is anyone who has a bigger pond, and a stocked one at that, than the business owner. Is there anyone you could invest in who has the potential of having a greater impact on your community than the "business missionary" who attends your church?

Oh, if only pulpit pastors would say to business leaders, "I want to teach you everything I know about building people and helping people follow Jesus. And I want to personally help you build your connection with the God of all wisdom and success! You are the missionary we are sending out every week! Let our volunteers come over and serve you in your business. Let our conventional church support what your business is doing as an extension of the church in our city!"

Pastor, how would you feel if your church was responsible for giving away thousands of Bibles a year in dozens of countries around the world? How would you feel if your church were able to place over a billion Bibles in public places where everyday people would pick them up and read them in countries where it is illegal to do church? That's what Bill Marriott and a group of businessmen called the Gideons have managed to do. Bill Marriott is simply a business leader who decided to use his business as a platform for expanding the knowledge of God. One way that he does that is to place the Book of Mormon and Gideon Bibles in every hotel room around the world. The Gideons are a group of businessmen who decided to use their business resources and platforms to place Bibles in public places. They started in 1908 when two Christian businessmen thought it would be wise to encourage commercially traveling business people to spread the Word through having them place Bibles in hotel rooms.

I remember the first time I went to China at a time when it was illegal to do church the way we do it in America. I checked in to a Marriott Renaissance hotel in Beijing and was shocked to find a Gideon Bible in the drawer of my hotel. Bill Marriott has a business that blesses thousands of people in China with great service and by giving them exposure to God's principles. The Chinese government looks away when he puts what could be considered "church missionary propaganda" in his business because his business is adding so much value to their country. They essentially say, "If your spirituality comes with excellent business that adds value to our society, then we will take both."

What if the next Bill Marriott was in your church, and you didn't even recognize that powerful force for expanding God's principles and presence in this world? What if the next Gideon-like business leader, with vision and capability to expand God's plans to rebuild society, was sitting in your church and you only recognized that person as having the missional capacity to simply donate money or serve as an usher?

There is a pastor of a church in Oklahoma City who recognized the power of business leaders to expand the church. The Green family are wealthy business owners who sat in Life Church and partnered with one of the Life Church pastors to start the Bible App, YouVersion, which has now passed a quarter of a billion downloads. Mart Green operates Hobby Lobby. He helps run the family chain stores and heads up his own business, Mardel. Mart has a passion for getting the Bible translated into every language. He started "Every Tribe and Language," which is giving free access to the Bible to hundreds of thousands of people around the world.

Why is This Important for Your Business Success?

You may not be at a place in your business or personal journey where you care too much about whether your business is considered a ministry or missional extension of the church. That's okay. I still want you to understand how embracing these concepts can add a lot of value to you and your business.

When I was a pastor, I rarely questioned that God was all for what I was doing. I was confident that God wanted me to be successful in my work and mission. Why wouldn't he? It was HIS church I was building. There was plenty of challenge and opposition in pulpit ministry, but through it all, I never questioned whether God was involved and committed to the success of my endeavors. Why wouldn't God be committed to my success? Why wouldn't he be involved in everything I did? I was doing his work. I was doing his ministry. I was on his mission.

What if business leaders had the same confidence that God was all in for their business success—that, as a business leader, I have the same right to the same supernatural assistance as does the pastor of a conventional church. God cares about the success of my business ministry just as much as God cares about the success of a pulpit minister! God cares about the missional effect my business has in creating value in this world as much as he cares about the missional effect of the church!

Embrace this reality. If you are in business, then your work is worship, and your results are the redemption of society. You are a minister with a world changing mission, and God cares about your success at least as much as he cares about the ministers in your local church.

If you find this a little awe-inspiring and maybe a little hard to believe, understand that God has been working closely with business leaders for thousands of years. As a minister with the marketplace as your mission field, you belong to a long and proud history of successful business leaders building the kingdom of God on earth. Let's look at that illustrious history in the next chapter.

PART 4
DOING WHAT CHURCH WAS DESIGNED TO DO FOR THE WORLD

CHAPTER 13

GOD'S PRIMARY PLATFORM TO PERPETUATE HIS PURPOSES

It happens in fashion and design: everything old becomes new again if you wait long enough. Similarly, the idea of God using the marketplace as a primary platform for transforming society is not a new concept. It has a long and successful, though often overlooked, history.

Business was the platform Jesus used for his ministry on this earth. The marketplace was the springboard for the growth of the early church. Jesus and his first followers didn't see working in ministry and working in business as two different things. To them it was one and the same.

Let's take a closer look at the role of business in the life and ministry of Jesus. God could have chosen to have Jesus be born into any family on earth. In fact, his cousin, John the Baptist, who also became a famous religious figure in history, was born into a very religious, priest's family. Doesn't that seem like an appropriate kind of family for God to choose for his son Jesus to be raised in on this earth too? It would make sense that Jesus would be raised in a religious, priestly kind of family and would discuss priestly things every night with his dad, right?

But no. When God decided it was time to show up on this earth with the ultimate demonstration of his character and values, to penetrate the kingdom of darkness on this earth with the kingdom of his light, to execute an in-person attack on the dominion of Satan on this earth, God decided to personally establish his rule and reign on this earth through business! With all possible strategy options available to him, he chose business.

Jesus was literally born in a place of business. There was no room in the local motels, so he was born in a stable–which was the equivalent of a garage or service station where the common vehicles of transportation (donkeys) were refueled and repaired. He was born into the family of a business owner. He was not born into the family of a religious or political leader.

His father Joseph owned a regional construction company. As near as we can tell from historical and biblical evidence, it appears that Jesus' father died when Jesus was an early teen. As the oldest child in the family, Jesus would have taken over as CEO of the family business. We don't know exactly how large Jesus' business was, but we know that at a minimum it created enough profit to provide for at least the eight people in his family and probably some relatives and widows and orphans too. So the grandest strategy that God could think of to establish his kingdom on this earth was to come to this earth as a business owner!

In fact, it is theorized that the reason Jesus spoke "Koine," a form of Greek, was because he had accompanied his father, Joseph, on business trips to commercial centers where "Koine" was the common language of commerce. The everyday language in the local community and businesses of Galilee was Aramaic, but the language of big business or international commerce was Koine Greek. As a businessman, Jesus spoke it.

In case you haven't thought much about Jesus being a business owner, let me give you a bit more background of the type of business that he owned. When Jesus' contemporaries referred to him as "the carpenter's son"[47] and as "the carpenter,"[48] the Greek word these peers of Jesus used is *tektōn*, which literally means builder, something like today's general contractor. Israel is a wood-scarce country, and that includes Nazareth where Jesus lived. In Nazareth, nearly everything was built out of stone. In addition, Nazareth was only a few miles from the ancient town of Zippori, or Sepphoris as it was called at that time. During the first century, this town was built out rapidly under the reign of Herod Antipas and would eventually be called "The Jewel of all Galilee" by first century Jewish historian Josephus. Herod's massive reconstruction project in Zippori would have required the help of every available and skilled *tekton* in the surrounding area, likely including Jesus' father, Joseph, and later Jesus himself. Their Nazareth-based business would have been in the perfect location to commute to work on Herod's huge stone masonry projects because there was a famous big rock quarry halfway between Nazareth and Zippori. Regardless of whether Jesus himself worked on Herod's masonry projects, it is highly likely that he visited and probably utilized this nearby ancient quarry in building his business. So this and other historical evidence indicates that it is most likely that, as a builder, Jesus was a stonemason.

Think about that. God himself chose to demonstrate what he

was like by showing up in person on this earth, as the owner of a regional stonemasonry company!

Could this also be why Jesus talks about stone and rocks so much in his teachings? For example, after some religious leaders rejected Jesus's spiritual leadership, Jesus shared a story about some bad tenants, and when he finished, he looked directly at them and said, "Then what is the meaning of that which is written: 'The stone the builders rejected has become the cornerstone'?"[49] When Peter recognizes Jesus as "the Christ, the son of the living God," Jesus spontaneously acknowledges Peter's important epiphany with an interesting play on words that is likely from someone quite familiar with types of stones. Jesus said, "You are Peter, and on this rock I will build my church."[50] In the Greek language that Jesus spoke "Petros," which is how he referred to Peter, meant "small stone or pebble." Then Jesus used "petra" later on in the sentence, which means "foundation boulder." Jesus essentially said to Peter, "You are Pebble, and on this big foundational bolder (that I am the Christ, the son of the living God) I will build my church." Later, when defending himself before the religious leaders, Peter used a stone masonry metaphor in reference to Jesus: "This Jesus is the stone you builders rejected, which has become the cornerstone."[51]

The majority of the time Jesus spent on this earth he was building a construction company specializing in stone masonry! His business experience provided him with metaphors for his message.

It appears that by the time Jesus was thirty years old, he had developed his business to the point where it was self-running enough that he had the freedom to pursue his passion for teaching about God's kingdom full time for three years. When he recruited his core leadership team to perpetuate his vision, he recruited 100% business leaders! Isn't that awesome! Not a single priest in the bunch. Matthew was a tax collector whose business model was questionable in integrity but successful in taking a large "commission" on taxes collected. Luke was a doctor in private practice. Several of Jesus' key leadership team were owners and operators of fishing businesses, since that was a primary driver of the economy and culture at that time (like Peter, James, John, and Andrew). The famous Apostle Paul owned a portable building construction company (tentmaking back then was not making little camping tents like we think of today—it was literally the way that many commercial and residential buildings were constructed).

After three years of Jesus' leadership training and modeling, these business leaders were able to launch a movement that has perpetuated his purposes around the world for a couple thousand years. Their success is evident in the long list of his followers' accomplishments, which were summarized in Chapter 6.

A Strategy to Transform a Nation

This concept of God using business and entrepreneurs as the core of his strategy to change the world started even before Jesus showed up on this earth. The Old Testament (the first half of the Bible) describes how God chose the nation of Israel to develop a model that would show the world what it looked like when society established a culture under his leadership and his values. God started this whole nation-transformation strategy with three great leaders who were to become fathers to the first of many nations that would follow God's plans for society: Abraham, his son Isaac, and Isaac's son Jacob.

Abraham, Isaac, and Jacob were three generations of prolific entrepreneurs. Most people who think about key characters in this famous story conjure up mental images of rabbis, prophets, and kings. The reality is, when God launched this strategy to create a model nation under his rule and reign, he chose to build it under the leadership of three generations of Jewish business owners.

God didn't launch this nation-transformation strategy with some holy prophet in the wilderness eating bugs and honey. He launched this strategy to create a holy nation with a business owner named Abraham, who passed his business acumen down to his kids.

Abraham, Isaac, and Jacob were very savvy and successful business leaders. The Bible tells us that Abraham had a lot of possessions[52] when God told him to "go from your country, your people and your father's household to a land I will show you".[53] In that agrarian society, land was the primary asset required for business success. God sourced great land for Abraham and let him know it should be a multigenerational business asset to be passed down to Abraham's descendants.[54]

Abraham was such a renowned business tycoon in that region of the world that the Egyptians showered lavish gifts on him to build an alliance with him. They gave him "sheep and cattle, male and female donkeys, male and female servants, and camels."[55] Abraham had 318 trained men in his household.[56] That is a major family business enterprise just in his household employees. Abraham was important enough by this time to be entertained by King Melchizedek, who served him the best food and wine money could buy.[57] He was a man of wealth, power, and influence through the good management of the resources God had provided for him—in other words, by being a good business leader.

Abraham's son Isaac was also promised many lands and many descendants. He was told to go to the land of the Philistines, the land of Gerar, and live there as a foreigner.[58] Even though there was famine and drought in the land, Isaac managed to have a good harvest. In fact, it says he "reaped a hundredfold."[59] He became so successful, multiplying his herds and flocks, that the Philistines stopped up his wells out of competitive jealousy!

Isaac's son Jacob had to escape the murderous wrath of his jealous brother Esau by running away to an uncle's home.[60] He had nothing but a walking stick with him, but by the time he and Esau met again years later, Jacob was incredibly prosperous. His strong business acumen multiplied livestock and made him "exceedingly prosperous" with "large flocks, and female and male servants, and camels and donkeys."[61] In fact, Jacob was rich enough that, when he met his brother again, he could give him the following gifts: "Two hundred female goats and twenty male goats, two hundred ewes and twenty rams, thirty female camels with their young, forty cows and ten bulls, twenty female donkeys and ten male donkeys," all delivered by some of Jacob's many servants.[62] That might be the equivalent in today's world of meeting a brother you hadn't seen in years and giving him a dozen Dodge Ram trucks, twenty Lamborghinis, and ten Teslas! You know you've got to have done well in business if that's the kind of gifts you give to an estranged relative to try to build bridges to a better relationship!

If anyone wonders whether God is all for business leaders and entrepreneurs, hopefully this will put to bed any doubt about that once and for all. God chose business and entrepreneurial leaders as the founders of his chosen nation, and he never told them to stop working their businesses, stop making profits, and to devote themselves full time to religious activities.

When that chosen nation didn't end up creating the model society God envisioned, he decided to do it Himself. The Bible says that God came to the earth in the form of a person named Jesus to show the world what he really intended for his society to look like. And GOD Himself showed up as a business leader! God showed up in the flesh as an entrepreneur running a business.

God has all wisdom and capability. Even if you don't believe in God, by very definition, God would need to have that type of unlimited strategic capability, right? So here is a limitless God, able to choose any strategy, any method, to execute his plan to redeem humanity and rebuild human society to his original intent, and what does he do? He leads a business!

Since God does what he does with intention, one could conclude that business was and is God's ideal vehicle to establish his kingdom on this earth! Business was and is God's ideal platform for serving people and serving his purposes in this world.

That's why God has been using business people for thousands of years. It is an undeniable part of God's strategy to transform the world.

With this clear strategy in mind, let's take a fresh look at the relationship between business and the church.

CHAPTER 14

NOT YOUR GRANDMA'S CHURCH

You might be wondering why we are talking about church in a book about building your business to build a better world. It's pretty simple. Church is seen by many as the ultimate best vehicle to build a better world. In fact, some church devotees might even call it God's only way to build his world. But in this chapter I'm going to explain how YOUR BUSINESS could be the best vehicle to build a better world.

In fact, allow me to propose an even more outlandish thought. What if BUSINESS is a more effective model for "doing church" (as church was originally intended) than the conventional institutional paradigm that has defined church for the majority of the world for the last eighteen hundred years? What if when you're building a business, you are actually building the church?

Crazy thought, eh?

So please buckle your seat belt and hold on for an unexpected ride. I'm posting a danger sign at the entrance of this road. If you're really into church, there is great danger that this chapter will push your buttons and challenge your paradigms. If you're not into church at all, there is also great danger that this chapter will push your buttons and challenge your paradigms.

If you've got the guts, read on!

Let me start by asking you a basic question. Answer honestly. What does church mean to you? For some it is a place that is focused on a set of teachings that have little relevance to everyday, modern life. For others it is a set of doctrines that they may or may not fully buy in to. For many of my millennial friends it is a weekly religious meeting where passive people sit and listen to professional music and a professional monologue, when they'd rather just listen to a podcast and go do something to change the world. For some, church is a place where they have felt judgment, control, or condemnation, and they never care to return. For some it is a group of like-minded people who add an important social component to life. For some it is a place to receive valuable spiritual teaching or to nourish their souls in expression of worship to God. For some it is the dream of an institution that is supposed to transform and improve every element of our society–an elusive and unfulfilled dream, but a dream none the less.

For me, church has meant many different things over the years. I grew up in a fairly conservative, traditional church setting where the church services had good, somber organ music and some solemn religious liturgy that my parents and grandparents had come to appreciate as a vital part of their spiritual journey and mission.

The first time I attended a church that had upbeat, contemporary band music, stage lights, videos, and a guy talking in street language about relevant topics, I remember thinking, "Well, this sure ain't my grandma's church!" But it became apparent that this church and the thousands of contemporary, seeker-oriented churches that flourished in the last few decades were reinventing the practices of church services to make the experience more relevant and transformational. Yet many church movement experts are now concerned that this contemporary church movement has run its course, as church attendance and participation is on a dramatic decline in many parts of the world. It seems that the conventional church as we know it is declining. Some well-known church experts are saying that it may not exist as we know it today for our great grandkids.

Just after last Easter, there was an article in the *Washington Post* that documented the rapid reduction of church attendance and concluded that if mainline Protestantism doesn't stem this decline, there will only be twenty-three Easters left until no one is in attendance. Although the author's math in that article seems to work out based on historic trends, I personally don't think church as we know it is going to disappear any time soon. But there is certainly an increasing number of people who don't associate themselves with or relate to the concept or structures of conventional church but who still consider themselves spiritual, and maybe even committed to the notion of building a better world for God.

If you are part of the 45% of Americans who don't consider themselves church-type people, this chapter is for you. If you are part of the 55% of Americans who say they attend church, this chapter may stretch you a bit. If you are part of the more than six million people in America who consider themselves "churched" people but who don't regularly attend or participate in church, this chapter is particularly for you.

What if THIS Was Church?

Recently, I became aware of the most remarkable world-changing church! The pastor and staff possess more influence, leadership skill, and far-reaching impact than I thought possible coming from this relatively small church in the Midwest. The pastor's team's ability to cast vision, roll out strategic plans, and efficiently execute them is legendary. He has been faithfully discipling leaders from inside and outside of the church for over twenty five years. The passion that the core leaders in the church have for people who aren't yet enjoying God's leadership in their lives is unparalleled. This fellowship invests substantial amounts of money into organizations that help people learn to follow Jesus in its city and throughout the world.

The generosity of this church and its leaders is off the charts. With only a few hundred members in their congregation, for several years they have provided over a million meals a year to families in their community. This congregation pays for hundreds of children to go to school absolutely free. They pay the full salary and benefits of several school teachers, police officers, and firefighters in their community. They even encourage financially giving to other organizations that are making a difference in society by matching member donations dollar for dollar up to $5,000 a year per member. And if the members volunteer time to serve in other charities, the church donates $10/hour to the charities they are serving in. The ripple effect of all these acts of social responsibility is having a profound impact on their community and throughout the world. If this church ceased to exist, there would be a huge hole in society.

It is easy to see why it is so attractive to join this church. It offers every married member an opportunity to attend top-notch marriage conferences and pays for the travel, lodging, food, and registration expenses of both spouses! It provides free personal financial training to help every adult learn to effectively manage their finances and develop financial freedom. And the church does a lot for those in their group that need help. For example, they have an educational fund that offers totally free college tuition to any adult that's been with them a year—a full-ride scholarship until they complete their college degree. The compassionate hearts of the church leaders also caused them to start a crisis fund for any member who finds themselves in a tough season, and who needs temporary financial assistance to get over the short-term hurdles.

You may be as surprised as I was that a church and staff would have such profound vision, generosity, and effective execution on social responsibility! The minister is a leader of leaders, speaking at every opportunity about how this remarkable story has all transpired. He has met with dozens of other ministers who want to model their ministries after this trailblazer. He is one of the most gifted, community-focused ministers I have ever known.

Here's what's mind blowing about this story. Get this. Most pastors across the church landscape don't even recognize this guy as a minister. Many would say he isn't "called," and most would also say he isn't even a pastor. His church's generosity and dramatic impact on society have never really been endorsed or even acknowledged much by other pastors or by the church at large. You want to know why? The reason is because this church is technically not a church. It's a business.

Now before you get upset at me for telling you a tall tale, let me assure you that every detail about this story is true, except the name of the organization and the fact that it is technically called a business instead of a church.

What if THIS Was Business?

What if we recognize business as having the kind of society-changing power that most attribute to church? The story I just told is about a business leader named Steve Trice and the business he founded 43 years ago, Jasco Products Company, in Oklahoma City. Those million meals are the ripple effect of providing income that feeds employees and their families. If we were to add up all the property taxes and sales taxes these people pay because of their employment, we'd see the profound ripple effect this business has on building a better community.

Think about it. Churches don't pay property tax, businesses do. The people in the congregation pay taxes from income generated by businesses, not the church. I've been involved in enough church-building programs to know that there are cities that don't want churches to buy prime real estate because they don't pay property tax and sales tax. It's often hard for them to get permits to build.

Steve Trice is not called a pastor by his employees or by his church. But think about the influence he has compared to the conventional church pastor. Business leaders have a captive audience for forty to fifty hours every week, compared to the thirty to forty minutes each week that conventional church pastors have with their people. Just by measure of time, that gives the business leader about eighty times more potential influence than their conventional church pastor counterpart.

Jesus was a business leader who built a team of other marketplace leaders who truly transformed the world! What if we embraced the reality that everything done for God doesn't have to be done through the conventional church? What if business owners saw themselves as pastors called by God to care for and lead their employees during the week as their part in establishing

God's ideal society on this earth? What if there really wasn't supposed to be the marked role distinction between pastors or priests and business leaders that is so prevalent today?

Although this isn't a common idea, it is not a new idea, as mentioned in the previous chapter. The last book of the Bible refers to this paradigm of common people functioning in the role of priests by saying, by saying that we are a kingdom of priests.[63] In the Jesus model, we are all the priests who bring the Kingdom of God (his leadership and values) to wherever we are in society. We are all kings AND priests under the new paradigm which Jesus inaugurated! How can paid church staff ministers and business owners be two separate classes if we are all a kingdom of priests?

That means that as business leaders, our business is our pulpit. Our business is our podium to expand God's purposes on this earth. We have the privilege of "pastoring" our employees, customers, and stakeholders to build them into better people and to build a better world. You don't have to leave your business and go on staff at a conventional church to be smack dab in the middle of the most powerful force to change society: your business.

David High in his book *Kings and Priests* tells the story of a man who owned a company with five hundred employees that managed real estate. This man went to his pastor and said, "I feel like God is calling me into full-time ministry. I'm going to sell my business and get a theology degree, then go to seminary and become a full-time pastor." He just knew his pastor was going to be so excited that he had "accepted the call" to go into full-time ministry!

Instead, his pastor asked, "How many employees do you have?"

"Five hundred."

"Do all of them have a spouse or significant other?"

"Yes, nearly all of them."

"How many of those couples have kids?"

"Well, nearly all of them."

"Well, it appears to me you've already got a congregation of two thousand people, and you already have a forty-hour work week, right?"

"Yeah."

"You have influence over them for forty hours a week. So what you're telling me is that you want to sell your business that has two thousand people under its influence in order to go to seminary for a few years and have almost no influence over anybody, to go take a church somewhere with one to two hundred people in it to try to build it up and speak to them one hour a week instead of forty hours a week? I think it's a bad idea for you to drop your business to go into the ministry full time. You're already in full-time ministry! You just need to recognize it!"

As business owners, I believe that God doesn't give us all these people to build a big business; rather, he gives us this business to build big people who build a better world!

I Thought Church Was Supposed to Transform Society

For years, churches that believe that Christ's mission included the transformation of society have performed many valiant attempts to change their cities or countries. There have been some spots of success. Yet few cities reach a tipping point where the predominant culture is God-culture. Why? Is it because the transformation of a city is not a worthy goal? Is it because that's not what church is supposed to do? Or is it that we just need to do more—more praying, more social programs, more giving, more outreach, more preaching and teaching?

Maybe. But let me pose a question. What if the church's lack of ability to completely transform culture is based on a deficient system? What if our current conventional church system is just not designed to transform culture? What if the system that designed church to be what happens in and through a certain place that meets at a certain time–what if that system is not how church was supposed to be designed to be effective at building a better society? What if the kingdom of this world will only become the kingdom of our God when the people of God are commissioned and equipped to live God's principles and perpetuate God's purposes in and through *the business of daily life*?

Followers of Jesus believe that the values and purposes of God should permeate every part of every community. This is the fulfillment of what Jesus said in what we call "The Lord's Prayer" when he said to his Father in Heaven, "Your will be done on earth as it is in heaven." Some of us who have hung around church a lot tend to spiritualize this, but what does it mean in practical terms? For example, what does it mean for the economy and for individual incomes? Do you think that in heaven there is special low income or slum housing, violence on the streets of gold, or people starving to death? Jesus said he was "anointed me to proclaim good news to the poor."[64] What is good news to the poor? It is not so much that you are going to live forever in this misery, but that you are not going to be poor anymore! This was the first thing Jesus said he was anointed and commissioned to do. In this Scripture, poor in the Greek literally means poor–people with no money! So, technically, if a church is doing the work of Jesus, yes, the effect would be good news for the poor.

What Impact Would Be Missed??

If the last church you went to or the last church you drove by closed its doors, how many people in the city would notice? How many people would be devastated because they knew that poverty and sickness would go up in that neighborhood? How many people would say there was no longer good news for the poor in that area of the city? How many people would be crying and mourning at the closure of that church? How many people would contemplate suicide because of the degradation of the quality of life and relationships in that city because of the church closure?

On the other hand, if a large employer shuts down, the effects are devastating! What would happen if Boeing or Microsoft shut down? What would happen if your business closed its doors? It would probably have a big impact on hundreds, maybe thousands of people. Families, the economy, and maybe the welfare of the community would be affected. Heck! When my favorite restaurant that only had three employees closed, I went into mourning! It was my favorite environment to have meaningful meetings and great food!

Last week I was reminded again of the powerful impact that a conventional church can have if it embraces this paradigm that its mission is to transform the community through the marketplace. I was having a lunch meeting with Kathy, who is one of the top executives of a very successful senior care company in the Midwest called Augustana Care. I was talking to her about having their company take over operational management of one of the senior housing communities we had built in the area. Our team had done extensive research and interviewed several senior care companies, and Augustana came out on top as the company most likely to provide the highest level of care to our seventy-some seniors who live in our assisted living and memory care community on the river near Mayo Clinic.

As I was doing my final interview and getting to know more about the company, I discovered a surprising 120-year case study that illustrates the dramatic impact a conventional church can have when it embraces business as a primary platform for expanding the leadership and values of Jesus in the community. I asked Kathy who started their company, and to my surprise she said that this top-rated company in this region was facilitated by a church! She said it was started by Augustana Lutheran Church in The Elliott Park neighborhood of Minneapolis.

I was shocked. I knew that church, or at least that church building. There is an old, beautiful, historical stone church near the location where we are developing a new hotel which we have branded, "The Elliot Park Hotel" after its surrounding neighborhood. The Augustana Lutheran Church building was built in 1883 and is a historic landmark in the neighborhood. One rarely sees any activity at that church, so I asked Kathy if there was still any connection between her company and that church.

She sadly described how the congregation had shrunk and eventually closed down and the church building had just been sold. How ironic. Here I am, choosing what we consider to be the best company in this region to operate one of our business units and take care of the residents in our assisted living community. This fantastic business was launched by a conventional church in the year 1896. Yes, EIGHTEEN ninety-six. Over 120 years ago! That conventional church has ceased to exist, and all that is left of it is a historic stone building.

But the business which that conventional church helped launch 120 years ago continues to serve God's purposes in this region in very powerful ways. The Augustana conventional church is no longer impacting lives; but more than 120 years later, the Augustana Care business ministry still provides shelter, food, care, and health services to thousands of seniors in this region. The Augustana business ministry continues to impact thousands of families every day in this community.

As I caught my Uber ride to meet with another developer, I

wondered what it might have been like to go back in time and talk to the pastor who built that beautiful stone church in 1883, who with his growing congregation started Augustana Care just over a dozen years later. If I would have asked him which one would have the greatest impact on this community –which one would build God's kingdom the most –I wonder what he would have said? When Lutheran pastor Carl J. Petri founded Augustana Care to help young women and seniors in need of room and board in the Minneapolis area in 1896, would he have dreamed that one day his beautiful church building would be empty and only known as a historic preservation site, whereas the business he started would be helping thousands of people experience the leadership and values of Jesus in their lives and families 120 years later?

Thank God there was a pastor and a congregation that had a vision to become salt and light in their community by starting and supporting a business that served people in tangible ways. As I was pulling in to my next appointment, I suddenly got great joy at the thought that the business that I am starting in this same Elliot Park neighborhood today could be creating an environment where vibrant hospitality and relationships can thrive 120 years from now. Maybe the things we will start doing now to foster socially-minded business ventures in this neighborhood will be making a difference 120 years from now. We will help fund and facilitate businesses that will be tackling systemic poverty and fostering businesses that will help create abundance in this community.

The concept here is that if followers of Jesus pray as he taught us to pray: that things should be *"on earth as it is in heaven"*, one of the things this looks like is the elimination of poverty. There is no poverty on the streets of gold in heaven. What does heaven look like on this earth? Well, I'm pretty sure there's no violence in heaven, there are no slums in heaven, and no one is starving! That's the way it's supposed to be on this earth. And doing business well is a well-worn path to bringing the good of heaven to this earth.

Even though there are many businesses doing very important work to build a better society, to bring characteristics of heaven to this earth, why is it that very few churches actually celebrate anything that business does as being done by the church? Why don't they celebrate it or even recognize it when a business leader in their church is having that kind of positive impact on their community? Why don't they consider all those good things a business does for society as a vital and core expression of the mission of the church?

Yes, I know. Using transformational commerce to rebuild the world for God doesn't look at all like your grandma's church. If you're a church-type person, the notion that business is a powerful platform to accomplish the purposes God intended for the church may not feel like church to you. It may be as foreign to you as a contemporary church with a rock band, stage lights and smoke would be to your grandma, who grew up only listening to pipe organ music. But just because it doesn't look like your grandma's church, does that mean it's not a valid expression of the church?

If you're not a church-type person, seeing business as a valid expression of church may be intriguing but it may not align at all with what you have seen or heard of church.

How did today's paradigms and expressions of church become so separate from the world and from people's day-to-day lives in business? Let's look at some eye-opening history to help understand how the whole notion of church started and how this great divide developed between business and church.

CHAPTER 15

HOW THE DISTURBING DISINTEGRATION BEGAN

How is it that society is so quick to bifurcate the good things the conventional church does for society from the good things business does for society? How is it that the good work people do in everyday life has become so disintegrated from the good work of God in the world? I believe it is a consequence of the dualism disaster. The dualism disaster is at the root of this idea that business is secular and worldly while religion is spiritual and godly.

What is the dualism disaster? Glad you asked. Here's some background.

Much of Western society's philosophical view of life is still strongly influenced by Greek philosophy. Plato was the primary Greek philosopher who promoted what is called dualism: that there are two levels of life. The upper level (called "form") consisted of eternal ideas. The lower level (called "matter") consisted of physical and temporary things. The upper level is considered distinct from and vastly superior to the lower level.

Plato placed work and business in the lower realm. (Keep in mind he was a philosopher who sat around all day talking about ideas, not doing business). Christianity got its start in the period of time where this philosophy was the accepted norm in society. Thus, the Christian church came to view business as worldly, carnal, and temporary because it deals with earthly things like money, which is here today and gone tomorrow. As Christianity spread throughout the world, this concept of dualism spread with it. The irony is that Christians who believe in God got this dualism philosophy from the Greeks, who got it from the philosophy of humanism. Humanism is the idea that humans are the center of the universe, not God. Go figure.

An opposing perspective to the dualism philosophy is the Jewish view of life Jesus would have grown up with and that he taught. This is based on the concept that humans are not the center of the universe; God is at the center. Instead of dualism, this leads to a philosophy of integrated unity. If there is an "upper level," the only thing in the "upper level" of the universe is God. So everything else, whether visible or invisible, tangible or intangible, is under God. God is integrated into everything. Instead of a spiritual realm that is separate from the physical or created realm, everywhere God's divine presence exists is a spiritual realm. And God, by definition, is everywhere. Since God's presence exists in business, then business is as sacred as a temple, synagogue, or church. Therefore, the work we do in business is as sacred as preaching a sermon or singing in the choir at church.

When I first started to realize this, it was quite disturbing because I had spent much of my life serving substantially in the conventional church. I poured thousands of hours into the ministry of churches, thinking this was my sacred duty, especially since I spent so much time pursuing "secular things" in business. If you are still in that vein of thought, I want you to know that what you have done and will continue to do in and through your local church is not bad. It is probably quite good. I just want you to know there is a whole lot more to this concept of "church" as it was originally intended than what we've been led to believe. It was never intended to be disintegrated from the good work we do in business.

What Jesus Had in Mind When He Started His "Church" Might Surprise You!

Regardless of what you have believed or experienced about church, I want you to know beyond a shadow of doubt that it was indeed Jesus himself who started this thing we now call church. But wait. What he started is probably not what you're thinking when you think of church. What he started was a revolutionary, completely non-religious movement that was supposed to be integrated to benefit every aspect of society. In fact, what he started was so radically different from the model of the "centralized church" at that time, the leaders of the institutional religion killed him for it. Let me tell you the real story of how Jesus started the church.

Here's how it went down. Jesus was asking his followers what people were saying about who he was. Peter said, "I know who you are. You are the Christ, the son of the living God!" That is when Jesus essentially said, "You got it Peter! You get the gold star! And it is on the bedrock of this big paradigm (that I'm the anointed, kingly leader who is the son of the living God) that I will build my church!"[65]

The earliest documentation of this story is in the Greek language that Jesus spoke. The Greek word "ekklesia" is the word that Jesus used, which is commonly translated into English as

187

"church." Jesus said, "I will build my ekklesia . . . "

What is this "ekklesia" that Jesus said he would build? Is it the same as what we think of when we think of "church" today?

To understand what Jesus meant, we need to understand what that word meant to those who heard it when he said it. Just like when I read a phrase in an old classic novel like "John was a gay person," I need to understand what the word "gay" meant to audiences at the time the book was written. Did the author intend for "gay" to mean homosexual, as it has come to mean today? Or did the author intend for "gay" to mean happy, as was the common meaning to his audience then? They are obviously dramatically different meanings. In the same way, we must ask the question, did "ekklesia" mean what it has come to mean most popularly today when we hear the word church? Or did Jesus intend for "ekklesia" to mean what it meant to his audience then? What if there are dramatically different meanings?

What did ekklesia mean to the Greeks, Romans, and Jews in the Mediterranean world of the first century A.D.? That was when Jesus first used this term to label the thing he would create for the purpose of rebuilding the world into God's ideal design for society.

What Ekklesia Meant to Jesus

In Jesus' time there were three institutions around which culture centered. Two were viewed as religious, one was viewed as secular.

The two primary religious institutions were the temple and the synagogue. These were the holy places where holy men read holy Scriptures and people came to hear about and worship God and practice certain religious ceremonies. The primary non-religious institution was the ekklesia. This was central to the form of governance that the Greeks and Romans used to integrate

Greco-Roman culture into the world.

Those were the three primary organizational systems that society at that time used to perpetuate culture–to create and duplicate certain values and norms of behavior under certain types of leadership. When Peter said to Jesus, "You are the Christ, the son of the living God," Jesus used this as a teachable moment to launch the system he intended to build society to follow his values and live under his leadership. He essentially said to Peter, "You got it! On this rock, this foundational concept, I will build MY ekklesia." He didn't say, "I will build my synagogue "or "my temple." He didn't say, "I will build another religious institution."

He said, "I will build my ekklesia."

Peter knew exactly what Jesus meant. How do I know that? Because Jesus didn't explain himself! Ever wonder why Jesus didn't give 101 lessons on how to plant churches? If the church as we know it today was so all important to Jesus, why didn't he give specific instructions on how to build great churches? How to select the right site? How to design the most functional building? How to choose the right staff? How to preach the best sermons? How to start churches with the best programming and coolest Sunday services so they become mega churches?

With all the emphasis that denominations and church networks place on church planting, with all the volumes of training materials and techniques available on how to do it, it has always puzzled me why there is very little specific instruction in the Bible on it. Why is that?

Could it be it's because when Jesus said, "I will build my ekklesia," Peter got it and so did the rest of Jesus followers? Maybe they knew exactly what the ekklesia in society was and how it was built. It wasn't a new idea. It wasn't a remake of some existing religious institution. Ekklesia was a well-known secular system. It was the system the Romans used to permeate every aspect of culture through the marketplace with the emperor's rule and reign. It was the system that was used to expand the kingdom of Rome.

The reason there were no teachings on it was because they got it! It was obvious to them! They lived in the Roman ekklesia system! They knew how it grew! He didn't have to explain it to them. They knew how it worked. The ekklesia that Jesus was referring to was commonly understood at that time to be a SECULAR system that the Roman government used to bring societies under the leadership of the Roman emperor and to embrace the culture and values of Rome. The Romans adopted that ekklesia concept from the Greeks and expanded it further as their all-encompassing system to bring the world under the rule and reign of the Roman emperor.

The Encyclopedia Britannica defines ekklesia as an ancient Greek assembly and says that such assemblies existed in Greek city-states and continued to operate throughout the Hellenistic and Roman periods. It's obvious that this kind of secular assembly to govern and build society has little resemblance to what we think of as church today.

When Jesus said he would build his ekklesia, it would have been as full of meaning as if someone in America said today, "I will build my own political party that will take over the leadership of this country." Jesus was referring to the prevailing system that was being used to shape society. He was announcing that he was going to rebuild society by building his own version of that same pervasive secular system—a version that would operate under his leadership and perpetuate his values and norms of behavior. They knew he was saying he was going to build his own self-governed body of people under the kingship and jurisdiction of Jesus.

This period of history was near the height of emperor worship. The common belief was that the emperor of Rome was a direct descendant of God (literally the son of God) and therefore was divine himself. Therefore, the emperor was said to have the divine right to rule anywhere his subjects went. Because of this divine right of kings, they believed that nothing could stop the expansion of Roman territory and rule. The belief shared among Roman citizens at that time was that anywhere there were two or three Romans gathered together in the name of the emperor, they were an ekklesia assembly and the presence and power of the emperor was there with them to give them the authority to expand the kingdom of Rome.

When Peter recognized Jesus as being the divine Son of God, that was a perfect cue for Jesus to announce that he was going to build HIS ekklesia that would rebuild the world the way God intended it to be, and nothing could stop its expansion. Later Jesus would say to these same followers that where two or three were gathered together in HIS name, there his presence and power would be with them to give them the authority to expand the kingdom of God.

From Salt and Light to Safety and Liturgy

In a later teaching about his kingdom, Jesus made it clear that his kingdom would come and be spread through the secular society like yeast in dough or salt in food, or like a light on a hill penetrating all the darkness. Jesus intended his ekklesia to permeate everything. Just like a little yeast permeates every part of the loaf of bread, and a little salt flavors the entire pot of soup, and a ray of light pierces and transforms the darkness, the ekklesia was designed to permeate every aspect of life. The ekklesia was to be the invisible element that impacts every aspect of business, every component of government, every part of your family, every part of media, education, and entertainment. In short, the ekklesia was intended to be a force so integrated into society that it transformed individuals, families, cities, and nations.

The Church in a Bottle

The church today has come to function more like a saltshaker dropped in the middle of mashed potatoes, storing its contents neatly in holy huddles. Church-centric programs are dropped in the middle of the mash of humanity but have relatively little impact on culture. For many, the church today has become more about joining a group where one can be safe from the influences of the world. For many, the church today is about going to a place where they can enjoy a comfortable liturgy or experience good programs. Something that was intended to be like salt and light has become more about safety and liturgy—and it seems to be losing its effect on society.

There is no question that church attendance in the United States is declining, as noted previously. There is a growing percentage of U.S. adults who say they are religiously non-affiliated. This non-affiliated group jumped up 7% in seven years. Those who say they are affiliated declined 6% in the same time period. Not only are Americans dropping out of their church affiliations, even their belief in God is toppling. The non-affiliated lost their belief in God by 9% over a period of seven years.[66]

This decline in religious faith and practice is due to many factors, but one of them could be that church is increasingly seen as a place with programs for certain people who need it rather than a practical force for good that meets the tangible needs of everyone in the city. The millennial generation is swelling the ranks of those unaffiliated with church. As a generation, they have a built-in longing to be part of a cause that makes a practical, positive impact on this world.

Could it be that this generation is the one best positioned to embrace what Jesus had in mind when he said, "I will build my ekklesia" as an integrated, organic force to transform every aspect of our world?

Please don't get me wrong; I'm not in any way proposing a business orientation can revitalize a dying church. I am saying the church was always meant to be salt out of the shaker, seasoning society. And business is perfectly positioned to be the ideal delivery mechanism for salty and savory solutions to transform real life in the real world.

For salt or yeast to be effective, they have to be out of the container. They have to be allowed to penetrate that which they are designed to influence. In fact, the more effective they are, the less visible they are. Salt and yeast actually disappear as they permeate. The more they penetrate, the more they disappear and the greater the effect. When yeast and salt are doing the work they are designed to do, they are invisible as a separate element. The only way to truly quantify their impact is by the look or taste of the food. When the ekklesia is doing its best work, it is fully integrated into daily life, invisibly infiltrating and influencing the rebuilding of the world into God's ideal design.

Out of the Bottle

We need to take the church out of the bottle. We need to take the people out of the bottle we call the church and put them back into the world. When God's people are building the ekklesia in the world, the more they penetrate the world, the less it looks like conventional churches with buildings, programs, liturgies, and labels, and the more you will see the difference in the world. The loaf rises–the levels of care and compassion in society rise, the economy rises, the core values rise, the level of creativity in solving world problems rises, etc. The taste of society is different. Instead of the taste of death and poverty, there is the taste of life, joy, peace, and prosperity.

Some good church folks might object here and say I shouldn't imply that church isn't church when it meets on Sundays. Is salt still salt when it is in the shaker? Sure. It is just not doing the work of salt when it is in the bottle. The impact of the church on Sunday when it is gathered for amazing teaching and worship is minimal, yet it is still part of the church. That is not the church working, though. The impact of the church happens between those meetings, when it is invisible; when it is being the ekklesia out in secular society. The church, as Jesus intended it, is doing its best work when there is no way to capture it or claim that work as a program of the church.

Oh, there are certainly some people who come to the church meetings and programs—who come into the salt shaker and are influenced greatly by the concentration of salt. That is marvelous. The paid staff of the conventional church have great influence when people come into the salt shaker of the church programs.

However, business leaders have a platform where they have influence as salt at least forty hours a week, transforming the taste of society. In the marketplace, we have the opportunity to be ministers all day, every day. What a business leader does every day in business has the potential of having greater impact on building God's leadership and purposes into society than almost any "religious" activity.

What if your business looked more like what Jesus intended when he set out to build his church (ekklesia) than the church that meets down the road on Sunday?

What Jesus began as a way of life that transformed society with God's values, has for most of the world become defined by buildings, events, and programs. It's time to reconstruct the meaning of church from being about a place and a program, to church being more like what you have the opportunity to do every day in business. In fact, I would go so far as to say that what you're doing in business is the primary platform Jesus had in mind for building his ekklesia.

Where Did the Word "Church" Come From?

You might ask, "If Jesus and his followers didn't actually use the word 'church', where does that word come from and how did it get so popular?"

When the word "church" appears in the Bible, it is translated as such from the Greek word "ekklesia" in most cases. Ekklesia is used 115 times in 112 verses in the Bible. All but three of the times ekklesia is used, it is translated as "church". Those three times are in one story about a public and political assembly of people where, ekklesia is not translated as church but as something that would have been closer to what the author and audience would have always understood it to mean—a non-religious, secular assembly of people. However, in these three verses, the Greek word is exactly the same as the other 112 times where it was translated as "church." This is a bit strange since the word "church" and its associated meaning didn't even come into existence until long after the Bible was written.

In 1526, William Tyndale completed the first English translation of the New Testament (the second part of the Bible). In these original translations, Tyndale translated ekklesia as congregation, a collection of people who gather for a purpose. The word "church" was never used once in that first English translation. As history progressed, conflicts escalated over the appropriateness of translating the Bible into common language until King Henry the VIII took jurisdiction over the Church and essentially kicked the Pope's influence as the head of the Catholic Church out of England. One of Henry the VIII's first acts was to further defy Rome by officially making it legal to print Bibles in the common language of the people. Over time, there became an increasing number of English translations.

Somewhere along the journey of various Bible translations, the word ekklesia started to be translated as church, most likely because that was the word that had come to be used for the strongest religious institution at the time, the Roman Catholic Church.

The English word church originated from the Old English and German word "kirche" meaning House of God or the Lord's House and clearly referred to a physical building. Based on the Greek Lexicon, it's unclear how the word church became included in the languages of the world as a replacement for ekklesia. This inaccurate translation of ekklesia as church changed the meaning from the original meaning, which was focused on groups of people assembled or called together for a purpose, to a meaning that was more focused on a place or a program. The truth is that ekklesia has nothing to do with the word "church".

Around 1604, King James of England commissioned a new translation of the Bible to be translated and printed in "modern English." King James engaged fifty-four translators to work on this project. They were given fifteen rules to follow. The third rule was as follows: "The Old Ecclesiastical Words to be kept, (namely, in other words) the word church is not to be translated as congregation."

King James required this because he had jurisdiction over "the church" at that time, and having over one hundred references to "the church" in the Bible clearly bolstered his political and personal power. This thing that Jesus himself started and his early followers lived and died for, was the very thing that King James had authority over! What's not to like about that, if you like power and control of society? The king had little control over a congregation of people, but he did have significant control over the institution of the church and its cathedrals.

The political leaders of the time apparently didn't want the word ekklesia to mean "assembly" or "congregation of people" as separate from the religious institution of the church because it would forfeit the king's authority over the people who were in that institution.

Fast forward to the 20th century, and ekklesia is still being translated as church in the majority of the hundreds of English translations that are available today. I took three years of ancient Greek at the university, and I enjoy reading old manuscripts in the original language to better understand the original intent of the authors. So I had known for a long time that the Greek word translated as church was ekklesia. I just assumed that was the right translation because, well, everyone was doing it. The first time it dawned on me that the word ekklesia might not have been intended by Jesus to mean what we think of when we say church, was when I was walking through Ephesus with my wife Shelley.

Epiphany at Ephesus

We walked into the ruins of that ancient city in Turkey, and there was a huge outdoor colosseum that seats twenty thousand people. I stood on the stage and spoke in my normal voice. Shelley, who had wandered up to the top of the colosseum, could clearly hear what I was saying. It had perfect acoustic design for excellent communication with large assemblies. While we were in Ephesus, I read the parts of my Bible that referenced things that happened in this city. I came across this story in Acts 19 that happened in the coliseum right where I had stood that day.

The jewelry and idol makers had a thriving business, making and selling stuff to honor the goddess of the city, Artemis. Paul moved into town and set up shop right next to these idol-maker

197

businesses. Paul's business became a powerful platform of credibility and influence, so that many people started to follow Jesus instead of worshiping those stone idols. One day the idol-maker union started a riot against Paul! The riot mob got so big, it pushed into and filled this 20,000 seat stadium.

It is in this story where I saw for the first time that the word ekklesia was used in the Bible in an entirely secular context, referring to the crowd itself. The crowd of Roman rioters that filled that colosseum is actually called the ekklesia. Not exactly what you'd picture when you think of "church"!

The second time ekklesia is used in a secular context in the Bible is later in this story when the city clerk comes onto the scene after two hours of rioting and says, "If there is anything further you want to bring up, it must be settled in a legal assembly (an ekklesia)."[67] The ekklesia here refers to the civil body in Ephesus, essentially a town council.

It is interesting that in these verses, because of the context, the translators are forced not to use the English word church and instead use a more accurate translation of what ekklesia actually meant at that time in that culture.

As you can see, in today's culture, we have arrived at an understanding and experience of church that is quite different from the concept Jesus had in mind when he said, "I will build my ekklesia." Jesus' idea of ekklesia was not about a religious institution that is disintegrated from and designed to protect people from the world. It was about a secular organism integrated with and designed to transform the world. It was about people expanding the leadership and values of Jesus into everyday life. It was about bringing the presence and principles of God into the real world.

The majority of people in the world, during most hours of most days, are gathered doing business in some way. This is where the modern-day ekklesia is designed to thrive best. As we'll see in the next chapter, this is how the ekklesia paradigm Jesus launched began to transform the world.

CHAPTER 16

A PARADIGM POWERFUL ENOUGH TO CHANGE THE WORLD

For purposes of this book, I am terming "the church as we know it" or the current dominant model of church, as "the conventional church." Conventional is not a derogatory term at all. It is conventional simply because it is based on or in accordance with what is generally done or believed to be the paradigm for church. The conventional model of church is the prevailing paradigm that church is largely defined by a certain group of people who regularly meet in a certain place and offer a certain set of programs that emanate in or from those people and that place.

The concept of the ekklesia as Jesus intended it is not at all what we have come to experience in most conventional churches today. If our paradigm of church was the original ekklesia

201

model, where the ekklesia is what happens out there 24/7 in the marketplace, it would be a GAME CHANGER and CULTURE TRANSFORMER! How could it not be?

With this paradigm, the church is not something we join or even start. It is something we are. It is the experience and perpetuation of Jesus' kingdom values and purposes wherever we are. So when we are working in a business as a follower of Jesus, we are working in a church.

Groups that gather together on Sundays could be a part of the church, but that is not what makes them the church. If the people are the church, then yes, when they gather together, they gather as the church. But they are not the church because they meet on the weekend and listen to songs and a sermon. The people who gather in local congregations and the people who go to work in business during the week are both "the church." They are the people of God called to perpetuate the values and leadership of God in the world. What happens on Sunday is not opposing or competing with what happens during the week in business. It is just *functioning differently* when it is gathered than when it is out in the marketplace.

THE EKKLESIA PARADIGM

The people of God are the church (the ekklesia).

They are the church when they are gathered on the weekend and doing the programs of the local church.

They are the church on the other six days of the week when they are in the workplace.

The church is not centered around a place or a person or a set of programs.

The church (the ekklesia) is an organism of people perpetuating the purposes of their Leader wherever they are.

The church is God's people acting as the dominant creators of kingdom culture in every community, gathering, and setting.

If you are a member of a conventional church, please keep in mind you are part of the church in your city. If you are a pastor of a conventional church, keep in mind you shepherd just a part of the church in your city.

Jesus is not the head of a building. Jesus is not the head of a place or a set of programs. Jesus is the head of his church, which he calls his body–a living organism. As in the Roman paradigm of ekklesia, where two or three are gathered together, there the power, presence, and principles of King Jesus are perpetuated through HIS ekklesia.

Now, wait a minute, you may say. What about that story where Jesus threw the merchant "money changers"[68] out of the temple? He said his father's house should be called a "house of prayer." Doesn't that show Jesus' paradigm intended the ekklesia and business to be completely separated? Doesn't that show some support from Jesus for the centralized, temple model of religion?

No, this is taking the words of this story out of the historical and literary context in which they were spoken in order to support a certain paradigm. In this story, Jesus is chastising a specific set of behaviors common in the temple model of that time. Religious leaders were trying to get people to come to that holy place to perform certain religious practices and give money at that place under the pretense that this was a requirement to belong to the group and have the favor of God. They took it a step further and were actually bringing business into the temple. This is the opposite of the paradigm Jesus intended. Jesus didn't intend to bring business into a holy place called a temple. He intended to bring the holiness of his presence in his people into the everyday life of the real world. He didn't intend to bring business into the temple. He intended to bring his temple (which he defined as the body of people who followed him) into business.

When Jesus said, "My house will be called a house of prayer" it didn't necessarily mean that he was referring to that particular temple as his "house." He obviously didn't live there. Those who see Jesus as God may interpret it that way now, but the people he was talking to would certainly not have acknowledged him as God. So they wouldn't have thought, "Oh, he's saying that God's house should be called a house of prayer, and this is God's house." Jesus was quoting from the Scriptures they had at that time, from the writings of Isaiah. If you read that section of the old Scripture that he quotes, you'll see it indicates that "God's house" is a place of prayer that includes the mountains, not just certain sacred buildings.[69]

As we've covered, there is nothing about the word Jesus used for his church that indicates that it is a house or a building. That was a concept added much later in history, perpetuated by the German word for church (kirche) which means house. Nothing Jesus said or did in this story indicates he was supporting the temple system or the notion that his church was supposed to be anything like what happened in the temples or synagogues of that time.

In other teachings Jesus makes it clear the "house of God" is wherever God is and wherever God's people worship or honor him. One time Jesus had an interesting conversation over a cup of cold water at a well with a woman who asked him who the true worshipers were. Jesus responded by talking about how people try to go to a certain place to worship but true worshipers are those who worship God wherever they are "in the spirit and in truth."[70]

We need to get away from the idea that only a building with certain rituals within it can be a holy place. Every place is holy when God dwells and is honored there, including the marketplace. The reality is that most people spend a whole lot more time in business than they do in a church building. It was with this powerful paradigm that the early church grew dramatically through everyday life in business.

The Ekklesia Grows from Centers of Commerce

Paul was a famous apostle who wrote much of the New Testament, which records what he did in building the early church. Yet Paul, this famous church builder, was not a pastor. He was actually a successful business owner. If you know much about him, you probably know that Paul was a tentmaker.

That may not sound like much of business to us today. It sounds like some small, home-based business in a back room with a little sewing machine. In the first century, though, most citizens were "Bedouins" or wanderers, who lived in elaborate mobile homes—finely made tents. Most stores were tents set up along the road. If a bakery café had a leaky tent, the entire business was at risk! As a result, a tentmaking business was similar to a modern home builder or commercial building contractor. It was a core commercial business that was vital to the success of society. So this most famous and highly effective builder of the early church was actually a substantial business leader.

In Chapter 13 of Acts of the Apostles (Acts for short), there is a story about how the ekklesia grew in the city of Antioch. By the way, here, as in most places in the Bible, it does not refer to the "ekklesias" *plural* in Antioch. Rather, it notes the ekklesia, singular, in the city. This is clearly different from our paradigm today where there are many separate churches in each city that all compete for people, time, and money. Acts distinguishes a gathering of people from the ekklesia in the city. It says there was a huge city-wide gathering on the Jewish Sabbath (what we call Saturday today). Here's what it says:

"On the next Sabbath almost the whole city gathered to hear the word of the Lord ...For this is what the Lord has commanded us: 'I have made you a light for the Gentiles, that you may bring salvation to the ends of the earth'... The word of the Lord spread through the whole region."[71]

This chapter starts by referencing "the ekklesia in Antioch." Again, the ekklesia was in the city, not on the corner of 8th and Main Street. Because the ekklesia was in the city, almost the whole city gathered to hear the word of the Lord.

The apostles clearly understood this concept because they explained that they were following the command of Jesus to be a light to the Gentiles. "Gentiles" was their label for non-religious people. In other words, these early followers of Jesus were following his instruction to bring the light and life of Jesus' ekklesia to non-religious people. This is how they were to bring salvation to the ends of the earth. The result of this paradigm of church was that the word of the Lord, the directives of the leader of this new kingdom, spread throughout the whole region.

How and why did this happen in Antioch? It was not because Antioch was the religious center of the world. It was not because a bunch of religiously trained church planters went there to plant churches. Antioch was a center of commerce, a very secular city. Like Silicon Valley, it was known for great innovations.

You would think that the church would grow fastest out of Jerusalem, which was the religious center of that region. It didn't; it grew fastest out of Antioch, which was the core commerce center. The whole city came out to hear from God on the weekend. Then a few verses later it says, "The word of the Lord spread through the whole region."

Paul spent most of his time in two places: Antioch and Ephesus. Why? Because Paul went to these great cities of commerce as a business person. He partnered up with Aquila and Priscilla building homes and places of business for people. He went about his business with the mindset he got from Jesus: "We're going to take the Roman ekklesia paradigm and take this message about the Jesus ekklesia to the whole city. Our business is our platform to perpetuate the presence and principles of Jesus." The result was that the whole region heard the word of the Lord.

This is such a different paradigm of church than how we operate today. If a church does reach out into the city, it is called outreach. But if the paradigm is that the church is in the city, then those things done to reach the city with the principles of Jesus should technically be called "in reach." The church is permeating every aspect of the city and in the marketplace *already*. What the people of God do in the city throughout the week is not a part of a program of the church, but it is the actual lifestyle of the church. It is the life of people who follow Jesus in the city.

Church members tend to talk about belonging to a certain church: "I belong to New Hope Church." Instead, we should be the *church in the city that belongs to God*. Saying that I belong to a church is directly opposed to the paradigm of church that Jesus first established. The church belongs to Jesus, and we are to be the church because we belong to Jesus. When our paradigm is: "I am the church in the city 24/7," then the entire city begins to belong to Jesus and come under his leadership.

An Early Failed Attempt to Centralize the Ekklesia Paradigm

Later in Paul's life, he made a valiant attempt at utilizing something much like what we see today as the common model for spreading religion.

Paul decided to spend three months teaching in the synagogue every Sabbath. The synagogue was the center of the Jewish religion. It was a holy place where holy men taught from the Holy

Scriptures. Sound familiar? Like most good entrepreneurs, Paul decided he would try something new. "Let's try building the kingdom of God by piggybacking on the existing weekly religious gathering to market this way of living (The Way)–this new society led by Jesus." The result of his three-month pilot program in a centralized "church-like" religious place? All kinds of opposition and negative PR for the Jesus way of living!

Here's the summary quote of the story:

"Paul entered the synagogue and spoke boldly there for three months, arguing persuasively about the kingdom of God. But some of them became obstinate; they refused to believe and publicly maligned the Way. So Paul left them. He took the disciples with him and had discussions daily in the lecture hall of Tyrannus. This went on for two years, so that all the Jews and Greeks who lived in the province of Asia heard the word of the Lord."[72]

Paul was used to things of God being taught weekly in religious places, just like we are. So he just did what seemed to come naturally. He preached his heart out for three months in the conventional "churches" and got opposition from the religious people and everybody else.

I'm sure Paul was just starting to fully understand this new paradigm himself. Maybe one day as he was teaching in the synagogue he said to himself, "Wait! Jesus said 'my ekklesia'! He didn't' say 'I'll build my synagogue!'"

As a result, Paul decided to move from teaching in the synagogue every week to teaching in a public lecture hall every day. It was probably a meeting space that was already used for secular assemblies of the Roman ekklesia. Here we see Paul embracing the paradigm that the ekklesia Jesus came to build was designed to grow through everyday life, through the public marketplace. Paul switched his strategy to perpetuate the culture of Jesus like the Greeks and Romans were doing it–through the ekklesia every day in the public, not in a private place for members only. He met in the public places daily in the same city with the same people he did business with every day.

The ekklesia was then and is today, the place where the non-church-goers and the non-religious were hanging out. That's where Paul focused his time.

The result? In just two years, the entire province of Asia had heard the word of the Lord! Paul went from beating his head against the wall and getting nowhere preaching to the private religious club "in the church" to being the church in public places every day. In two years the whole continent heard what it was like to live with Jesus as their life leader (Lord).

The ekklesia continued to take the world by storm in the early years. They were blessing people, giving favor to them, and doing miraculous things for them! They fed people, met all their needs, and healed them–now those are causes for viral marketing! Acts says there was not a person with unmet needs in the early movement of the ekklesia.

By 300 A.D., the church had taken over Rome. The ekklesia of the emperor was overshadowed by the ekklesia of Jesus. It got to the point that the Roman emperor ended up seeing this as an opportunity to embrace more power and authority and began to usurp control and authority over the church. The Roman Emperor Constantine essentially declared, "We're all Christians."

Thus began the demise of the ekklesia as an organic movement of people who penetrated every aspect of society. Instead, it devolved into a hierarchical institutional paradigm that became increasingly focused on power, money, and centralized control.

Certainly most churches today would not have this motive or focus. But this historic shift from a movement of people to a centralized institution had an indelible impact on church as we know it today.

The church as we know it today has been unable, despite its best efforts, to perpetuate the leadership and values of God into every aspect of society and it is, in many ways, an unsustainable model for most of the world. That means the prevailing current paradigm of church can't work to deeply impact the majority of humanity.

Let's take a closer look at why.

CHAPTER 17

SO MUCH MORE THAN BUILDINGS AND MEETINGS

Our affluent society in America is one of the few cultures in the world that can sustain the funding needed to fuel the conventional church model. Our model of conventional church works best in the more affluent places in America and Europe. The majority of the world doesn't have the resources to build churches effectively based on this model.

If church planting as we think of it is the key to taking the world by storm for Jesus, again, why isn't there more specific instruction on how to plant churches in the Bible? There's no instruction like "You gotta get your core team in place and make sure you have a great worship leader and a fantastic children's pastor." Not only is that not in alignment with the essence of the ekklesia model Jesus had in mind, it is also true that this method of church planting can only be done in a relatively affluent culture.

For example, it doesn't work very well in the majority of Africa or India because, tactically, it requires tons of money! When the church in the West institutionalized, it got money! It became hugely wealthy. The increasing value proposition became, "Let's attract more people and more success by our big edifices and by our great programs."

America is one of the relatively small segments of the world where this conventional model of the church has worked for generations –where you can build a building, hire full-time staff to run it, and have quality productions that capture people every Sunday. You need an affluent society, with the majority of the people relatively rich, for this model to work over time. We build buildings that sit empty several days a week, often on quality real estate locations. What other business can afford to do that?! We hire staff to run programs that primarily serve people one day and an evening or two a week. We exempt churches and church properties from paying taxes, but not all countries have our tax structure. Taxes might be prohibitive in some countries. For all these reasons it's really not a sustainable business model, and it's only manageable in the affluent societies that comprise about 20% of the world's population.

That means millions of people cannot be served by this model, and millions more live in countries where it is illegal to "do church" in this conventional way.

What Happens When it is Illegal to do Church

What's interesting is that today the church is growing the fastest and strongest in places where they are not doing church in the "conventional church" way. In recent years I have taken several business trips to China and have seen first-hand how the underground church in China is growing like crazy through the marketplace and through everyday relationships. The church in China looks a lot more like the strategy Jesus had in mind for taking the world by storm. It is a church for the most part without buildings and with minimal programs or paid professional pastors. The ekklesia is growing faster in China than it ever has in America. Now the largest atheist nation in the world is on track to become the largest Christian nation in the world. It looks like this could happen in the next seven to ten years. There are more Christians in China than in the U.S. now!! That's in a country where it is literally illegal to do church the way we do it in America.

As I have asked many Chinese Jesus-followers why Christianity is growing so fast in their country, the answers are fairly consistent. The key is not some particular method of church planting or some specialized techniques. The key to the success of the church in China is a completely different paradigm of church than what we have in North America. They say, it's not about what happens in or emanates from a certain place where we meet on Sundays. The prevailing paradigm of church is that we are the church in the community; we are the church when we are doing business and living our everyday lives.

This unconventional but very accurate model of doing church in China is growing in spite of the dire lack of great buildings, great children's programs, and great worship teams. In fact, when most of the church in China gathers together in houses, they can't even sing or worship out loud. In many locations, they mouth the words without sound so no one around them in the neighborhood can hear them or know there is a gathering of the church going on. The country with the greatest church growth in the world uses a strategy that does not depend on meeting in a great place with great lighting or great music on a great stage.

In North America we have justified our more program-centered church because our culture of affluence is entertainment-driven.

To attract attendees you need stage lights and professional quality music, drama, video, and attention-grabbing programming.

Don't get me wrong. I love that stuff and have spent much of my life helping churches create those attractional factors. I'm highlighting that this belies a less-than-ideal, less-than-highly-effective paradigm of church. It's still the conventional centralized model of church that says, "Our priority is to get people to come to the church. To do that, we need to have a cooler production. But get them to come to church, we must. Because what happens in and through and from this place is what church is all about. Coming to this place is how they get saved, how they become better people, how they learn to serve God, and how they get protected from the evil of the world."

The church in the West often looks a bit like a pond. The majority of those who swim into that pond swim in it once a week for an hour so and maybe dip in once or twice during the week. The hope is that we, the believer fish, will get our non-believer fish to come check out the pond so the pastor can cast the net in the service and catch a few more fish that can be trained to come stay in the pond.

For most churches, the programs that happen in the pond (within the building and programs of the church) are the only place, or at least the primary place, they are currently casting nets to catch new unbeliever fish. Most church people think they need to get unbeliever fish to come to church, and they hope they like the church enough to swim in the pond until they are "caught". If unbelievers don't like the people who have invited them to the pond, that's okay as long as they like the church. But most people aren't inviting their non-religious friends to come to church because they are embarrassed. Or they just know that their unchurched friends won't relate to what goes on in the church.

In China people aren't invited to come to a pond. The pond is flooding the country to penetrate every aspect of life, especially through business. On one of my trips I learned about an atheist business owner who had about four thousand employees. One of his business owner friends helped him learn to embrace the values and leadership of Jesus in his life and in his business through the friendship developed during their many business interactions. Naturally, that business owner began to live Jesus' values and follow his leadership in his own company. Within just a few years, the majority of his four thousand employees became followers of Jesus. If you ask them what church they are a part of, they name their business. If you ask them who their pastor is, they talk about one of their co-workers as a friend and spiritual mentor.

People from the West have a name for churches like this. They call them "Boss Churches." Business leaders like this who follow Christ realize that they have this incredible bait that brings non-believer fish to swim in their pond forty hours a week. The bait is a paycheck and a cause that adds value to society, to the environment, or to people in some tangible way. They simply use their pond—their business—as a place to establish Jesus' leadership and values in people's lives and thereby transform society.

I was having lunch with an attorney in China who was a founding partner of one of the largest law firms in the country. He is very tied in to the communist government. He himself was not yet a follower of Jesus. But I asked him why the government had not stepped in to keep these business owners from influencing people to become followers of Jesus. In many cases the government overlooks the practice of encouraging employees to take time to gather together on breaks or before or after business hours to talk about Jesus. They are even allowed to pray and encourage each other during paid business hours—essentially to have a church gathering. The answer the attorney gave me spoke volumes about the practical power of the ekklesia. He simply said this: "The communist government is very pragmatic, and these boss church businesses are creating so much value for society, in many cases setting the pace for excellence or productivity or employee satisfaction or growth, that they don't want to do anything to mess with a formula that is creating such good value for society." That is what the church is supposed to look like. It should be such a positive culture-creating force and adding so much value to society that everyone in the world cheers it on.

Culture Protector or Culture Creator?

I grew up believing that the world was the enemy of the church and therefore the world was my enemy. I learned that the Bible says, "Do not love the world or anything in the world"[73] I interpreted this to mean, "The world is evil but the church is a safe haven from that evil." It is true that the enemy of God's rightful leadership on this earth has used the things in the world to pull people away from God. The Bible also says, though, that we are to be in the world but not of it.[74] We are to live like lights in the world of darkness but not identify ourselves as belonging to the darkness.

Conventional church has come to be a critic of the culture of the world and a safe haven of protection from it. In stark contrast, ekklesia by definition is to be a culture creator, not a culture critic. It is designed to be a culture programmer, not a culture protector. The ekklesia is people called forth to transform culture, not to create a sub-culture. The ekklesia exists in culture to take charge of culture.

If you research history for a vehicle that would be an ideal platform for shaping culture, you'll see that business has been the dominant force behind building societies and shaping culture throughout time. For example, the famous Silk Road was a trade route that started operating several hundred years before Jesus' birth. It connected East and West. Although it was mainly used for transactions and transportation of silk, it spread ideas too, including philosophical and religious ideas. The Silk Road was a powerful force in the cultural development of Asia, India, the Middle East, Europe, and Africa. In some ways, this business trade route affected almost every human life, then and now.

Throughout history, the marketplace has been a gathering place, where people got together and exchanged ideas and information as well as goods. The market was where the people were; it was a social place in addition to a place of business. It was where people swap their stories as well as their supplies. Business has always been at the hub of human existence, the centrifuge of cultural values and norms. So wouldn't it stand to reason that God would want to spread his values and norms through this epicenter of culture creation?

So Does this Mean Death to the Church?

It's important that you understand my intent here. My intent is not to encourage anyone who is going to church to quit going to church or to abandon their precious church community. My intent here is not for anyone who is engaged in church to move away from it. My intent is to encourage everyone to move toward what Jesus intended when he announced that his followers were to be the ekklesia to perpetuate his values and purposes into every aspect of business and life. I'm not putting down the many good things that have happened and that will continue to happen in and through conventional churches. God knows there are many people who would never hear the good news about Jesus, many who would never find a place of meaningful community, many who would never experience the wonder of worshiping God in unity with like-minded people, many who would not have tangible needs met, if it wasn't for the great work many conventional churches do. What has and will happen there can be very good. I'm just saying that there's more.

We can be a bit more of what Jesus was hoping for when he launched his ekklesia. We can be more like what it looked like when the message of Jesus took over entire continents in the early ekklesia. For those of us who are involved in conventional churches, is it possible we have settled for just the "good" we experience instead of going for the "more" that Jesus has in mind? As we know, good is often the enemy of the best. Let's not let satisfaction with the good that has been, keep us from the more that can be.

Why Do We Get Together?

Is there still a place for the conventional church gathering in this ekklesia paradigm? Absolutely! It just might look and feel a bit different. When you look at the early ekklesia, when people got together, everyone brought something to share.[75] That sounds a lot more like my weekly staff meetings than my weekly church service! What if church functioned a bit more like a weekly staff meeting does in our businesses? When the staff gathers it's to connect more directly and in person with their leader and with each other. Staff meetings exist to equip, train, resource, and coordinate to be effective at doing the work during the week!

For years I have had staff meetings every Monday. These weekly staff meetings in my business are a time for all the staff to do strategy updates, and to share progress, plans, and discuss coordination and synergy opportunities. The staff also receive input from their team leader on current priorities and perspectives based on the leader's ability to see the bigger picture.

What if when the church gathers, we see it as a time to hear from the big boss–from God Himself? What if we see it as a time to share what everyone accomplished last week, what the strategies are for this week, and how can we coordinate together so we can maximize our efficiency this week as we go out and do the work of the ekklesia in the marketplace?

In business, when we gather for staff meetings, we act differently than when we go back to our offices and work stations. In church, when we gather on the weekend, we act differently than when we go back to our places of ministry in the marketplace.

- In business, we are staff not because we are in the staff meeting, but because we do the staff work during the week. In church, we are not doing church because we show up for the weekly meeting. We are the church because we are doing the work of the ekklesia to transform our part of the world during the week.

- In business, though the staff can hear from me through email and other methods throughout the week, the purpose of the staff meeting is to hear from their leader in a concentrated and focused fashion. In the ekklesia, though, we can all hear from God throughout the week as He interacts and communicates with us in real time, the purpose of the church gathering is to hear from God in a concentrated and focused fashion.

- The purpose of my staff meeting is to make sure everyone on the team has the resources and training needed to do the work the rest of the week. It is also to celebrate the business wins from the previous week, and to coordinate the strategy for the upcoming week. Likewise, the purpose of a gathering of the ekklesia is to make sure everyone on the team is equipped and empowered to do the work that needs to be done all week, to celebrate the kingdom wins from the previous week, and to coordinate and synergize strategies for what we are going to accomplish in building God's purposes into our society during the next week.

So when we gather, it is to connect more directly in person with "the boss" and to equip, train, resource, and coordinate, to be effective at doing the important work during the week. There is the staff gathered and the staff doing business: the staff meeting and the staff working. As we often say in my office, "When we're meeting, we're not working." But we still meet so that we can work better.

What if that was the paradigm when the church gathered? There is the church gathering and the church working. There is the church meeting and the church doing business the rest of the week. What if when the churches (people on God's team) gather, they do it to take intentional time to connect with the boss (God) and to make sure that everyone is equipped and resourced and has coordinated efforts to get the important work of the church done in business during the week?

We apply a similar concept in my family. We have family gatherings where extended family gets together most every week. Then the individual families and members go and do life and business throughout the week. We are still family. We are not family because we gather. We are family gathered and family working.

In the same way you will not be in church because you go to church on Sunday. You are not in church because you gather. You are in church on Sunday and you are in church working the rest of the time.

Training Camp, Super Bowl or Fantasy Football?

There was a pastor who said, "Listen, our worship services

on Sunday are our Super Bowl every week." One of his staff members raised his hand and said, "I beg to differ. Our Super Bowl is six days a week out there in the community, and this is training camp." I love this staff member's paradigm shift, that the Sunday gathering is the training camp and pep rally to go out and play the game that's played six days a week.

Maybe that shift would start an explosion in the popularity of the ekklesia, a bit like what happened when fantasy football entered the sports scene. Football went from thousands of people in stadiums watching a few people playing on the field once a week to over forty million people playing football during the week outside of the stadium! My hope would be that church will go from thousands of people in sanctuaries watching a few people on stage once a week to millions of people engaged in the game of transforming culture during the week in business and everyday life.

Take a minute and think about what it would really look like if you were part of a group of people who "did church" in this way, where it was about so much more than the building and meetings. What would it be like if you were part of a group that gathered regularly like staffs do to celebrate accomplishments and coordinate the work of rebuilding the world through the marketplace? Imagine how exciting it would be to gather together with like-minded world changers to celebrate what happened in the last week to transform your city!

Don't you think that would add vitality and excitement to the whole concept of church—actually having a tangible impact for good on the world each week? What might it look like if you embraced the talents and tactical work of your business as tools to transform your city? I'll show you an exciting example of what this looks like in the next chapter.

CHAPTER 18

SUPERNATURALLY POSITIONED TO TRANSFORM THE WORLD

In the church I grew up in, we gave spiritual gifts evaluations to learn how we could best serve in the programs of the church. It was not a bad thing. Good church programs need good church volunteers serving in the right roles. Identifying roles that someone can serve in where they are doing something they are particularly good at is a solid human resource management practice.

Spiritual gifts are exceptional capabilities that seem to come naturally to the one with that strength. Christians believe these gifts have a supernatural origin. For example, someone may have the gift of teaching, administration, healing, mercy, speaking in other languages or leadership. Outside of the Christian community, people might refer to someone who seems to have an innate, out-of-the-ordinary capability as "gifted" in that area. In the church, these gifted capabilities are seen as inspired by God with their primary purpose as serving in God's church.

At the extreme, I have heard teachings where pastors insinuate that something is only a "spiritual gift" when you use it in the ministry programs in the church. Imagine if instead, the spiritual gifts evaluations and teachings of the church were focused primarily on finding your sweet spot for the service/ministry/ work you do in the marketplace during the week when the church is not gathered? What if, when the church gathered, we flipped that around and identified and nurtured those gifts and talents each person could use to build God's values and leadership into their daily lives in business?!

The reality is that many of the spiritual gifts listed in the Bible can be more powerfully applied in the marketplace than in the programs of the conventional church. For example, the gift of "apostleship" (which is really an entrepreneurial and pioneering capability) is actually more applicable in the marketplace than in the programs of the conventional church. If you're a truly gifted apostle like the famous Apostle Paul was, you start things and get them running with effective people and processes, and then you move on to start something else.

Well, the reality is that you can't have a lot of people like that in one conventional church. Just from a practical standpoint, because it is one organization, you can't have a lot of apostle leaders without causing conflict or confusion. Yet this gift of apostleship is most powerful in building God's kingdom when leaders use it to go start new ventures in the marketplace.

When I was a kid it was in vogue in the church circles I was a part of to post a certain sign above the exit of the church building for people to read as they left. The sign said, "You are now entering the mission field." With this ekklesia paradigm I am proposing, the new vogue would be to replace those church building exit signs with signs reading: "You are now entering the church (ekklesia)."

This would remind us every time we leave a gathering at a church building that our platform to transform the world is where we are the rest of the week. And where are we? The truth is that we are in business. We may gather with other followers of Jesus once or twice a week, but we spend most of our waking hours in business.

There is an old Jewish saying, "Business is Life." Those three words say a lot. Business is where a lot of life happens. Business is what creates and drives a lot of what we experience in life. And the ekklesia Jesus came to build is designed to influence and infiltrate a lot more than what we've believed it could.

The ekklesia is a collective group of people called to change the world in everyday life, primarily through business. The weekend event that most people now call "church" is simply a gathering of the different parts of the ekklesia in the city or region that meet during the week. And your business is exceptionally well positioned to be the primary platform for expanding God's ekklesia in your city! As a business leader, you are exceptionally well positioned to fulfill Jesus' dream to build his church and all the powers of evil can't prevail against it. As a business leader, you are supernaturally positioned and supernaturally gifted to rebuild the world.

Let me give you an example.

Pastor Daniel's Story

Are there many examples of business leaders who really embrace their business as a vehicle to rebuild their world? Yes! It is happening more all the time.

Let me introduce you to Pastor Daniel. Yes, he really is

225

a business owner, and yes, he really is called "Pastor" by the employees in his business and by many people in his city. I'm not saying that it is necessary for a business leader to be called "Pastor" to fully embrace this paradigm. However, in this case, it is a clear cue that the idea of business as a platform for building the ekklesia (church) is alive and well.

Shaji and Shiney Daniel started Agape Home Healthcare out of their home twenty years ago. They worked with Shiney's mother (who is an RN). With little to no money, they started providing nursing services out of their home to other people's homes. Their business grew and grew, and they added employees and kept adding employees until they reached over two thousand people on their team. They are now considered the largest home health provider in the state of Texas.

It's also noteworthy to mention they grew their business the hard way. They have not grown through mergers and acquisitions. They hired every employee one at a time. They are gifted entrepreneurs, leaders, and administrators. They view these supernatural abilities as their God-given gifts to enable them to build better people and a better city in and through their business.

I first got to know Pastor Daniel a few years ago, when I was involved in developing a senior care community in Forney, Texas. In the process we did market studies on the surrounding market. I kept hearing about the strong revitalization of the neighboring city, Mesquite, and a few times it was in conjunction with the name of a business called Agape Home Healthcare. I heard about the huge company BBQs and banquets to which they invited the people of the city. I heard about all the families this business was supporting with their business services and by providing literally tons of food and even toys every year. My curiosity got the best of me.

The first time I walked into the beautiful home office of Agape Home Healthcare, I asked the receptionist where Shaji's office was.

She looked puzzled for a moment and then replied, "Oh, do you mean Pastor Daniel?"

I said, "Is he the same Mr. Daniel that is the CEO of the company?"

She laughed and said, "Yes, of course, Pastor Daniel started it!"

That was my first clue that something was different about this CEO's paradigm of business. When I sat down in the executive suite in front of Pastor Daniel, I asked him what church he was pastor of and whether he was a pastor there before he started this business. He just grinned and told me that he was the pastor of this business. He described how this business was his ministry. He said for many of his employees, this is the closest thing to church that they will ever experience. He told me how he is intentional at building community among his employees and deliberately giving them time and space to support each other's needs and dreams.

As he gave me a tour of his newly expanded headquarters building, we walked into a room that was a sea of well-designed cubicles with hundreds of people working diligently. Of course, many of the employees don't work in the office because they are providing care for people in their homes. Most of the employees show up at the office in the morning to check-in before they go out to the homes at which they will provide care services.

Off to the side was a large open area. Pastor Daniel described how every morning they facilitate a time of prayer when employees can be prayed for and can pray for each other. Although it is optional, most employees join in for this time of prayer. He described how there have been many times when people just showed up for this kind of support when they were going through a crisis in their lives, and this became their number one support group.

I remember asking one of his managers what the best part of working there was. He launched into describing how excited he has been to help lead a couple of high-impact humanitarian trips with large teams of employees from the company to support orphanages and impoverished people in India. I asked how he was able to get so many people from the company to take time off work to go on a mission trip like that.

He chuckled and said, "Oh, it's pretty easy when the company pays their way AND gives extra paid vacation time to go. Our only challenge is that we have a waiting list of people who want to go! Now it is more of a reward for great team members, who get selected to go on these trips. Of course, the life-changing stories and deep camaraderie that people come back with after these trips makes everyone else want to be able to go on the next one."

This is such a great example of what I am talking about! This is what the ekklesia is supposed to look like! Shaji and Shiney Daniel have truly embraced their business as their platform for building God's presence and values into their city. Pastor Daniel, as CEO of a successful business, is truly a pastor of the ekklesia in the city of Mesquite.

Pastor Daniel grew up in India, where he wasn't surrounded by a concept of the conventional, centralized, model of church. In his home town, it was hard to even come up with the money to build a special hut for Christians to gather in, let alone to pay a full-time professional pastor. So the prevailing paradigm was that following Jesus meant you brought his leadership and his values into every relationship and every situation in everyday life. You were considered a "pastor" if you took on the responsibility to shepherd or mentor other people who were learning to follow Jesus. So in Pastor Daniel's mind it was just a natural thing for him to take some spiritual responsibility for those within his business. Nobody told him he should be a pastor, but he saw himself as the guy who was responsible to shepherd anyone within his circle of influence. That's how he was used to doing it in India. So why not in Texas? And if it can work in Texas, why not in your business?

What if dozens of other business leaders in this same city began to see their business as the primary vehicle for building God's presence and principles into their city? More importantly, what if every conventional church in this city began to see these Jesus-following business leaders as the primary expression of the ministry of their church? What if pastors of conventional churches began to see business leaders like Shaji Daniel as being every bit as much of a pastor as they are? What if pastors of conventional churches began to view businesses like Agape Home Healthcare as a campus of their church? What if conventional churches poured as much time, money, and energy into seeing God's presence and purposes thrive through the spirited businesses in their community as they do in building the programs of their church?

It wouldn't be long until the entire city was transformed to live the principles of Jesus. It wouldn't be long until all of society was living the abundant life that Jesus intended. It wouldn't be long until the supernatural power and presence of God was permeating every aspect of our world.

PART 5

IMPLEMENTING THE MASTER SYSTEM TO TRANSFORM THE WORLD

CHAPTER 19

THE MOST RADICAL LEADERSHIP INITIATIVE EVER

We live in a society today that seems to spin toward fragmentation, complexity, and even chaos. Nothing is more needed than a clear and compelling system to bring life together into something with cohesive meaning and vision. I believe God has designed such an all-encompassing global system. And you and your business are in a position to implement it.

What I am proposing is perhaps the most radical leadership initiative ever announced on this planet! It is an initiative to replace and rebuild the present state of society with a new world system. What I am proposing here is that you consider the reality of a complete system for rebuilding society. I am proposing that you embrace your leadership role in business as a comprehensive platform to perpetuate this ideal system for society.

You are perfectly positioned to bring in this new world system.

Yes, you! You can change the world! That's not just some flowery motivational speech. For real, as a business leader, you can change the world! You will!

The business leaders throughout history who have made rebuilding society central to their cause have left the greatest life legacies. The most influential leader in the history of this world, Jesus, made rebuilding society the central emphasis of his entire life's work. Like every good leader, he was extraordinarily clear and consistent in the language he used to describe what is central to his cause. He called this new world system the "Kingdom of God" or interchangeably the "Kingdom of Heaven."

He used those phrases over one hundred times just in the records we have of his teachings. Everything he did and taught as a business owner and as a world leader centered around making this new world system a reality on this planet.

I suggest that his going down in history as the greatest world-changer ever is largely because his primary motive for building his business was not just serving customers well or making a profit. His primary focus, his driving reason for being in business and in life, was to build a better society, one where people lived under the leadership of and with the values of God.

This was his life purpose. He called it the good news. It is the only thing he ever called good news. He went out preaching the good news of the kingdom of God.[76] This was the theme of his mission.

At one point Jesus stated his life mission in these words: "I must give the good news of the kingdom of God . . . for that is what I was sent to do".[77] If the highest impact business leader ever–the greatest world-changer ever–thought this was that important, then it seems this notion of building the Kingdom of God would be a focus worthy of consideration for any leader who aspires to make an impact on this world.

Every great leader who has clear purpose, over time becomes identified with that purpose. Martin Luther King is essentially synonymous with equal rights. Jesus is essentially synonymous with the Kingdom of God. The Bible asserts that Jesus was God who lived among humans to demonstrate what God–the God of the Kingdom he was so passionate about–is really like. In fact, Jesus himself said, "Anyone who has seen me has seen the Father."[78]

When we see his attitudes and actions, we see what God thinks and acts like. When we see his character, we see the character of God. When we see his relationships, we see the relationship system of God. When we see how he treats people, we see how God treats people.

The good news is that if this is what God is like, then God is a very good God. He is trustworthy. He is loving. He is always in a good mood and always out for our good. In Jesus' person, we see this is what God is like. In Jesus' teachings and life, we see what God's kingdom is like.

If There Is a God, He Must Have an Ideal System for Society

Some who are reading this may not be convinced there is a God. If that's where you're at, just play the "what if" game with me for a minute.

What if there is a God? What if there is a supreme intelligence that, at a minimum, designed and originated the universe? If there is a God, it stands to reason his impact would be global. If there is a God, it stands to reason his kingdom–his rule and reign; his influence and domain–would be a total kingdom for the total world.

It just wouldn't make sense that God would be a partial God ruling over just a part of the world. It wouldn't make sense for such a total God to have dominion over the spiritual realm but not the material realm, or have influence over churches but not businesses, or have an ideal system for individual lives but not for the collective society. A good God, by definition, must have designed an ideal system for all of society (his kingdom) or not be God at all.

It is the same way that a good business owner, by definition, must have a system for his total company, not just one product, one person or one division in the company. An ant with a system for building its ant colony could arguably be more god-like than a God without an intentionally designed system for how individuals and society should ideally operate! If there isn't a God that has designed an optimal system for society, there should be!

Many of the most sophisticated scientists these days conclude there must be an intelligent designer behind the complex micro and macro elements of the physical world. For example, one of the twentieth century's leading atheist philosophers, Anthony Flew, who often debated Christians publicly, eventually renounced atheism based on scientific evidence of an intelligent designer. Check out his book, *There Is a God*, where he explains the reasons he came to believe there is "a divine source" because of the "world picture" that has "emerged from science". He makes it clear that this belief in God was for him no leap of faith but rather doing what he had done for half a century as a philosopher: "Follow the argument where ever it leads." The evidence led him to the logical conclusion that there had to be a creator and designer of the natural world. Albert Einstein was asked whether he believed in God, and he said that no serious scientist could study the universe and not see a unifying, brilliant, and intentional design behind all that is.

The odds that something as complex as the atom or the solar system just happened by chance are far less than the odds of an intelligent designer's involvement. Design is detected through logic that filters out chance or natural law necessity. For instance, when you look at an iPhone, logic says this is not explainable on the basis of chance or automatically functioning natural laws. We know from looking at its specific complexity that it was designed by an intelligent agent. Heck, unless you're a dumpster diver, you know the last meal you ate had an intelligent designer behind it! In fact, the greater the complexity and the more specific the outcome of the complexity, the less the likelihood that event or that thing came about by chance. It must have been designed to be that way.

In *A Meaningful World*, authors Benjamin Wiker and Jonathan Witt say:

> We circle a star that is neither too big nor too small, neither too hot nor too cool. Additionally, if we were allowed to go shopping around the galaxy for the star with the best type of electromagnetic radiation for organic life, our Sun would be hard to beat. Our Sun is the golden mean, a metal-rich G star, providing us with the necessary elemental materials, but it's not too metal-rich. If a star is too metal-poor, it cannot even make planets; but if the original 'birth-cloud' out of which a star is formed is too metal-rich, then it produces a planetary system that is a disorderly jumble of planets and comets colliding, tugging, and flinging planets out of the habitable zone. In contrast to such chaos, our system has . . . an improbably high number of planets with nice, well-behaved, and nearly circular orbits . . . that near-circularity not only ensures that planets aren't smacking into each other or disturbing each other's orbits, but that we on Earth enjoy a relatively narrow range of temperature fluctuations. A significantly more elliptical orbit would drive us above or below the narrow biological temperature range, [and] the smaller the temperature range needed, the more difficult it is to attain and maintain.[79]

How could all this be by accident? It isn't. It's by design.

Although much more can be said on this subject, if you do your research, you will find that belief in an intelligent designer—belief in God—is not based on ignorance of science or natural law but rather based on deeper knowledge of these things. Truth be told, those who ignore these indications of an intelligent designer are simply relying on their bias that there is no God and therefore everything—even the most improbable, biologically-favorable occurrences—must happen naturally. They are not relying on science and sound reasoning wherever it may lead.

So here's my point. Doesn't it stand to reason that the same intelligence that designed the tiny, but uber-complex individual atom and its complex interaction with every other element of the physical world would have designed a plan for individuals to live their lives? Doesn't it stand to reason that the intelligence that designed the stars and the planets and made sure their courses were orderly enough to keep human beings alive would have designed a plan for people's complex interaction with everyone and everything around us? Doesn't it stand to reason that there must be an ideal system for BEING, both within each of us and within all of society?

My hypothesis here is that Jesus came to demonstrate to the world that ideal system for society (The Kingdom). From the platform of a business leader in his community, Jesus taught and modeled this ideal system for society. In so doing he left us a clear model to rebuild society.

The Ideal System for Building Society

It is indeed good news that God does have a system to build the ideal person and the ideal society, and we have seen it! There is a case study that we can learn from and follow!

He could have delivered his ideal system for society in a complex set of operating manuals. In fact, there were some attempts at something like this earlier in the history of his interactions with humankind as recorded in the Old Testament of the Bible. There we see many rules and regulations given to try to make society function better. When they were followed, better societies resulted.

Yet these rules and regulations were not consistently followed any more than employees can be convinced to perfectly follow operating manuals someone else creates. God could have announced his system for society with a powerful publicity campaign accompanied by thunder and tornadoes and shouted, "Follow my system or else." If he is God, he certainly has the authority by force of legislation to build his kingdom in this way. But that would not create free and empowered people. It would only create slaves who follow out of fear. Based on the risk God took in allowing freedom of choice and what it has cost him, he appears to place a high value on our freedom to understand and choose his kingdom systems for success.

While God's system is a total one for doing life, it is not a system that brings bondage. When you follow this system fully, you find total freedom.

History has shown that in any political totalitarianism system like fascism, Nazism or communism, people lose freedoms. But if you totally follow the system of God's kingdom you gain total freedom. In fact, the freest people throughout history have been those who have lived the values of the kingdom (including following its restrictions) in order to enjoy a life released from the controls of ineffectiveness. God's kingdom ways are simply the most effective ways to live. It's in our very design.

History and science have proven that lasting positive change within individuals and within societies does not happen best by imposing legislation or by powerful dictates. Sustainable success happens best by personal discovery and inspiring leadership. So God chose to embed the principles of his kingdom into the very fabric of human systems so we could discover it on our own adventure through life and also by learning from others throughout history.

This is how we get to the point of adopting these principles as our own because they embody the self-evident, most effective way to live. In this way we get to discover that the success principles of the universe and the success principles of our very being are indeed the success principles of God's kingdom.

As an accelerator to that discovery process, God himself chose to show up in person on this earth in the form of a human being who was named Jesus. In that magnificent manifestation of authentic kingdom living, we see the undeniably attractive nature of the character of God (the king) and the undeniable value of his system for society (his kingdom). We see what the God of "the kingdom" looks like in human form and what his system for society looks like in human relationships.

If you want to know what God looks like, look at Jesus. God relates to people like Jesus related to people. God leads like Jesus. Jesus models the kingdom of God in living color! His life and teachings are the perfect illustration of the kingdom. God allowed us to see his kingdom in operation in a real person. Jesus' entire life, even to the very end, is an illustration of what the system of God's kingdom looks like when lived out. As was noted in an earlier chapter, the followers of Jesus have fanned out throughout history and geography to give us visions and concrete examples of the kingdom in operation from hospitals to art, architecture, government systems, charitable endeavors of all kinds, transcendent music, and other noble and worthy endeavors. It's a fabulous sight!

You've gotta love God's genius strategy in all this. God snuck up on us in disguise, as a baby born in a hardworking general contractor's home. This child grew and as a teenager took over leading the family business and became the best builder of society the world has ever seen. Now this same world-changing leader is in a position to be an ever-present mentor, coach, and an unlimited resource center for any leader who chooses to live for his purposes and under his leadership.

This is how God builds his kingdom, in and through people. First he showed his kingdom in and through Jesus, and now he will manifest it in and through you and me.

What Is the Kingdom?

The kingdom is doing life God's way, under God's leadership. It is God's ideal system for society as seen in the life and teachings of Jesus. It is the Jesus model experienced throughout all of society. It is the ideal plan to optimize humanity. It is God making both the individual and society his realm and reign. The kingdom of God is designed to replace and rebuild the current ineffective world order with God's world order. Jesus is both the model and the architect of this new world we are building.

It starts in the individual and permeates all of society. Experiencing the kingdom of God begins by embracing a whole new paradigm of life—what the Bible sometimes refers to as a new birth where you push "reset" in your mind and allow it to be reprogrammed by the values and perspectives that Jesus modeled. The characteristics of the kingdom are best understood in the character of Jesus.

The kingdom happens to the degree people and societies are following Jesus. It brings heaven's system of life—the eternally sustainable success system of life—to earth now, literally creating heaven on earth now. It is a total system for life.

It is worth noting that experiencing the kingdom of God fully requires a comprehensive loyalty but it is a loyalty which results in complete freedom. As noted before, following God's restrictions results in much more breathing space and happiness in life—freedom from a host of problems and ills!

There is simply no situation in our lives, our businesses, or in society that would not be better if the values and actions of the kingdom were applied. In fact, I challenge you to imagine what the world would look like if everyone in the entire world and every societal system fully lived out the values of Jesus. Then I challenge you to think of any other competing world view, or societal system that would come anywhere close to producing the ideal life that you would dream of living.

Imagine a world where individuals, families, governments, and all of society consistently modelled and perpetuated the core values and key outcomes of the kingdom. Envision a world where individuals and all of society are characterized by love, joy, peace, patience, kindness, goodness, gentleness, and self-control. Imagine economies where everyone was driven to continually find better ways to understand and fulfill the needs and desires of others. Picture what relationships would look like if everyone defined and lived out a quality of love that was always patient, always kind, never rude, never boastful, always hoping for the best, never giving up, and doing what is best for others regardless of rewards or ramifications. Daydream of a world where success is defined based on how well one demonstrates and experiences that kind of love. (Jesus said that love was how the world would recognize his followers.) Envision what relationships would look like if the primary thought on every individual's mind, the primary question that governed societies was: "What does this kind of love require of me?"

Whether or not you believe in God, I think you can see that it would be a better world and a better society. People would be happier and well cared for with such a worldview prevailing. If you were to engage the best minds throughout history and ask them to design the ideal society that you would like to live in, I can't imagine anyone coming up with anything better or more exactly as humans were designed to be, than a society where the

Jesus model pervades every aspect of life. THIS is the Kingdom of God. THIS is a lifestyle worth giving our lives to experience and perpetuate. It is for THIS reason God chose to enter the human experience as a business owner named Jesus. THIS was the central focus of the life and teaching of Jesus.

Why can't we as business leaders see our business as the platform to build THIS kind of society–to build the kingdom of God–right here, right now, right where we are? Imagine a city, a nation, living fully under God's rule and reign. That is what the founders of America intended. In fact we declare it every time we pledge allegiance to our flag: "One nation, under God." What if we actually believed that and made it so?!

Could it be that business is the primary process God intends to use to take dominion over this earth through his people? What if business is God's chosen vehicle to bring his kingdom to this earth? What if you are the one to do it? What if you are in your position because you are destined to rebuild the world after God's ideal pattern?

We don't have to wait for someone else to do it. We don't have to wait for some future political or global event to change the world. We don't have to wait for some future heaven to happen.

The kingdom system is God's plan to rebuild society now. Many Christians see the kingdom as something that only applies to their inner experience now and to the future "coming of the kingdom" when they are in heaven. But they think the kingdom has little to no practical impact on the world here and now.

What if the kingdom was intended to take over here and now? What if it was supposed to become the norm in our time? What if it was God's system to bring health to every social, political, and economic element of our society today? What if the kingdom was designed to be the absolute universal order of things right now?

What if you are destined to start rebuilding the world, right now? What if you are destined to bring heaven to earth through your business now? If so, how do you do it?

You start by embracing the leadership paradigm of the kingdom in your own mind and in your own business!

CHAPTER 20

THE NEW KINGDOM LEADERSHIP MINDSET

What I am proposing here is a new mindset for most leaders. It is not the typical motivational mindset of: "The more successful I become, the more I get to do what I want, the more I will have, and the more others will serve my needs." It is: "The more successful I become, the more I get to influence the world for good, the more others will have, and the more I have the privilege of serving others' needs."

The paradigm of the pre-kingdom world is that the leader exists to be served. The multigenerational, world-changing success of JC International demonstrates that the paradigm of the highest impact leaders is that they are the hardest working servants. In fact, throughout historic Jewish culture, the greatest leaders were the greatest servants. As mentioned in an earlier chapter, even in Jewish societies today, business owners with many employees are given significant honor. This is not done to flatter them and win their favor. It is specifically to honor them because they serve more people than others do.

Jesus highlighted this paradigm of leadership when he said to his followers, "You know that the rulers of the Gentiles lord it over them, and their high officials exercise authority over them. Not so with you. Instead, whoever wants to become great among you must be your servant, and whoever wants to be first must be your slave— just as the Son of Man did not come to be served, but to serve, and to give his life as a ransom for many."[80]

This is perhaps the most fundamental characteristic of leaders in the kingdom. They have the mindset and take the actions of a servant. They are not servants who just follow what everyone else tells them to do. They are expected to rule, but as a servant of those that they rule.

Notice that Jesus expected his followers to be rulers—to be great and highly influential leaders. He was just asking them to do it in a new way, in the kingdom way.

That, as with many other kingdom principles, is the opposite of the world's way. If you want to be first, be the last. If you want to be the leader, be the servant. From this vantage point, Jesus became the greatest by serving up love to people, even to people that were wickedly brutal to him to the point of torturing him to death.

I don't know about you, but I don't anticipate nearly that bad of treatment from the people I work with, and I still have a hard time wanting to stay in the servant mindset all the time.

The truth is, though, that every self-centered leader is an unhappy leader. If your happiness is centered around pleasing yourself, then you will never be pleased with yourself, and no one else will be pleased with you either. In companies with CEOs like these, the boss may be universally flattered, but he or she is also universally disliked.

Every self-centered business ultimately becomes an unsuccessful business. Every business that focuses on meeting its own needs first rather than seeking to meet the needs of customers or clients first will eventually not have any customers.

The Selfishness Implosion

Selfishness sooner or later implodes. Things fall apart. Once responsibility to others is thrown out the window, profits and happiness are soon to follow. Let me give some examples.

I've had a fair amount of experience in the legal world through my businesses over the years. I've had as many as five full-time, in-house attorneys on staff. I've spent hundreds of thousands of dollars on legal fees for single transactions. Some of that money has been well spent and some of it, well, let's just say I wonder who actually profited the most from the transaction. Over the last years, I've noticed that some law firms have changed in their customer centric focus.

Derek Bok, an attorney and former president of Harvard University, writes about how many law firms went from being places dedicated to serving their clients to places dedicated to making huge profits. One way they did this was through emphasizing "billable hours." Attorneys were pressured to rack up thousands of billable hours per year.

Did this lead to better service for the clients? No, it led to lawyers providing more services than necessary, at a slower pace than usual, to rack up those hours. It led to abuses too, Bok said, with attorneys "padding" their hours to bring in more profits.

Yet, in spite of more profits, lawyers reported more unhappiness in their work than ever before.

Researcher Deborah Rhode, writing in the *Fordham Urban Law Journal*, found that the pressure to put in more and more billable hours for greater profits leads to great stress for lawyers, including physical and relational consequences. It has led to alcohol and drug abuse.[81] Under such pressures, lawyers also may find themselves tempted to bend the legal rules and standards to please wealthy clients. The consequences can really get steep then, and lawyers worry about them.

Many lawyers went into law because they had high ideals about serving society. A traditional way to satisfy this idealism, in addition to giving good and fair service to clients, was through pro bono work. Pro bono work is when lawyers provide some legal services for free, especially to those who cannot afford to pay. Yet, under pressure to rack up billable hours, attorneys had no time for pro bono work.

Rhode says that an important way for partners in a law firm to serve society and their own employees is to make time and space for pro bono work. This is because lawyers have said that their pro bono work is the most satisfying part of their work lives.

Another example is the atmosphere that has prevailed in the financial markets in recent years. Our real estate company has worked with some of the largest financial institutions in the country before, during, and after the great recession. It has been interesting to see some investment banks and lenders that started out great become weak or collapse and some remain strong and even grow. There are always many reasons for a collapse, but a common theme seems to be that these companies end up focusing more on serving the bottom line than on serving their customers.

In his 2012 *New York Times* article "Why I Am Leaving Goldman Sachs," Greg Smith concluded that the culture of Wall Street had changed from serving the client to serving the profit margins of the financial institution. Smith said, "Culture was always a vital part of Goldman Sachs' success. It revolved around teamwork, integrity, a spirit of humility, and always doing right by our clients."[82] That culture changed, he said: "I attend derivatives sales meetings where not one single minute is spent asking questions about how we can help clients. It's purely about how we can make the most possible money off of them."[83]

Is it any wonder that so many financial firms like this have experienced so many challenges in recent years?

A business centered upon selfish interest eventually implodes. That's because it is going against the fundamental principles of the kingdom; the intrinsic laws of the universe. An individual or group can only do that so long before decay, decline or destruction of some sort comes about.

This is because we are not built to be the center of the universe. Whenever we try to be the center of the universe and make our business and/or our life revolve around our needs and wants, we go against the endemic global operating system. The universe isn't built around you or your business, and it won't back you if it's all about you. Sooner or later there will be some sort of implosion or collapse.

The system of God's kingdom is built on the principle that the one who makes it their priority to meet the needs of others first will have the greatest influence. That's why God is at the top of the food chain. He is unquestionably the greatest servant. He serves up a million things we didn't even work for and that we hardly notice. Every brilliant sunrise, every beautiful flower, and every breath is evidence of this. A further dramatic demonstration of the servanthood nature of God is seen in the life of Jesus. He served people even when it resulted in his death.

You have probably heard the saying: "Power corrupts, and absolute power corrupts absolutely." I have sometimes worried about whether the power coming from having ever-increasing leadership influence would put me at risk for this corruption from power. I don't know of a thoughtful leader with character who hasn't pondered this risk carefully. My conclusion has been that the greatest mitigation of that risk is knowing and honoring a self-giving God who stays smack dab in the center of my world. The life of Jesus puts a million-lumen spotlight on the character of God, revealing the absolute self-giving, others-focused nature of his kingdom. The most absolute power in the universe went so far in demonstrating self-giving love that it killed him. Because of that self-sacrificing love, he has been promoted to the highest position of honor in the universe.

I can be subordinate to that kind of God. I can even bow low in honor and respect before that kind of God! It's not because I have to. It's because I can't help it.

I believe this is my greatest safeguard against the corruption of power, and it keeps my influence going strong.

Try it. If you bow low before a God like that, it helps you stand tall even in the greatest leadership role while at the same time keeping the humble attitude of a servant. Sustainable success, satisfaction, and happiness follow, because you have the power of the king and his kingdom behind you.

The Selflessness Explosion

Jesus' vision was that the others-focused values and blessings of the kingdom of God would penetrate every aspect of our culture. Again, this was the central message of Jesus' leadership when he was on this earth. His teaching centered on the kingdom of God. It was front and center in his mind.

We pray about what is front and center on our mind. When my kids are sick, that's what I pray about. We pray for what we care about most. If you ask me on Super Bowl Sunday what I am praying for, I might say, "That the Seahawks win." But then if you ask me what I am praying for the next Sunday, it might be something else.

When Jesus' followers asked him to teach them to pray, he responded with what we now call "The Lord's Prayer." They asked twice. One request is recorded in Matthew and the other in Luke, and as near as we can tell, those two events occurred about a year and a half apart. Jesus' answer to their request to teach them how to pray like he prayed was consistent over that time.

At the beginning of his two model prayers, Jesus says to God his Father, "Your Kingdom come and your will be done on earth as it is in heaven." Jesus was clear what the coming of God's kingdom looks like. It looks like God's will being done here on earth just like it is done in heaven.

What is God's will? Jesus summarized it well when some religious leaders asked him what was the most important thing of all that God requires of humanity. Jesus responded by saying that everything God had expressed about his will up to that point could be encapsulated in two simple statements: Love God with all you've got. And love people as you love yourself.[84]

How do you think the will of God is done in heaven? Half-heart-edly? Just by individuals and not by the society of heaven? Surely it must be done on both the individual level and in the total social system of heaven. That's how it is meant to be on earth too, infiltrating every aspect of human life and activity, including and especially business. God's will is that our simple love for God and love for people would cause an explosion of selflessness that transforms society.

Go with What's Woven into the Fabric of Life

For over two thousand years since Jesus built his business and set in motion a system to rebuild the world, anyone and everyone who embraces the leadership and norms of his kingdom (his system for society) inevitably has a quality of life, regardless of circumstance, that is out of the ordinary. Those who do not, live less than optimal lives.

In reading this, some might think I am suggesting the imposition of some type of religious burden or restrictive way of life on them. Actually, quite to the contrary, I am simply suggesting that we get serious about aligning our lives with the systems that are built into the very fabric of how society is designed to function.

An early follower of Jesus named John says it this way: "In fact, this is love for God: to keep his commands. And his commands are not burdensome."[85] When you first read this, you might be thinking, "Wait, aren't all commands burdensome?"

Think about this. Let's say you just worked in the hot sun for two hours with no water, and your mouth is parched. I command you to get a drink. Is that a burdensome command? Is that a restrictive requirement? Why not? Because your body demands what I am commanding!

God's system for doing life in his kingdom is not burdensome. It is liberating! His commands (the things he asks us to do based on the example or teaching of Jesus, or based on the directives he gives us in our own minds) are not burdensome. What he commands is what the very nature of things demands. What God requires of us is what the universal systems for success, built in to the fabric of the universe, require for success. It is all for creating an abundant life. That's why Jesus said, "I have come that they may have life, and have it to the full."[86] Most people think Jesus' primary focus was to extend the quantity of life into eternity. However, the vast majority of his focus was on extending the abundant, Kingdom of Heaven quality of life into this world.

When we live within the demands of the kingdom, we are simply fulfilling what our human nature demands for true fulfillment and sustainable success. The commands of the kingdom and the demands of human nature are made for each other. When we live successfully within the kingdom, we live successfully within our true selves. When we live within the kingdom, we become the dominant force in every situation. It is not because we are trying to be dominant but because the things we think and do are the very things the situation demands.

This means the kingdom of heaven is within us. It is in the very laws of our being. The kingdom of heaven is also among us; it shows up in the relationships we have with others. It is endemic to our very nature as people and as society.

It is how we are wired to be, from the inside out. It is like our internal operating system that came from the manufacturer. If we try to load programs or actions that conflict with that internal operating system of the kingdom within us, things just don't work right, and they may eventually crash. If we align our lives with the kingdom operating system within, everything works better. Life and outcomes are more robust and sustainable.

In fact, life within the kingdom creates such sustainable success that it leads to an abundant eternal life. Yes, eternity is a long time to sustain success, but that is how things work when we live out the values of the kingdom.

The Royal Law

One of these kingdom values is what the biblical writer James calls the "Royal Law." James said, "If you really keep the royal law found in Scripture, 'Love your neighbor as yourself,' you are doing right."[87]

This isn't some man-made rule he is referring to. This is a non-negotiable universal principle of the kingdom. It is a "royal law," a "kingdom law." It is a law of the universe from the king who designed the universe. It has automatic benefits and natural outcomes with no external force or manipulation required. Its consequences are as predictable and as non-negotiable as the law of gravity. The quality of our life goes up or down according to how well we live out this "royal law," this non-negotiable principle of the kingdom.

This is true in our individual lives, our businesses, and our whole society. To go against this law is like turning a normal healthy cell into a cancer cell. It is still a cell, but instead of serving your body, it demands that your body serve it. Inevitably, it destroys that which it seeks to be served by. No matter how much those cancer cells multiply, they are destined for failure and destruction.

The right thing morally, the right thing according to the kingdom value system, is always the right thing producing the best relational and economic outcomes in the long haul. When you follow the way of Jesus and love your neighbor as yourself, you are set up for success in business.

You still have free will. You don't have to love your neighbor as yourself. Yet if you don't, you won't be successful in life or in business. The right thing in the kingdom value system will always produce the best relationships over the long run. When you follow the way of Jesus and forgive others, letting go of wounds and bitterness, blessing those who curse you, loving those who hate you, doing good for those who don't deserve it, you will have strong and fulfilling relationships. You will have stronger relationship-based leadership influence than you could develop through any other means.

You don't have to do this. Yet if you do, you will have more abundance in every way. It's just the way the universe is designed to work when you apply the new kingdom leadership mindset in business and in life.

CHAPTER 21

FREEDOM TO FOLLOW AND FLOURISH

Scientific studies repeatedly prove that the kingdom way is healthy for mind, body, and spirit. Plant yourself firmly in the kingdom, and your life will grow healthy fruit. When your life is filled with what the Bible calls "the fruits of the spirit" (love, joy, peace, patience, kindness, gentleness, and self-control),[88] the very cells and organs of your body benefit. When you experience the opposite outcomes, like hate, anger, bitterness, and self-centeredness, your body begins to break down. The heart can even suffer a meltdown or heart attack.

The peer-reviewed, scientific journal of the American Psychological Association published a study by university researchers who measured what happened to people engaged in the experiment when they harbored resentful, grudge-bearing, hate-filled thoughts toward people who had caused them harm.

They also studied subjects who took a fresh perspective on their enemies and tried to understand them and forgive them.

The researchers found that when people were unforgiving, they felt terrible: all stirred up, sad, angry, and out of control. Their facial muscles were tense, their sympathetic nervous systems were aroused, and their heart rates and blood pressure rose. The researchers said those who are chronically unforgiving, resentful, blaming, accusing, et cetera may have chronically higher heart rates and blood pressure, which may lead to serious cardiovascular events. On the other hand, those who are forgiving, patient, kind, peaceful and able to control themselves with peaceful and gentle thoughts, even toward those who have harmed them, exhibit the opposite physiologically.[89]

Researchers have also found that people who are lonely and isolated die earlier than people with happy and fulfilling relationships. These findings were presented at the National Academy of the Sciences.[90]

What kind of people have happy and fulfilling relationships with a network of other people? It is not the nasty, unforgiving, grudge-bearing, resentful types. It is forgiving, loving, patient, joyful people. Such people may not believe or know they are exhibiting the fruits of the spirit or living kingdom values, but because they are, they live more blessed lives, even impacting their overall health.

Whenever the values of the kingdom are implemented in society and human relations, things become better. Whenever those values are ignored, society gets worse. Jesus said when we seek the kingdom way of life, all the other things we want will be added to our life.[91] But if we seek our own life as the center, all the other things end up getting subtracted from our life. The degree to which the world is not as it should be today is a direct correlation to the degree to which the values of the kingdom and/or the leadership of the king has waned. So when we repeat the prayer that Jesus taught his followers to pray and say, "Your kingdom come", what we are essentially saying is "May the ideal design for society come."

It is so fulfilling when you finally discover the principles of God's kingdom are the very principles that flow from your own being and from the universe to make life work best. When we live by those principles, it is like finding life as it was always meant to be–it is like coming to a comfortable and fulfilling home after being away for a long time. It is like flowing with the river of the universe instead of swimming upstream. I'm sure this explains why so many who followed Jesus over the centuries describe this experience as a homecoming and as life as it was meant to be.

I remember when I started getting to know the amazing lady who has been my wife for over thirty-five years. I heard her describe the close relationship she had with her dad with words like, "My dad and I have such deep love and trust for each other that I would feel horrible if I went against what he wanted." She wasn't following her dad's wishes because he legislated it but because of the love and trust between them. It was most natural for her to follow her dad's wishes because of love and trust. Clearly, it was unnatural for her to go against what he wanted. That would make her feel horrible. It was built into her nature to experience love and trust rather than to disobey and dishonor.

In the same way, we are all designed to have and enjoy good relationships through living in alignment with the values of our God. It is in our nature. Living the kingdom way is the natural way for human beings to live.

Restriction from Failure and Freedom to Flourish

The values of the kingdom are life-giving barriers, protective-mechanisms to keep us from destroying ourselves and diminishing society. Any restrictions they may seem to put on us are restrictions from failure. Their real purpose is to bring freedom. That is why these kingdom values are also called "the perfect law that gives freedom".[92] These values of the kingdom are principles that apply to everyone, everywhere in any culture or circumstance. They are universal laws built in to the very fiber of how human society is ideally intended to flourish.

As a private pilot, I am free to fly pretty much anywhere and anytime I want as long as I fully embrace all of the laws of aerodynamics and the Federal Aviation Administration. Freedom as a pilot comes from adherence to a set of principles and laws that govern flying and the universe. For example, while I am free to jump out of my plane without a parachute, the law or command of gravity will quickly show me that my freedom is subject to the consequences of natural law. My freedom of movement will very quickly be compromised–I will likely die or, at best, be laid up for months with a lot of broken limbs. Obeying the law or command of gravity actually ensures my freedom to live and move. Likewise, freedom as a human being comes from adherence to a set of principles and laws that govern the kingdom.

Here's a little experiment you can try just in case you're not buying into the inherent value and freedom of living in the kingdom system. Try this. For an entire month, go out there and do your very best to make sure that every thought, feeling and action is the opposite of what Jesus modeled and taught as the system for society. Be mean to people every chance you get. Lie, cheat, steal. Only focus on your own interests and needs. Don't give a rip about anyone or anything else but yourself. Go ahead. Be a leader and organize a movement that is passionate about perpetuating complete impurity, total hate, fierce selfishness, and unwavering dishonesty.

At the end of the month, I'd like to ask you one question (if you're not in jail or dead): So how's that working out for you?! It's pretty self-evident, right? It wouldn't work at all, would it? Build an entire society on those principles and it would disintegrate rapidly!

Think about what your imaginary experiment means. Every person who lives by any of these anti-kingdom values is essentially a parasite on society. Every dishonest person is a leech on some other person whose honesty keeps enough positive things happening for the dishonest person to be able to have the opportunity to suck life and value from society. Every selfish person is a leech on some generous, others-centered person who keeps enough value creation going in society to keep things functioning. Any attempt to live life against the values of the kingdom of God, as demonstrated in the life and teaching of Jesus, just misses the mark of how life is designed to optimally work. It just doesn't make any sense. It is just dumb!

By the way, many good religious folks refer to going against God's will as "sin" with a connotation that it is some mystical indelible black mark on your life. The word Jesus used that is translated as "sin" in most Bibles literally means "missing the mark". (The Greek word is *"hamartia"*. *"ha"* means "miss" and *"martia"* means "mark"). Sin is not some guilt-ridden, scary, religious thing. It is simply missing the mark of living life as life was intended to be lived at its best.

Choosing to Right the Wrongs!

So how does all this apply to your life and your business? It's simple. There may be aspects of your life that you intuitively know are missing the mark of God's ideal system for living a completely fulfilling and abundant life. You can choose to continue missing the mark. Or you can choose to redirect your focus toward the target of living life as it was meant to be lived. It's your choice.

You don't have to look very hard to see many aspects of society that are missing the mark of God's ideal way of living life. You can choose to continue doing business as usual and let that be 'their problem". Or you can choose to redirect some of the focus of your business toward righting the wrongs of society. It's your choice.

Today's millennial generation is driven by causes. There are more socially-minded business leaders in this generation than ever before. According to the 2018 seventh annual Millennial Survey by Deloitte, 73% of the more than 10,000 Millennials questioned believe businesses can have a positive impact on the world. "The message is clear: Young workers are eager for business leaders to be proactive about making a positive impact in society... Millennials want leaders to more aggressively commit to making a tangible impact on the world... One silver lining is that far more millennials believe that business leaders are making a positive impact on the world than government or religious leaders."

At the same time, there is even more of a trend toward socialism than ever before. Yet socialism is a system of forcing social justice and transformation by government decree. It isn't voluntary. It doesn't come from the free choosing of the human heart.

God's answer to socialism is business leaders who think: "Through my business I am going to choose to bring God's rule and reign to bear on my circle of influence. I am going to make what's wrong, right through my business and in the way that I conduct my everyday life."

Let me give you an example.

Michael Brown founded Michael's Transportation Services with one bus in 1982. Today it has grown to include a fleet of over one hundred buses with more than one hundred employees in three Bay Area cities. He has more than a thousand clients, including nearly every school district in the Bay Area.

I first met Michael in the hallway of a leadership conference in the Bay Area. I had heard about the significant impact his business had made on the community. He had been asking the same questions that I was asking, only several years sooner: "Does what I do every day as a business leader really matter to God? Can my business really make a transformational difference in the world?"

I had this conversation with Michael at a time when I was wrestling with whether or not I should continue being a full-time CEO or if I should start a church as a pastor. I remember Michael telling me how he discovered that God did indeed have a specific need and purpose for him to be CEO of his business. He believed God had a specific plan for him to build God's kingdom in Michael's region in a way that Michael could fulfill only as a business leader. Michael went on to tell me once he realized that, he chose to dedicate his business to God's purposes. Over time, he went a step further and began to really consult God on every aspect of his business.

He said to me, "God is now the chairman of the board, Jesus Christ is the CEO, and the Holy Spirit is our legal counsel. I now take it as a serious responsibility to manage the business platform God has given me in a way that builds his kingdom in my region of this country."

The first thing Michael said he did was to begin looking at his business not just as a way to make money by providing good service, but primarily as a vehicle to bring positive transformation to society. That was the pivotal moment where he chose to begin his journey as a Level 3 business that rebuilds the world. He began asking God to show him how his business could be used to solve some very real and practical problems in his community and break the cycle of what was going wrong in Vallejo, California.

One thing that was clearly wrong in Vallejo was it had one of the highest recidivism rates in the country. Nearly eight out of ten inmates went back to jail after serving their initial term. Then they served longer and harder sentences in a never-ending cycle. By default many prisons end up being training programs for criminals and perpetuate things that are very wrong for society. Michael realized for inmates to rejoin society as productive members, they needed specific skills and training.

He used his business as a platform to make this wrong right. He developed Michael's Transportation Services Training Academy to give convicts the skills and certification needed to have a successful career as soon as they left prison.

Michael describes that this was no easy task. Some of them had very few skills, had never held a steady job, and often had rough social skills as well. But Michael got his employees on board with building beyond business and then with using their business as a platform to solve this endemic community problem. They went beyond providing basic job skills training to help these inmates understand and apply principles of the kingdom that would create sustainable success for their careers and their lives.

The results have been astounding. Dozens of inmates have been trained, with 100% placement for jobs. Former inmates now add tremendous value to society. That's a wrong made right. That's the kingdom of God being built through a business.

Now those former inmates are learning to live for others, to live within the freedom of the laws of the kingdom. Because one business leader decided to dedicate his business to rebuilding the world God's way, those who were once in bondage are now flourishing in the freedom of following the leader and principles of the kingdom.

CHAPTER 22

WHO AND WHAT IS INCLUDED IN THIS INITIATIVE?

During the Christmas season a couple years ago, my family and I experienced a dramatic illustration of what it looks like when the kingdom of God comes near. Throughout that year I had made a few trips to China, focused on developing relationships with people who might be interested in co-investing in our U.S. real estate projects. In that process I began to develop a close relationship with a billionaire from Beijing who had a real passion for using his business as a platform for improving society. He is literally investing billions of dollars to turn impoverished villages into thriving cities with strong ecosystems. I'll call him Chairman X for the purposes of this story.

As Chairman X was doing his due diligence on our company and team, he decided to bring his key leaders, including some of his family members, to visit our headquarters in the U.S. During his last night with us, we hosted a home-cooked meal and shared some good relationship-building time between our teams. I invited my wife and kids to join us if they wanted to. Of course they did, if for no other reason than just to meet a billionaire.

At the end of the meal, I asked my kids if they would be willing to share a couple songs. I'm blessed with a wife who is very musical and who has helped us raise kids who love to create and perform music. So all four of our kids got up and sang a couple of traditional Christmas songs.

As they were doing this, I noticed out of the corner of my eye that there were tears welling up in Chairman X's eyes, as well as in some of his team members. I knew it wasn't because of the words my kids were singing or even the familiarity of the tunes. They didn't speak English, and they had no familiarity with our Western tradition Christmas songs. They didn't even recognize the tunes and probably didn't like the music style because it is so different than theirs. I also knew from previous conversations that Chairman X was a devoted follower of the Confucian philosophy and founder of one of the premier private traditional Confucius schools in the country. So I knew that his emotional reaction had nothing to do with Christmas sentimentality.

At the end of the second song, Chairman X stood up and asked if he could say a few words to me and my family. The speech he gave floored us. He talked about how he had never felt such love and joy and unity as what he experienced and witnessed in our family. He said we had totally changed his perception of family in America. He said they strive for this kind of love and unity in families in China but it is extremely rare to see. He said after experiencing the dynamics of our family, he knew we shared the same values and vision for what is ideal in life. He said that what he saw was the fulfillment of what he believes is the foundation of success in business: mastery of self, then mastery of the family.

After his kind speech, with tears still in his eyes, he asked my permission to hug each of my kids. I learned later from his personal assistant that in almost twenty years of being with the man all day, six to seven days a week, she had never seen him cry or show the emotional connection he did when hugging our kids.

When I was alone with my family, we all asked each other, "What just happened there?" No one could be that affected by words and music they don't understand. No musician is that good. Our conclusion was that what we just experienced was the Kingdom of Heaven coming near. When someone experiences God's principles and leadership lived out in relationships in the family and in business, it has a profound effect. Language and culture don't matter. When people see and experience the love and unity of kingdom living at a new level, it is a profound spiritual experience.

Since that time, Chairman X and I have become great friends and business partners. We have spent many hours on flights visiting various projects discussing (through a translator) the similarities between the teachings of Confucius and the teachings of Jesus. We agreed to read each other's books of guidance. He gave me my first copy of the Analytics of Confucius, and I gave him his first copy of the Bible. I have learned much from him, and he says he has learned much from me. When I see the love and respect with which he treats his thousands of employees, when I see the millions of dollars he gives to fund education for those who can't afford it, when I see the ecosystems he is building to eliminate systemic poverty in China, I am convinced much of what Chairman X does is bringing the kingdom of heaven to earth. He does not call it that, of course, but that is what he is doing. The common bond that unites us in life and in business is that we are both seeking to establish God's kingdom on this earth.

This reminds me of what Jesus said when he started his

public teaching on these subjects: "'The time has come,' he said. 'The kingdom of God has come near.'"[93] Then he went on to demonstrate by how he lived his life and by what he said, what it looks like to live in the kingdom come.

Results Matter in Relation to the Kingdom

As we discussed previously, the church as society labels it today is quite a bit different from what Jesus had in mind when he started what he labeled as the ekklesia. The ekklesia was a secular system embedded into the fabric of Roman society, intended as the primary vehicle to establish the rule and reign of the Roman emperor. The Roman ekklesia was not the same thing as the kingdom of Rome; it was only valid or valuable to the extent it established the kingdom of Rome. There were other things that established the kingdom of Rome that were not considered officially part of the ekklesia but played a valuable role in establishing the kingdom wherever it spread.

In the same way, the ekklesia Jesus established was intended to be a primary vehicle to establish the kingdom of God. The ekklesia or even any conventional church today only has validity to the degree it is actually establishing God's kingdom. The ekklesia of Jesus is not the same as the kingdom of God. And the conventional church or the religion of Christianity are certainly not the same as the kingdom of God either. In fact, unfortunately, many conventional churches and much of Christianity have lost the focus on the kingdom of God almost completely. We know this based on results.

The nation of Israel, which had a unique invitation by God to demonstrate his kingdom principles to the world, lost the kingdom because it had no kingdom results. Jesus said, "Therefore I tell you that the kingdom of God will be taken away from you and given to a people who will produce its fruit."[94] The litmus test of whether you have the kingdom of God is fruit; results; outcomes of the kingdom. This elevates the kingdom above being identified with any particular group, church, movement, religion or nation. It is available to everyone but not synonymous with anyone except Jesus and those who produce the kind of life and societal results that he produced.

Could it be possible that one could be a non-church-member and more a part of the kingdom than the most dedicated church attender? Could it be possible that one could even be a non-Christian or non-religious person and be more a part of the kingdom of God than the most religious person you know? Could it be that even those who see themselves as atheists could have elements of the kingdom of God written on their character and evidenced in the parts of society which they impact? That without even knowing it or calling it by that name, they are experiencing and even perpetuating pieces of the kingdom?

Jesus said not everyone who called out to him and called him "Lord" would be a part of the kingdom of heaven. He said: "Not everyone who says to me, 'Lord, Lord,' will enter the kingdom of heaven, but only the one who does the will of my Father who is in heaven."[95] Could it be that the kingdom of God includes anyone to the degree they do what God wants them to do in their corner of the world to make what's wrong in the world right, to make things on earth as they are in heaven, to establish God's kingdom?

The kingdom of God excludes no one except to the degree they exclude themselves. Inclusion or exclusion in the kingdom is not based on the issues that seem to drive acceptance or rejection from most religions—issues like doctrinal distinctions or religious rhetoric or practices. It is based on a choice to follow the leadership and values of Jesus.

Could it be that the kingdom is not limited to any religion or race? Could it be that it is something larger than any particular culture or nation? Could it be that it is available to anyone, anywhere on equal terms? Jesus, as the architect of the kingdom, was certainly not tying it to any religion. In fact, it was largely because he didn't tie his kingdom and its message to the prevailing religion of his day that those religious leaders tortured and killed him. They did not see his message about the kingdom as supporting their religion. It confounded them to see he was not setting up a new religion over and against their religion. He was talking about and living principles that were above and beyond any religious or cultural traditions. That means anything that is good and from God in any religion, race or nation could be preserved and not lost in his kingdom.

I will say that Christianity, as an organized religion, has a unique platform upon which to build God's kingdom. After all, it is founded by and named after Jesus Christ, the embodiment of the kingdom. However, I don't believe God wrote some type of exclusivity clause into the organizational documents for Christianity, giving it sole possession of the kingdom of God. In fact, when Jesus came, the Jews thought they had exclusives on the kingdom of God. He burst their bubble badly and universalized the kingdom of God.

In the same way, I believe he is bursting the bubble of organized Christianity and making the kingdom of God accessible to anyone who demonstrates they are being led by the king and his values. Being a part of God's kingdom may or may not include being a part of some church or religion. Jesus didn't make his kingdom and the church one in the same. He never said, "Thy kingdom come, thy church be developed on earth as it is in heaven." He said, "Thy kingdom come, thy will be done in earth as it is in heaven."[96] He made his kingdom and his will synonymous. Doing his will (living life based on his leadership and values) is the litmus test of being in the kingdom.

Throughout history, whenever the kingdom and the person of Jesus are separated, whenever the kingdom becomes something other than what Jesus demonstrated in his life and teachings, it has taken on all manner of distortions. One of the worst demonstrations is the Crusades. This is an example of what it looks like when a group thinks they have a corner on the kingdom but are missing the leadership and values of the king. In that case people tried to bring the kingdom by force, and they only created generations of hate and conflict.

Another demonstration of the dangers of limiting the kingdom to the conventional church is in the story of Genghis Khan. Khan asked the Pope through Marco Polo: "Please send us a hundred teachers, well learned in the seven arts and well able to prove that the way of Christ is best." Two teachers instead of a hundred were sent to Genghis Khan with this message: "Become politically and ecclesiastically attached to Rome." Bummer. The universal Catholic church of Rome (catholic means universal) didn't offer the universal kingdom of God. Instead they offered a political and ecclesiastical (read "conventional church") attachment to Rome. Genghis Khan didn't like that offer and instead accepted Islam and spread bloodshed and violence through abuses of that religion wherever he went.

What is the Kingdom Really Like?

So what is the Kingdom of Heaven like? If Jesus' primary passion was for everything on earth to be as it is in the kingdom of heaven, wouldn't it be cool if we could have a clear picture of what the kingdom of heaven is like?

What do you think of when you think of the kingdom of heaven? What picture comes to your mind? People floating on white, fluffy clouds playing golden harps? Magnificent mansions lining streets of gold? If those are the pictures that come to your mind, you're in for a surprise. The Bible records ten times where Jesus said, "The Kingdom of Heaven is like . . . " and in every instance, the picture Jesus painted had something to do with business leaders doing business!

Check out these illustrations Jesus gave of what the Kingdom of Heaven is like.

JESUS' ILLUSTRATION	BUSINESS TYPE
Like a farmer who planted good seed in his field[97]	A farming business of a land owner
Like a mustard seed which a man took and sowed in his field[98]	A spice business of a land owner
Like a treasure that a man discovered hidden in a field. In his excitement, he hid it again and sold everything he owned to get enough money to buy the field.[99]	An investment business
Like a merchant in search of fine pearls.[100]	A merchant or jewelry business
Like a fishing net that was thrown into the water and caught fish of every kind.[101]	A commercial fishing business
Like the owner of a house who brings out of his storeroom new treasures as well as old.[102]	A home-based business or family estate manager
Like a land owner who went out early in the morning to hire laborers for his vineyard.[103]	A vineyard/winery business
Like a king who wanted to settle accounts with his servants.[104]	A lending business
Like a king who prepared a wedding banquet for his son.[105]	A multigenerational wealth dynasty
Like yeast which a woman used in making bread. She put a little yeast into three measures of flour and it permeated every part of the dough.[106]	A bakery business

This last illustration of the Kingdom requires a bit of explanation, as at first glance you might think this was about a woman baking a loaf of bread for her family. "Three measures" is the usual translation for the original Greek *tria sata*, which is a little over a bushel of flour (1.125 bushels). That's a huge amount of flour; 144 cups to be precise! Assuming a loaf of basic wheat bread uses 5 ½ cups of flour, that is enough to make 52 loaves, each weighing about a pound and a half. At 16 slices per loaf, that's 832 slices of bread! This is clearly a commercial baking business.

The kingdom of heaven is like a woman who wants to do more than feed her family. The kingdom announced by Jesus is like a woman who builds a business to feed her whole village! And she puts a small amount of something invisible (yeast, which could represent the values of the kingdom) that permeates every aspect of what her business does to serve her village.

Jesus was clearly casting the vision that his kingdom was a lot like doing commerce. In all these illustrations, Jesus clearly connects building business with building the kingdom of heaven.

One might even conclude from all these vision casting talks that when Jesus pictured the kingdom, he pictured commerce being done well. Is it too much of a stretch to think that Jesus' vision for his kingdom looks a lot like capitalism done well? Compassionate capitalism or conscientious capitalism is the most effective system for weaving the kingdom of heaven into the fabric of this earth.

Sure, there are abuses and misuses of capitalism just like there is of any good thing. I am obviously not referring to the type of capitalism that exploits, uses or abuses people or resources for greed and gain. That abuse of capitalism does not create sustainable success in any way. I am referring to the form of capitalism that is good because its driving motive is to create

271

value for others. Its method is to serve people so well that they choose to give certificates of service which we call money. When done well it is living kingdom principles in such a way that it elevates every aspect of society.

Could it be that doing business well was Jesus' primary plan for building his kingdom on this earth? Could it be that doing commerce well is your primary calling to bring the kingdom of heaven to your part of the world?

The reality is that your business can be a perfect vehicle for expanding the values of the kingdom. Over and over, throughout history, we see God seeking to connect with humans on this earth, and he does it by meeting a tangible human need. God provides food for the nation of Israel "mana"—and used that as basis for them to revere him. Jesus provides health care to sick people and then says, "Follow me."

The first topic on God's mind when meeting with humanity is providing a solution to a pressing need on earth. His primary focus is to fix something that is not "on earth as it is in heaven." God doesn't just step in to circumvent humans to provide those solutions to human needs. His pattern is always to ask some human to provide a solution to that need. Then he steps in and gives those leaders direction, resources, and authority to address a specific need in order to bring his kingdom to this earth.

If Jesus were here today, I think he might say the kingdom of God looks a lot like the many senior-care leaders who work hard to build businesses that assist seniors with the acts of daily living while conveying genuine care, respect, and dignity. I wonder if he might say the kingdom of heaven looks a lot like what our apartment property management company does when we create safe, quality places people enjoy and where they experience love. (Our slogan is Places. People. Love.) I wonder if he might say the Kingdom of God looks like what my good friend Jim is doing. He has devoted twenty years of his life to inventing an energy solution that will save people money and significantly reduce the carbon footprint of energy production lower than any energy source currently known. I wonder if Jesus might say the kingdom of heaven looks like what my wife does in her health coaching business, where she is bringing health and healing to solve previously unsolvable, chronic medical problems. I wonder if he might say it looks like what my son-in-law does in his mental health practice to foster holistic healing to emotions and relationships. I wonder if Jesus might say the kingdom of heaven looks like my daughter's health café and juice bar that is making it easier and more popular for people in our town to be healthy, whereas a few years ago, we were ranked the fourth most obese city in the nation. I wonder if Jesus might say the kingdom of heaven looks a lot like what my other daughters are doing when they lead yoga studios and retreats that help people have a safe space to connect with their inner spiritual and emotional lives while bringing health and strength to their bodies? (Many of these people would never step into the door of a conventional church!) I wonder if Jesus might say the Kingdom of heaven looks a lot like the business my son leads that helps young people who have dropped out of college find purpose, alternate means of education, and specific paths to contribute value to society. I wonder if Jesus might say the kingdom of heaven looks like what one of our strategic partners in Minneapolis does when she gives away 100% of the profits of her company to feed the poor in that city? (She has given away over one million dollars so far.) I wonder if Jesus might say the kingdom of God looks a lot like what another one of our strategic partners does to incubate businesses with specific social causes? I wonder if Jesus might say the kingdom of God lookslike what my dear friends in the Wilkinson family have done over the last twenty years inventing a completely new bread-baking technology that will provide significantly healthier and higher quality bread at a much lower cost to millions of people around the world? In the process they donate a portion from each loaf sold to build wells for people who are dying from lack of clean water. I wonder if Jesus might say the kingdom of God looks like what my nephew, Ryan, is doing to revolutionize fashion clothing manufacturing (an industry that has one of the most harmful impacts on the environment) by using recycled, organic, and sustainable fabric made in factories that provide a true living wage and reduce the international economic orphan crisis.

Who and what gets included in this grand kingdom building initiative? I think Jesus might congratulate any business that is honestly meeting real needs of real people as being the superstars on center stage.

CHAPTER 23

HOW THE KINGDOM COMES— YOU MIGHT BE SURPRISED

Jesus was on his way to Jerusalem. He had recently become hugely popular and there was a big crowd following him. These people were going to try to crown him king as soon as he got to Jerusalem. Jesus knew this. In fact, the Bible says Jesus told the crowd a story specifically because they thought the kingdom of God was going to take over their world that very day, when he got to Jerusalem. Jesus tells the crowd this story to correct their inaccurate understanding about how the kingdom of God actually comes to the kingdom of this world.

Are you ready for another paradigm buster? If you've got a religious bone in your body, this might even offend you. The kingdom doesn't come the way you think. Here's the story Jesus told:

While they were listening to this, he went on to tell them a parable, because he was near Jerusalem and the people thought that the kingdom of God was going to appear at once. He said: "A man of noble birth went to a distant country to have himself appointed king and then to return. So he called ten of his servants and gave them ten minas. 'Put this money to work,' he said, 'until I come back.'

"But his subjects hated him and sent a delegation after him to say, 'We don't want this man to be our king.'

"He was made king, however, and returned home. Then he sent for the servants to whom he had given the money, in order to find out what they had gained with it.

"The first one came and said, 'Sir, your mina has earned ten more.'

"'Well done, my good servant!' his master replied. 'Because you have been trustworthy in a very small matter, take charge of ten cities.'

"The second came and said, 'Sir, your mina has earned five more.'

"His master answered, 'You take charge of five cities.'

"Then another servant came and said, 'Sir, here is your mina; I have kept it laid away in a piece of cloth. I was afraid of you, because you are a hard man. You take out what you did not put in and reap what you did not sow.'

"His master replied, 'I will judge you by your own words, you wicked servant! You knew, did you, that I am a hard man, taking out what I did not put in, and reaping what I did not sow? Why then didn't you put my money on deposit, so that when I came back, I could have collected it with interest?'

"Then he said to those standing by, 'Take his mina away from him and give it to the one who has ten minas.'

"'Sir,' they said, 'he already has ten!'

"He replied, 'I tell you that to everyone who has, more will

276

be given, but as for the one who has nothing, even what they have will be taken away.[107]

What does this story tell us about how the Kingdom of God is actually built in society?

A mina was a monetary unit in that society. It was equivalent of approximately three to four months' wages for a six-day-a-week worker back then. In round numbers, one mina would be worth about $15,000 in today's economy. So the CEO in the parable gave each of these ten employees the responsibility for $15,000 of capital. What did he tell them to do with it?

He didn't tell them to protect it, guard it or watch over it, start a ministry with it, or build a synagogue with it. He didn't tell them to donate it to the poor. He specifically said to do business with it, to put it to work. This was business operating capital or venture capital that each of these leaders was supposed to use to do business while the CEO was out of the country. Yet while the CEO was on this trip, there was essentially a hostile take-over of his empire. His key leaders, though, to whom he had entrusted his operating capital, continued to do business even in this hostile environment. (In case you haven't connected the dots, Jesus is giving an allegory about himself as the CEO who left this world in our charge until he returns as king of the entire world.)

When the CEO returned from his trip, he asked his division leaders for a report on the profits they made. One created enough profit in business to earn a ten multiple on the original capital. He turned the $15,000 into $150,000. Another earned a five multiple and turned the $15,000 into $75,000. Another one made no profit at all.

During the investment period, this CEO had become king of his own kingdom. He had the authority to lead every city in his empire. He then gave each of his successful business leaders authority over entire cities in direct correlation to the profit they made in business. The leader who earned a ten multiple in business was given authority over ten cities. The one who earned a five multiple was given authority over five cities. What about the guy who didn't earn any profit in business? Well, let's just say he got voted off the island with nothing.

Let's talk about that last guy for a minute. The last guy obviously misunderstood the king's paradigm for success. This last employee essentially just kept the money that was entrusted to him safe in his pocket (literally in a handkerchief). He didn't risk losing it by investing it to create more value. He just played it safe. At least he did not lose the investment. In many investments I've made, I would have been happy with at least the return of my capital.

Yet this guy clearly misunderstood the king's method of measuring success. The king's method of measuring success was not just returning the original capital, but putting capital to work to add value and increase capital. The king's measurement of success was multiplying money.

The basis for the guy's misunderstanding was that he misunderstood the king's character or values. This third leader was stingy in protecting what he was given instead of taking the risk of giving to get as free market capitalism requires. The reason he gave for doing this was that he believed the king was an austere man who takes out what he did not put in and reaps what he did not sow. This loser in the opportunity to influence society, accused the king of being anti-capitalistic. He accused the king of not seeking to make profit based on the value of what is given. He completely misunderstood the king as essentially being a socialist who values receiving something without having provided value.

That this was an obvious misunderstanding of the king is made clear in the king's response. The king told him that if he really thought the king was like that, he could have at least put the money in the bank and earned some interest on it. The king took the money from this last guy and gave it to the one who got a tenfold return on his investment.

What was Jesus' point in this interesting story about capital, investment, and character?

I have read and heard this story many times over my lifetime. Yet I missed the real point until I recently saw WHY Jesus told this story. He told it specifically to let his listeners know how the kingdom of God was supposed to come.

ROI for the Kingdom

Through this parable, we understand the kingdom comes to people who accept God as their leader. He gives them resources to do business. They then manage and multiply money on behalf of the king to expand the king's kingdom. Those are the people the king gives dominion over cities!

When I was growing up in church, most every talk I heard on this story spiritualized "minas" as referring to my talents or spiritual gifts. The message I got was that how well I used my singing or speaking talent (usually in serving the programs of the conventional church) would be the basis for whether King Jesus would be pleased with me and entrust me with more spiritual responsibility in the church. Yet the story Jesus told is about real minas! Real money! Jesus was literally talking about doing business and making a profit!

To those who make a tenfold profit in business, the king says, "Okay, you've proved you have what it takes to take charge of ten cities!" This is the part that just blows my mind! Jesus is saying, "I'm going to Jerusalem. You think I'm going to be king over Jerusalem because you put a crown on my head and sit me on a donkey, but here is how the kingdom of God comes! It's when I, the king, trust you, my servants, with money and you multiply that money in business. That's how you gain kingdom authority over cities."

The people who are faithful at managing and multiplying money will be the ones who will take dominion over cities on his behalf. They will make his kingdom a reality in those cities. That's how the kingdom of God comes.

If you want to build the kingdom of God in a city, if you want to see God's kingdom come to a city, Jesus is saying, "Do business in a way that multiplies money. Increase the value you bring to society in a way that society pays you more money and you make more profit."

In Jesus' paradigm of thought, if you do business in a way that turns one dollar into multiple dollars, it means you have the kind of kingdom leadership capacity to influence entire cities on behalf of the king. When Jesus said, "You turned one mina into ten, so I'm going to trust you to have influence over the people in ten cities," it was with the full understanding of how business works and what it took to get a tenfold increase in capital.

Think about it. Jesus knew the only way you could multiply the net worth of your company by tenfold in a year was by serving a bunch of people really well! You did a bunch of good for a bunch of people in a bunch of places. You met a lot of needs. You loved a lot of people well. That's why Jesus trusted that this guy who did business in a way that increased net worth by ten times could lead ten cities. He knew that the same heart, the same principles and practices that create profit by doing business well were the same that would benefit entire cities. Jesus is saying, "Because you are faithful at managing and multiplying the resources I have given you, that demonstrates that you have what it takes to make my kingdom happen. It happens when I entrust my followers with money and they multiply that money by putting it to work to build a better world."

Scorecard of Service

As I pointed out earlier, money is a certificate of service. The way we handle money is a scorecard of service, a scorecard for how much value we add to society. Could it be that Jesus intended that the ability to do business in a way that multiplies money would be a scorecard for leaders in his kingdom? Could it be that his kingdom appears in direct correlation to the way his followers serve society through business? Could it be that having a profit in business is a measure of one's ability to have dominion over the opposition to the kingdom of God in a city?

As business leaders who follow Jesus, we make profit under the direction of King Jesus. Then he gives us influence and authority over cities, one city at a time. Eventually his kingdom will appear in entire nations. The end of the story is that King Jesus will take back full control of his empire, planet earth, and all nations will welcome him as their supreme leader.[108]

When I read this story and understood this for the first time, I wrote in my journal: "I clearly need to look at the process of building business to multiply money as a much more spiritual and honorable thing. It appears to be a litmus test Jesus gives for whether I am living under the rule and reign of Jesus, whether I am in the kingdom of God, whether I am part of bringing the kingdom to this earth. Building the kingdom of God is directly tied to building financial wealth. According to this Scripture, those who build financial wealth will be put in charge of cities—to take dominion over cities for the kingdom of God. Wow!"

What Did Jesus Come to Save?

Right before Jesus tells this story about the ten minas, he says this: "The Son has come to seek and to save that which was lost."[109]

Through my old lens, I had always interpreted that to mean Jesus came to seek and save the people who are lost. Yet it literally says "That which was lost", not "Those who were lost". What was Jesus' point? What is *that* which was lost? Adam lost dominion over creation, and Jesus came to seek and save the lost dominion. We have lost God's rule and reign on this earth, and Jesus came to reestablish it–God's rule and reign! THE KINGDOM! The kingdom of this world became the kingdom of Satan. Jesus came to make the kingdom of this world the kingdom of our God.

Stories like *The Return of the King* in J.R.R. Tolkien's The Lord of the Rings series are allegories about the restoration of the kingdom of God on earth. That which was lost is regained; the power of evil is broken and a good, fruitful, prosperous, happy, and proper kingdom is restored under the wise and rightful ruler.

In the story of the minas, Jesus essentially says, "Do you want to know how my servants are going to regain dominion over this earth and over cities? They'll do it by being faithful in and good at managing and multiplying money. The better you are at managing and multiplying money, the more influence you'll have to take dominion over the transformation of cities for my kingdom culture–to bring my values, my principles, my ways of doing life, to entire cities."

Remember, that is what the ekklesia Jesus started was supposed to do anyway: to bring his leadership and values–his kingdom–to entire cities and nations through the marketplace.

The Kingdom Is Hiding in Plain Sight!

For years we have tried to transform cities through the ministries of the conventional church, through programs, prayer, preaching, outreach, and every possible means. But we have missed the most obvious possible means, the one God himself used when he decided to personally come to this earth to bring his kingdom. He came as a business leader. He made the kingdom of heaven appear on earth by doing business. When Jesus talks about giving authority over cities, he is clearly referring to the influence that comes from business leaders doing business well enough to multiply money.

I firmly believe that when the business leaders and the conventional church begin to see business as its primary vehicle for the transformation of society—for bringing the good news of the kingdom of God to their city and to this world—we will begin to see unprecedented progress.

As a side note, I want to tell pastors that the mina they have so often hidden in a handkerchief is the business leader sitting in their congregation, whom they have not empowered or identified or endorsed or celebrated as being in a position with high potential to build God's kingdom. Pastors, you've been given the opportunity to shepherd and celebrate these high capacity kingdom-builders, and you've rarely done it. You have those people handing out programs at the door of the church or rocking babies in the nursery, and you celebrate that as their ministry! I'm not saying those things aren't ministry, or that they aren't important to the effectiveness and good work conventional churches do. Yet the average pastor has business leaders sitting in the congregation who have demonstrated they have what it takes to take dominion over an entire city for God. The average pastor doesn't even recognize their business as ministry, let alone as a God-ordained platform to bring the kingdom of heaven to earth.

Don't wrap your mina in a handkerchief! Help the business leaders in your church embrace their high calling to build businesses that openly and intentionally implement God's principles and God's leadership into the daily fabric of the life of their company and their people. Learn how to support them in aligning themselves and their business environments with God's values and purposes in the world. Then everything they do in business can and will exert influence to make the world a better place, a place that is a bit closer to the way that God would have things be. Then they will be using their business to bring God's kingdom to earth. Then your part of the ekklesia in your city will begin to do what it was designed to do–permanently transform society to live under the rule and reign of Jesus.

The Goal of History

The first branding message that was given by the marketing campaign of heaven that was sent to premarket the birth of Jesus was: "He will be great and will be called the Son of the Most High. The Lord God will give him the throne of his father David, and he will reign over Jacob's descendants forever; his kingdom will never end."[110] The simple brand message was this, "Jesus is setting up a kingdom that will never end."

At the culmination of this earth's history, when the angel in charge of branding calls for an advertisement for the effectiveness of this campaign, a huge crowd of raving fans will shout: "The kingdom of the world has become the kingdom of our Lord and of his Messiah, and he will reign for ever and ever."[111] The zenith of end time events, the seventh trumpet, is when the kingdom of this world has become the kingdom of our God.

There are many views on the historical and prophetic sequence and timing of these prophecies in Revelation. But one thing is clear and agreed upon by all views. The goal of human history is for God's authority, leadership, and values to pervade all society.

The pop song that the entire world will be singing is this: "Great and marvelous are your deeds, Lord God Almighty. Just and true are your ways, King of the nations. Who will not fear (respect) you, Lord, and bring glory to your name? For you alone are holy. All nations will come and worship before you, for your righteous acts have been revealed."[112]

Here again we see a picture of what it looks like when the goal for the history of this earth is complete. The theme song of humanity is that God's ways, his values and his principles, his way of conducting life are right and true–that his way is the best way. Everyone acknowledges Jesus as their leader, their God, and the king of all nations. The outcome is not just that he is king of my life or your life, the outcome is that he is king of every nation: king of the nation of America, king of the nation of Israel, king of the nation of China, etc. The goal of history is society's transformation to follow and honor God as the king of all nations. Wow! God's goal for history–the endgame–is that all nations will come and honor him has their leader!

Your Choice: Build your Kingdom or a Kingdom that Never Ends

Maybe you have never thought much about the kingdom of God or how it appears. Yet maybe now you see that even though you may not have called it by that name, there have been times where you have seen it in action. There have been times where you have entered in and experienced or even helped to create a unique abundance of life. If those times have been few and far between, now is the time for you to make a choice to enter fully into that kingdom way of life. Now is the time for you to commit to build a kingdom that never ends.

It starts with you being the one to choose to live your life based on Jesus' values and leadership. It starts with you being the one to enter the kingdom. The good news is this: entering the kingdom, living life as God designed it, is available to anyone and everyone. There is no unaffordable entrance fee. It is not based on birth or privilege or situation. It is not based on what you have or have not done in the past. It is not based on how good you are or aren't.

It doesn't matter what you have or what you have accomplished. It has nothing to do with your worthiness, only your willingness. It is simply based on a decision—the decision we make to follow the way of Jesus and the principles of his kingdom, for which we were meant to live. It is something we receive because we decide to receive it.

Like all great gifts we receive—gifts we truly did nothing to deserve—our devotion and our desires become bound to and influenced by the giver. This bondage of devotion is not a burdensome duty but a breath of brand new freedom—freedom to live as we were designed to live—freedom to cooperate with the designer of the universe to build a better world.

Make the choice that will change your life, change your legacy, and change the world. Simply choose to live by the principles of the kingdom of God and choose Jesus as your leader, your king. It makes sense for anyone to live by and promote the principles of God's kingdom, because they work.

Don't stop there. Embrace the presence and power of Jesus in your life. Embrace the presence and power of the king. Choose to belong to team Jesus.

When you belong to team Jesus, the resources of the king and his kingdom are available to you. This is great news. You have at your fingertips God's total solution for humanity's total needs—and you are his man or woman of the hour to build his kingdom on this earth!

PART 6
FINDING THE FUEL YOU NEED TO BUILD A BETTER WORLD

CHAPTER 24

THE FUEL OF FAITH THAT FORMS THE FUTURE

You may be a business leader who doesn't identify yourself as a person of faith, and you're wondering how all this talk about God's kingdom and how a chapter on faith fits into the formula for success in business or even in life. Just hang in there, and read the rest of this chapter. I think you'll see that the kind of faith I'm talking about is very different than the religious notions of faith you might have heard about.

The kind of faith I am talking about has nothing to do with religion. In this chapter, I'm not talking about religious faith. I'm talking about a powerful paradigm that is a prerequisite to turning your vision into reality. I'm talking about a faith that is the fuel for forming a better future. I'm talking about a principle of success that has helped leaders create the best and brightest innovations which have formed the history of this world. The kind of faith I'm talking about is the foundation for success in business and in life.

Every person who has achieved great success saw something that could be better, something that could be done differently. Most others could not see this. Successful leaders developed the ability to see what is not as though it existed–they had a vision of something that did not yet exist but they believed could exist. The greatest innovations, the greatest successes, come from those rare people who can see something which is not yet a reality as clearly as if they could hold it in their hand. Those people had the ability to see a vision so clearly and believe in its accomplishment so fully that in their minds, it was as if it already existed. That is the kind of faith I'm talking about in this chapter.

Faith, by definition, is the ability to see what is not as though it were; the ability to hold in your hand what is not yet real. Faith makes something so real, it's as if you could feel it in your grasp.

In case you're wondering where I'm getting this definition for faith, it's from a couple thousand-year-old letter from Paul to the Hebrews at the beginning of Chapter 11: "Now faith is confidence in what we hope for and assurance about what we do not see."[113]

Check the history books. Every successful human being who has created a legacy, or had an impact on this world in a dramatic way, had a vision that required faith.

Hopefully, you are coming to embrace the reality that your business is a powerful platform to build a better world. If you are going to do more than just believe it; that is, if you are going to crystallize a vision that will galvanize you into effective action that will turn that vision into a world changing reality, you need to understand and develop this quality of faith that has fueled world-changers throughout history.

Almost every book on success talks about the importance of having a vision. Vision, by its very nature, requires faith. In fact, it is impossible to have vision without faith. A mental vision, is seeing something that is not yet there. That is the first part of the definition of faith. The last part of the definition of faith is seeing that desired future AS IF IT WERE ALREADY THERE. Vision is seeing something different for the future. That's the starting point of faith. Faith builds on that to include the absolute certainty that that future is real.

If the word "faith" turns you off because it sounds religious, then call it something else. Please know, though, that you cannot have a worthwhile or inspiring vision that is significant enough to compel you to passionately pursue it unless it's something significantly better than what exists now. What's more, you won't perform the persistent actions needed to overcome the challenges on the way to that vision unless you have the faith to believe beyond a shadow of a doubt that the vision will become reality.

For instance, say I had a vision that I could be a superstar NBA basketball player. I could say I have that vision. I could write that vision down. I could declare it out loud with great vigor. But I'm not going to be passionately persistent in pursuing the actions required to overcome any obstacles to accomplish that vision because—well, because I don't really believe I could do that enough that I can touch it, taste it, and feel it in my mind's eye. Heck, I hardly ever watch NBA basketball, and at my age and stature, I doubt I could even get close to dunking a ball once.

You see, vision that creates passion and persistence requires faith. Faith is being so sure something will happen that you actually take action on it with passion and persistence. If you have faith, it's as if it were already there. So why wouldn't you take action on it? Why wouldn't you persist until you succeed?

For example, say you inherited a brand-new Tesla from your late, great uncle Bob. The title is already in your name. All you have to do is figure out how to get it from Hawaii to New York.

I bet there are not many obstacles you wouldn't persist through to get there to pick it up and take possession of such a beautiful, dream car. If all the standard car carrier vessels went on strike, I bet you'd still find a way.

On the other hand, let's look at a slightly different version of the same scenario. Say you had a picture (a vision) of a new Tesla in Hawaii that you really wanted, but there was a contest over the will and it wasn't in your name yet, but if you got it to New York, there would be a better chance you might be able to take possession of it. In that case, you wouldn't spend as much to bring it over because you don't see it is yours yet. The point is that we will always be more persistent and passionate about overcoming obstacles when we have faith that something is already ours; we just have yet to take possession of it.

It is this type of faith that substantial business endeavors demand. It is this quality of faith that building a better world demands. There have been a number of times in my entrepreneurial ventures where I have tackled big visions that demanded big faith: starting new businesses, inventing new products or services, taking a business to a whole new level. These require vision, faith and persistent action.

I've done a fair amount in the real estate business sector in the last dozen years. The majority of the companies in our niche of real estate went out of business during the Great Recession in the late 2000's. Our company had a near-death experience, and if it wasn't for the undying faith of my partners and our team that "We will find a way," we wouldn't have made it. There were several times where we had done absolutely everything we could humanly do. We had run out of solutions. Yet solutions materialized that could only be explained by supernatural intervention. It seemed God honored our dogged faith and persistence to survive and succeed.

An Impossible Acquisition Vision that Required Ferocious Faith

Not long after the worst of the Great Recession, we tackled what then seemed like an absolutely impossible acquisition of a portfolio of nearly 1600 apartment units in Dallas and Houston, Texas. Most people in our company thought we were crazy. Even my two partners, who are men of great faith, wondered whether this was just a pipe dream. We were still recovering from the impact of the recession. We were about to tackle the largest acquisition we had ever done, at a time when our financial strength was the weakest it had been for many years.

When we first put it under agreement to purchase, I must admit, it seemed a bit far-fetched. But the more due diligence we did, the more we became convinced we could add significant value to these thousands of residents and these communities. These properties had gone without much attention for years. Many of them looked like they were run by a slum lord. We became passionate about what we could do to create value and developed a detailed plan that allowed us and all of our team to see and taste the vision.

I still remember feeling butterflies in my stomach when we gave the huge, non-refundable deposit. It was a bit like jumping off a bridge and hoping the bungee cord is really attached. We only had a month to come up with millions of dollars, and we had no clue where that would come from. The closer we got to the deadline, the more I think even the non-praying types in our office started to pray!

At one point we taped a big circle on the floor at the entrance to the elevator in our main lobby. Some of us had just read the book *The Circle Maker* by Mark Batterson. In it, he tells the story of a village that had been experiencing months of terrible drought. There was a man who had such audacious faith that he drew a circle in the dirt in the middle of the village and declared boldly that he was not going to leave that circle until it rained. It eventually rained before he and others in the village died of dehydration. That circle on the floor of our lobby was a reminder to all of us that we were taking a stand and believing that somehow, some way we were going to come up with the capital to buy these properties.

There were many times the whole deal was going to blow up, and we were going to lose everything the next day. Then some solution would materialize, often just in the nick of time. Faith caused us to be persistent in our actions to find solutions and overcome a myriad of obstacles.

When we had our gong-ringing ceremony in the office, as we always do to celebrate the successful closing of a transaction, there wasn't a person in the office who didn't know one thing for certain. What had started out as an impossible dream became a reality because of the individual and collective ferocious faith of our team. That faith produced dogged persistence in overcoming obstacles and finding solutions and allowed the miraculous interventions where God's super powers made up for where our natural abilities fell short. Today our whole team is proud to say there are thousands of people who have living conditions that are now much safer and nicer. We have been able to create significant value for residents. As a result we have received more value than we had forecast to ourselves and our investors.

A Scary Development Vision Required Crazy Faith

In the last few months, I've had the opportunity to experience another significant success that required more faith than anything I've done in business before. That means it was a bigger, scarier, and seemingly more impossible vision than anything I'd tackled up to this point.

A couple of years ago, we found an opportunity to participate in the redevelopment of an entire city block on the edge of downtown Minneapolis. It was part of a larger vision to bring new vitality and significantly upgrade that area of the city. The opportunity was to build a boutique hotel and farm-to-table restaurant that created a unique, high-quality lifestyle experience for the city and for travelers. It also included a component of social entrepreneurship, partnering with a company that gives away all of its profits to feed the poor. It included participating in the development of an innovation center and incubator for businesses that exist for the purpose of building society—a center for social entrepreneurs. Obviously, it was in perfect alignment with my passions.

The more I learned about this opportunity, the more I felt in my gut that this was something we were supposed to make happen. The only problem was, it was about three times larger than any development we'd ever been involved in. We had no capital reserves available to fund it ourselves. It was focused on an asset class we had never been involved in. It was a scary vision. But we started down the path, in pure faith, not knowing how we'd do it. Still, we knew it was a project that was going to happen, and we could be the ones to do it.

Yet everything seemed to be more complex and harder and to take longer than we had anticipated. We were not able to hit some key contractual deadlines and had to risk more money to negotiate and pay for extensions.

We ended up proposing the project to over fifty construction lenders and got turned down by all of them. But we kept believing it could get done. One lender—that needle in the haystack—finally had enough faith in us to agree to provide the construction loan. Yet after we paid the big fee to engage them and they started doing their due diligence, they decided that our financial strength wasn't enough for this type of loan.

We took several trips to Asia, looking for investors to partner with us. Eventually we found one company that agreed to it. We had a signing celebration in Beijing the first week of November. But by the end of November, before the money was transferred out of China to the U.S., the Chinese government announced that they were placing a moratorium on significant investments from China into the U.S. Fifteen million dollars of our investor equity fell through within a few weeks of when we were required to close on all the funding and start construction.

All we could do was have faith that somehow we would find a way. That faith gave us the passion to persist in making call after call, going to meeting after meeting, taking flight after flight. In the meantime we were spending hundreds of thousands of dollars on architectural plans and other development costs that are required to keep a project like this moving forward. That was money that we had not budgeted to spend because the other capital sources were supposed to have come in long before.

We kept spending money like it was all going to happen, but some of our key vendors started to question whether this could ever get done. They started to back off on doing more work. Yet we kept moving forward in faith that we'd find a way to make it happen.

At one point we had just a few weeks left until we reached the end of our deadline to purchase the land. We had to either do it by that date or we would lose the entire opportunity and everything we had invested in it.

We had to show proof of funds within the next week. We didn't have it. We were about to lose everything, and I was about to lose my mind. I had already lost my peace of mind. I was super stressed! On top of this business stress, I was dealing with personal financial stress because we had purchased a new dream home and had gone for months without an offer on our old home.

That weekend, I took some time to sort out my thoughts by journaling and inviting God to communicate with me to build my faith and give me guidance on what to do.

JOURNAL: APRIL 22, 2017

"I feel pretty stressed. I have needed peace this week. There have been too many times this week where I have lost my peace and went to the space of worry and even fear. The causes are mostly related to the Marriott development funding issues. _____ (the construction lender) said that after further study, our balance sheet did not qualify us for the loan. So frustrating when their credit committee initially approved it, having seen our balance sheet! And now they are saying that although they had our financial statements, they hadn't really studied them . . . that their approval was with the understanding that they wouldn't go forward if, after further due diligence, they determined otherwise. We would never have gone this far down the road and spending millions that are fully at risk in this project if we would have known this was going to be an issue.

We have already gone to over fifty lenders to find this one that was willing to do this loan. So we don't have a lot of back-ups. Kym, our main contact at this lender—the one who got it approved and had her reputation on the line to make sure it actually funded—just announced that she is leaving the bank. Yesterday was her last day. Not good!

On top of this, we had a major challenge with _____ (an investment firm) that had told us they would put in the $15M we have been looking for to replace what our Chinese investor was going to put in. Out of the blue, they told me they would only do it on the condition that we bring in another major investor with a lot of hotel experience.

Our very experienced operating partner, Coury Hospitality, isn't at a place where they can invest the millions the investment firm is asking for. I've made tons of calls to experienced hotel operators, trying to find one that would invest, but if they do have the money to invest, they want to take control of operations. I have made a commitment for Coury to be our operator, so it just wouldn't be right to replace them, even though we have the legal right to do that. But at this point _____ (this investment firm) is our only option for the additional $15M we need and they are requiring this.

So what do I do, when the only option for survival requires me to break a commitment with someone who has done nothing to deserve that? I know, just do the right thing. I will tell _____ (this investment firm) that we just won't change operators to meet their requirements. But then we are without any option for the $15M we need. And if we don't get that, we lose everything.

In addition to these challenges, we had a three-hour call with _____ (our major investor) who had committed to invest $5.7M, and they are getting cold feet to even follow through on their commitment because the deal structure changed again. They said they would need to present it to their Investment Committee again, and the projected returns are down from 25% to 20% IRR.

So basically, almost all of the capital we need and thought we had in place for this project is now falling apart. The real stress comes from the fact that we have now invested most of the company's operating reserves into this one development project because its funding has been delayed so much. We've had to keep spending money to keep things moving forward and demonstrate that we really are committed to make this vision become reality. Now, if we don't have the full funding in place to close by May 17 (which looks 100% impossible right now), we lose those millions we have invested in this project and put the entire future of the company at risk.

Okay, when I write that, I can see clearly why I've been feeling the stress I have.

In addition to these challenges in business, I am feeling the pressure of having lost my home equity credit line last week because I didn't know the bank didn't set it back up on auto pay after our identity theft like they said they would. Now I find out I didn't get notice on late payments because they didn't have our new address. So they shut it down. I was counting on that for extra cushion to help cover any major unexpected expenses and in case our house or land takes a lot longer to sell than we are hoping. The reality is that we have not received any nibbles, let alone offers, on our old house. Nada. The extra expense of multiple mortgages is eating into our reserves.

Right now the circumstances seem overwhelming, and the odds of success seem impossible."

Now, I often do what I call "two way journaling" where I ask God a question, pause to see what thoughts come to my mind, and type those out as if God is speaking those words to me. It's a simple practice that over time has seemed to help me capture God's direction and empowerment more specifically in my life.

TWO WAY JOURNALING

So what do you have to say to me about all of this, Jesus?"

First, just rest in my care and embrace the peace of my presence. Then calmly and with faith, pursue next steps to solve each of these issues. This is a great opportunity to grow your faith.

Okay, where do I start?

First, let go of the stress and start with embracing peace that comes from knowing that I am with you in this. When I was on this earth I faced many challenges and the storms that I faced were significant in their own way— different than yours—but also significant. When I was on the storm on the sea with my followers, do you remember that all I had to do is say, "Peace, be still," and all was calm? What I said to them was what I say to you: "Why are you afraid, when I am with you?"

I am with you, Lonnie. I am the creator of the universe. I am the one who brought you into this world and gave you the upbringing and platform and talents that you have to do what you are doing now. I am with you. I am the one who knows no limits. You've gotten a lot of no's from people lately. I never let the word "no" stop me. There is nothing that I can't do. There is nothing that is good for you and for my kingdom purposes through you that I can't do and won't do. I am with you. Just keep that in mind. I am the one who gives you wisdom and creativity. I am the one who softened and hardened the hearts of rulers throughout the history of the world. I am the one who is with you.

Okay, I think I get that. But right now, my reality seems pretty overwhelming. Everything keeps changing, and not a lot seems to be working as planned right now. What do I focus on next?

You have been focused too much on the ever-changing circumstances and ups and downs of challenges and opportunities. Those things are all fickle and will always change. One day, one hour, things will be looking great, and the next, not so great. Yet I am always great, and I am always with you. Let that be your reality. My promises and my presence are always a "Yes". That doesn't mean that you will get a yes to everything you want when I am with you. It does mean that I am the ever present, unchanging, stable "yes" in your life! I am the stabilizing power that is a constant in your life. Focus on me. Focus on my words and the words that are written about what I said, like "My peace I give to you" and "With God, nothing is impossible". Let those consistent words permeate your mind.

But it shouldn't be this hard. I thought I was going down a path that you were leading. Why are there so many challenges?

This is all part of your training. Training is always for good purposes. This training will increase your faith and persistence. This is training you to focus on me and listen to me. I am training you to tune out those circumstantial stresses and distractions that could keep you from living in abundance internally and externally, all day, every day. This training is helping you see and live beyond current circumstances so you can be more persistent in pursuing visions I give you. Just keep going on the journey with me. Hear my promptings and take action on them. Don't try to figure it all out first. You would only need to figure it all out if I wasn't with you, but I am with you and I've got it figured out. Trust me! I do!

Discipline your mind to stay focused on me. I am the master of making something out of nothing. I am the master at making beauty out of ashes. Discipline your mind to stay focused, not on what is but on what can be and will be.

Wow. That's a powerful perspective. Help me embrace that mindset, because that's certainly not natural. I need your help to even have a shot at keeping that mindset. I would also like something–just give me anything a bit more specific to these current challenges.

I will get this Marriott done, and it will be a place that will make God look good and build my kingdom. We will be successful at this. You will sell the house and the orchard land around it for a good price at the right time to the right people. Trust my timing. Trust my wisdom. Even though you have gone now for four months and no one has even come close to making an offer on your house, you still have about four to five months of the extra cash you set aside to cover a potential shortfall. You've told me that everything you have is mine to use as I want, so it's my cash and I won't waste it unnecessarily. You have at least a month to get your house under agreement. Trust me. You will get it under agreement by the middle of May and close in June.

God not only gave me conceptual encouragement and support in the situation, as he often does if I listen long enough, he gave me specifics as well. I reminded him he told me I should trust him and calmly take the next steps, and I simply asked: "What are the next steps?" This detailed list is what flowed out of my fingers as I listened and typed:

PERSONAL FINANCES:

Finish sorting stuff to keep or sell at the estate sale this weekend. Be ruthless and minimalistic. You don't need stuff as much as you think you do. Others probably need that stuff more than you do. Within a couple weeks, the estate sale will be done and your house will be cleaned out. Then you can do another open house, and it will sell.

Talk to Norm about maybe leasing the orchard to your neighbor until it sells, as you might want to be prepared to hold it through this summer.

Marriott Development:

Do a new proposal to _____ (major equity investor) that he can give to his Investment Committee that will give them reason to want to go forward with their $5.7M investment.

Work through the bank's financial statement concerns and get the loan broker involved, if needed, to find a solution that will get them comfortable moving forward with the construction loan.

Talk to Nate at Marriott confidentially about the pressure _____ (the investment firm) is putting on changing operators. Marriott could give you specific challenges they would have with involving a new operator that hasn't been approved, and you can communicate that to the investor. Also, get your legal counsel's view on the challenges with changing operators.

Call _____ (the investment firm) and tell them you won't change operators and why.

Call the _____ (the land seller) and explain the specific challenges and ask for understanding and more time . . . yes, even though they said they wouldn't do that.

Get a term sheet from _____ (the investment firm) with an option that doesn't include changing operators, even if it means you'll have to do some other things you don't want. If nothing else, getting a new term sheet will at least buy you some more time with _____ (land seller).

Okay. Any final thoughts for me, God?

With all of those next steps in mind, now remember: don't let circumstances or what does or doesn't work on these plans, interrupt your awareness of my presence. Don't let circumstances cause you to pull back on your faith. That will just get you off track and flounder. The track you are to be on is connecting you with me. It's connecting you with my ability to step in to do things that you can't so you experience me even more. It's connecting you with challenges that help you in hearing from me, living with me, living my purposes. My purposes are grand and strategic and long term—eternal. At the same time, my purposes are also in the minute, in the small decisions, in the little actions, in the hallway conversation, in the call or text with someone who needs encouragement. My purposes, whether grand or granular, can only be lived out when I am living with you in the moment. You can only be on purpose when you are on point with me. You are actually most on point with me when it feels like you are on the edge of failure. That fosters fearless faith.

The clear confidence and direction I got from God got me through the next week. It bolstered my faith and gave me a basis for action toward the vision. I told the investment firm we wouldn't change operators, but to my dismay, I wasn't able to negotiate an alternate solution. They backed completely out of the deal. I thought I would be rewarded for doing the right thing, but no. Now I had a $15M hole to fill in a week and no options left for doing it.

I must admit I had a few words with God, wondering what in the world he was up to! I hit my knees at the end of that week of fruitless negotiations and told God again that I firmly believed this was a vision he wanted and that it was going to happen, but I desperately needed a breakthrough–and now!

Early that next Monday morning, a bipartisan omnibus spending deal was filed by the United States congressional leadership to postpone finalization of the budget and fund the government through the end of September. This deal included a list of other bills that would be postponed, including an initiative related to changing the regulations related to immigrant investments in the U.S. Months before, I had spoken to a multibillion dollar firm that made investments in the immigrant investor space, and they told me our project was too small for them. In addition, they weren't taking on any new funding projects until the regulations changed at the end of April. On May 1st, when I learned the regulations did not change at the end of April as planned, I contacted this huge company and asked if they would reconsider their rejection of our project.

This company is the best and by far the largest immigrant investment platform in the world. Normally they only work with much larger groups like the Ross Perrot and Donald Trump enterprises. They hadn't been taking on new business, though, during the last couple of months because of the pending regulation change. On the day I called, they had a space in their pipeline for a deal that could happen immediately. Since our project had been all cued up for funding and was ready to go, and since the regulatory changes were delayed, they had just enough time and just enough money available to meet the $15M shortfall. They did say they would only do it if we could execute on this in the next few weeks! It was at a much lower cost and with better terms than any other source we had seen for this $15M tranche of capital.

God's timing did prove to be perfect. Our faith-stretching vision that produced persistent action materialized in a miraculous solution.

Oh, and after having had our house on the market for almost half a year without even a nibble, we got it under agreement to sell by the middle of May and sold in June—just like God told me.

What's Your Faith-Requiring Vision?

What faith-stretching visions are you pursuing right now? If you don't have a vision that takes your breath away, you're not stretching your faith, and you're not living to your full potential.

You've probably heard questions like the following before, but go ahead and take a few minutes to free your mind to answer:

"If failure were not a possibility, what would you do?"

Go ahead and think of one answer to that question. What would you do if you knew you couldn't fail?

Or, if you have any entrepreneurial inclinations, answer this question:

"What would you do if you had unlimited resources to meet some important need in society ten times more effectively than is currently being done?"

Free your mind to dream a bit. Write down the thoughts that flow into your mind. Don't edit them.

Whatever you just answered, create a vision and begin to place a demand on faith. Your answer to questions like these is a kick starter for faith! Here's how.

Answering these questions creates vision. Vision is the ability to see some preferred future; the ability to see something that does not yet exist. The real value of vision is that it creates a platform for faith. In fact, I would go so far as to say that vision requires faith. Faith, like vision, is seeing something that doesn't yet exist, but faith takes it one step further. Faith is seeing what doesn't exist AS IF it already existed. Faith is being so sure that something will exist it feels as if you can reach out and hold it in your hand already. Faith is being so sure that something is going to happen that there's no chance it's not going to happen.

Every great vision requires that kind of faith to turn it into reality. Vision will just stay vision until the right action is taken toward accomplishing it. If you have faith that the vision will become reality, you see that vision as so real you can already taste it and feel it. If it is that real, why wouldn't you act on it?!

I've had many people tell me about visions they have for some area of their lives. But if they aren't taking action, I know they don't have faith in the vision. In fact, we can know whether someone has faith by the consistency of their actions toward that vision. That's why the Bible says, "Faith without deeds is dead."[114] It is because, if you truly believe a vision is going to happen, you will demonstrate that belief by taking action.

Faith is the fuel that will rocket you to success, but it must be ignited by the actions you take. Put your faith into action, showing you believe in the end result, and God will take you to whole new levels in your business and your life.

"Act and God Will Act"

This robust statement of faith was made by one of the most

intriguing figures in human history: Joan of Arc (1412-1431). This visionary seventeen-year-old girl led the armies of France at a time when grown women were expected to tend only to hearth and home.

Joan was convinced that God was telling her to fight for France, so she cut her hair short, donned armor, and set forth to talk to military leaders and the prince. Her job, as she saw it, was to convince them to listen to her battle plans for victory and to let her lead and inspire the troops.

If this teenage girl had any doubts about her vision or her abilities, she sure never expressed them. On the contrary, she was at the forefront of battles, lifting a siege around Orleans, and bringing about miraculous victories.[115] Yet the French army was so used to defeat, the leaders sometimes hesitated before Joan's action-oriented faith. When one French high commander held his troops back, Joan gave him a piece of her determined mind: "Whether you like it or not," she told him, "the soldiers will charge, and they will win." She then led the troops herself, into battle and on to victory.[116]

This great patriot of faith followed her vision all the way to her death. Her impact on history is such that there is a new movie or play version of her life every few years, even now, almost six hundred years after her death.

Action is faith expressed in an outcome.

There is nothing that makes God happier than to step in and act in response to the faith and hard work of someone who is doing everything he or she possibly can to pursue a worthwhile vision!

What Makes God Do the Happy Dance

When our kids were young and something particularly exciting happened—like the announcement of a surprise day on the lake or something—they would do this little dance where their bodies just jumped all over the place in uncontrollable, pure pleasure. We came to call that "the happy dance."

Have you ever wondered what it takes to please God? If you have, you probably haven't wondered what it takes to make God so excited about something that he does the happy dance! You might even be one of those who were raised with a view of God that says God is never pleased with humans, that there is nothing we can do to please God. Yet we do know there is something that does please God. The Bible says that without faith it's impossible to please God.[117] The corollary is that faith is very pleasing to God.

If I said, look, without something cold and sweet after a meal it's impossible to please my palate, the corollary would be that with something cold and sweet after a meal, my palate is very pleased! In fact, my kids often did the happy dance when they found out they were getting something cold and sweet like their favorite ice cream for dessert! So, if it is impossible to please God without faith, then with faith—well, could we say that God is so pleased by faith he does the happy dance?

If you want to please God, you need to have a vision about creating something that does not yet exist. In this book we're challenging you to have a vision for your business to create something that doesn't exist, something that needs to exist to make this world a better place. You now know that your business exists to make the world more like God wants it to be, to build God's kingdom.

When you have a vision for something that is better than what exists now, in any area of life or society, that pleases God. Vision, producing faith, pleases God. God gets excited about great vision! He does the happy dance in heaven!

If you have ever lived your life wondering if God is unhappy with you because you didn't keep some law or rule, I have great news for you! Keeping rules is not what makes God most happy!

It's not about whether you did or didn't do this or that. It's not about whether you went to church, or whether you cussed or drank too much. God wants to know whether you have a clear and compelling vision for something better than what now exists. God wants to know if you have the faith to create action to make this vision happen.

Do you have a vision big enough to require a faith that sees past obstacles and compels persistent action to make that new and better future happen?

Some of you may not consider yourselves big dreamers, especially when you compare yourself to others. Listen, there's no rule about how great the vision needs to be or how much faith is required. The point is that you need a vision big enough for you that it requires tremendous faith for you.

The size of the vision will look different for every individual. If the homeless person on the street has a vision to get a job that makes minimum wage, that's a big vision for him or her, and it requires faith. It pleases God as the homeless person takes action on finding a place where he can serve humanity for minimum wage. It pleases God as much as when my good friend Jim takes action, as he has for the last fifteen years, on a vision to invent a perpetual energy source; that is, a source that produces more energy than it uses. Both have a vision that requires faith and produces action to make the world a better place. Both make God just as happy. Both have found faith—the fuel that feeds a future of success!

CHAPTER 25

CHOOSE THE CHALLENGING PATHWAY TO SUCCESS

Let me start by asking a basic question you might think is rhetorical, but I'll ask it anyway.

How much do you want to be super successful in business and in life so you could literally say your life is perfectly complete and you lack absolutely nothing? On a scale of 1-10, with 10 being that you'd do anything for that kind of outcome, where would you place yourself?

Would you like to know how to get to that point? What if I told you there was a predictable formula to create that kind of a life? If such a formula existed, would you be willing to follow it? Let me show you this little-understood formula that can be traced to creating that kind of success over the last couple thousand years for those rare people with the courage to follow it. Ready?

Here it is, one of the most succinct and accurate systems for creating success:

"Consider it pure joy my brothers and sisters, whenever you face *trials* of many kinds, because you know that the testing of your *faith* produces *perseverance*. Let perseverance finish its work so that you may be mature and complete, *not lacking anything.*"[118]

I love how this quote ends: "mature and complete, not lacking anything". Who wouldn't want that?! Being a fully "mature and complete" person–fully grounded, with no insecurities, and emotionally, psychologically, financially, socially, and personally complete–who wouldn't want that? "Not lacking anything" means having everything you could ever want in your life, including all the things money can and cannot buy. Sounds like success to me!

If you want that kind of success, see if you want to volunteer for what it takes to get there. Here's a simple, but somewhat scary, two-step formula.

Step one. Have lots and lots of problems, all kinds of trials! Oh, and look forward to those challenges with joy. Chew through challenges with joy!

It doesn't say that challenges will be fun. It doesn't say challenges are a joy. It says, "Consider it joy." The challenge may be a pain but you can choose to consider that pain a joy.

When I work out, it's often a pain. My muscles hurt, but I have learned to consider it joy because I know that pain is producing a good result. The burning muscles are not a joy. They are a pain! But I consider the burning muscles a joy because I know that is the only way I'll get stronger.

Step two. Embrace your challenges as a treasured tool to test, refine, stretch, and strengthen your faith. Every challenge, by definition, presents a gap between the current reality and the desired one. That gap is a prerequisite to exercising faith, because faith is the ability to see what is not yet there. Faith is the ability to fully embrace what is on the other side of the gap–your desired reality–as if it were already there. A challenge is something you see that is not the way you want it to be. It requires faith to see past it. Faith is to see over, around, under or through the challenges to your desired future reality.

Here's the brutal reality. You can't have faith without challenges. Faith is a muscle that requires challenge and resistance in order to develop and get strong. When faith is being tested and stretched, it sometimes feels like muscles tearing. Yet every time that happens, your faith becomes a bit stronger, and you become that much more prepared for even weightier challenges. That kind of faith is the prerequisite for persistence. People persist in a direction to the degree they have faith that they will arrive at their desired destination.

I remember the first time my mentor, Paul Monson, invited me to go out with him on his boat. I thought, "Yeah! Let's go do it!" I was thinking it was a little ski boat or something. I pulled up to the marina and walked over to the dock and he pointed to this humongous yacht!

He was such a humble, understated man. He had never even mentioned his yacht. As I was walking up to this floating palace, I noticed the name on the back, as every grand boat has. The name of Paul's boat was Persistence.

I said, "Paul, why did you name your boat 'Persistence'? That's not like a cool, sexy lady's name like most boats have."

Paul then went on to tell me the story of how he had learned that persistence is the key to success in business and life: that every successful business and individual had a big enough vision that it presented significant problems requiring great faith to overcome. The gem hidden in that process was the development of undaunted persistence.

It is ultimately persistence that keeps you taking action toward your dreams, and that is what produces success in any area of life.

That was the first time I really connected the dots. If you want success, you have to want challenges so you can build faith that gives you the strength of persistence which knows no defeat.

If you want success, you want challenges. If you want greater faith and stronger persistence, you want more challenges. Success is guarded by challenges, and challenges qualify us for success.

Pathways to Challenges

There are three primary pathways to challenges.

1. You can have challenges that are caused by poor decisions and actions or by lack of decisions and actions. For example, you decide to sleep in, and you miss an important business meeting. It causes a challenge in your business. Or you don't take action to continue to improve your relationship with your spouse and put him/her first, and your marriage starts to have challenges. Or you have a big dream and start chasing it down the path, but you don't have a plan or don't count the cost and you end up in a big challenge.

The challenges most people face fall in this category. And yes, overcoming challenges in this category does require faith and persistence to overcome and can lead to success.

2. The second category of challenges are those which are created from things you have no control or influence over. You didn't choose the family you were born into or raised in. You didn't choose an inherited physical handicap you might have. For most people, challenges in this category are a relatively small percentage of the quantity of life's challenges. Since you have no control over the creation of challenges in this category, some find it easier to be joyful

in facing them. At least you don't have to feel guilty about your role in creating them, and sometimes they can be used to create unusual success in life. These challenges can be considered all joy. From them, you can expect all good, faith-growing, success-producing outcomes.

3. The third pathway to challenges is going after a vision that is so huge, it naturally creates all kinds of challenges you must overcome before it can be achieved. Say you start a new business to go after your dream of providing a higher quality service to an industry. You pursue inventing a new product that will meet an important need in society more effectively. You set a goal that takes your breath away because it seems so much more than anything you've done before. When you choose this third pathway to challenges, you get the same benefit of testing and growing your faith. You also get the benefit of the possibility of turning a dream into a reality.

If you want to take full advantage of this formula for success, be intentional about pursuing this third pathway for success.

The first two pathways to challenges can still be used to develop faith and persistence and to become more mature and successful. With them, though, you are more likely to just end up surviving instead of changing the world. Choose the pathway of doing hard things that will make the world a better place—and you'll experience hard, stretching challenges and very sweet victories.

Choosing the Challenges that Change Your Life

There were several points in the many months of developing our Marriott Autograph hotel that I felt like I was on challenge overload. In fact, there was a particular point where I came as close to having a panic attack as I ever remember. It was the week we had to either fully fund the $50M, buy the land and start construction, or we would lose the contractual right to buy the land. The land sellers had made it clear they were ready to give the opportunity to a different company. That meant we would lose millions of dollars we had invested in the project, with no hope of recovering it. We passed the deadline to close, so we were in default on the contract. Legally, we had forfeited the deal and lost everything.

After much negotiation, the land seller finally said they would allow us to cure the default if we gave them a lot of additional, non-refundable money and would close by May 17. In the next sentence they admitted they knew that was impossible. That same week, Marriott International told me they were going to give notice of default on our franchise agreement because we had missed the agreed-upon construction start date. They had several other companies that were begging to build in this market. Marriott made it very clear they were not willing to talk to me about extending the franchise agreement until we had all $50M in hand and until we had the land back under control.

Having had plenty of opportunities to stretch my faith muscle over the years, it takes a lot to get me really stressed these days. When this all came to light on May 12, though, I experienced a level of internal panic that literally took my breath away. I got little sleep that night. I woke up early in the morning and went to the best place I know to find possible solutions to impossible challenges. I sat down and asked–no, I practically begged–God to speak to me. I was at the end of my rope and at the end of my ideas. I had reached the end, end, end of my natural abilities and resources. It had been nearly five months since our primary equity source had backed out on us. Our project team and I had been working endless hours for many months on this challenge.

I was at the end of having a clear perspective on all this. It felt like the challenges were stifling me. I was underwater with no snorkel. I was gasping for air but only sucking in water.

I just wanted out—out from under the weight of this oppressing challenge. I wanted an easier life. I was starting to kick myself for taking on such a crazy vision that caused such gigantic challenges.

All I asked was that God would give me a new perspective on this so that I could get my head straight to fight another day.

This is what God gave me on that day as I asked him to give me his perspective and flow his thoughts through my fingers as I typed.

JOURNAL: MAY 13, 2017

It occurs to me this morning, as I reflect on my week full of huge challenges, that I can choose how I look at these challenges. I can look at them as stressful things to avoid or I can eagerly embrace them as opportunities to learn and grow. If I truly choose the latter, I won't be complaining about these challenges to others or even in my own mind.

Most everyone has peaks and valleys of challenges in life. The reality that occurs to me now is that most everyone can also choose the nature of the challenges they face.

It is not that we choose the specific challenge we face. Yet we certainly choose the nature of the challenges we face. The challenges I have been facing this week are the result of my own choosing. I have chosen to pursue a big dream to build a $50M Marriott Autograph hotel that our company did not have ANY experience or capability to do. It is multiple times larger than any development we've even been involved in, and we've never been involved in a hotel in any way.

To go after such a stretch goal and the choice to continue to pursue it despite the myriad of obstacles has generated many highly complex challenges. Many of those challenges are threatening the very existence of the company and the livelihoods of hundreds of people. That's the reality and I've got to face it.

I could sit here and feel stressed about these challenges, or I could be excited that I got to choose them and about the fact that somehow, some way, the very process of dealing with and overcoming these challenges will change my life and the lives of others for the better.

Just for the purpose of contrast, to solidify the perspective I want to have on this, I'll take a minute to imagine a different set of challenges that I could choose. I could choose to do the same thing that has always been done. I could choose to keep the company doing the same thing, the same way. That would result in its own set of challenges. At some point, doing things as we always have could even result in a threat of potentially going out of business.

I could choose in my personal life not to pursue new and aggressive goals, not to pursue new visions that require faith and hard work. If I did that, I could end up with a different set of challenges like a few of my friends have right now—where they face the challenge of relationships falling apart because there is no personal growth happening. Or if I didn't choose aggressive new goals, I could end up like a few others I know where they face the regular challenge of not knowing where they will get enough money to pay their rent or their next grocery bill. They choose those challenges that change their life in that way, just like I choose the challenges that change my life and are causing me to put energy and focus on solving them.

A tree gets strong by being exposed to the challenges of the wind and the rain. The stronger and more recurring the storm, the stronger the tree becomes. A sailor gets better by sailing in the storms, not in the calm. This is a law of life. If a tree could choose its challenges, it might choose to grow up in a greenhouse nursery with perfect climate control. Yet that tree would choose the challenge of having a ceiling on its growth, feeble roots, and a weak trunk so that it could never actually thrive in the real world. An ignorant sailor wannabe might choose to sail only in perfectly calm water so as never to face the challenge of strong winds or angry waves. In doing so, that sailor would choose the challenge of staying in one place, the challenge of boredom, and even the threat of eventual starvation as resources ran out.

I just read Isaiah 43:2 where God says to us, "When you pass through the waters, I will be with you. And when you pass through the rivers, they will not sweep over you. When you walk through the fire, you will not be burned. The flames will not set you ablaze."

I noticed that it doesn't say, "When the waters come out of nowhere and pass over you . . . " as if you were just an object caught up in a storm. "When you pass through the waters" implies movement, motion, choice, because you are exercising the will to pass through the waters. In essence it says, "When you choose to pass through the waters, I will be with you." It doesn't say, "When the river comes out of nowhere and floods you, it won't sweep you away." It says, "When you pass through the rivers," as if you had made a willful choice to go through those turbulent waters. In essence it says, "When you choose to pass through the river (on your way to somewhere of your choosing), it won't sweep you away." This is the same with the fire. It doesn't say "When a fire starts around you and engulfs you in flames, it won't burn you up." It says, "When you walk through the fire, you won't get burned." It takes some will, some deliberate choice, to walk through fire.

Whether you like those situations or not, you are putting one foot in front of the other and walking through them, using your willpower. So God is clearly saying to me in this verse that when I choose to go somewhere that takes me through a challenge, he will be with me and keep me on my path through the waters, the river, and the fire, and he will keep any of those challenges from destroying me.

So here's my new declaration today. I am choosing the challenges that change my life. I am choosing the challenges that will change my world. I choose challenges that make my life and the lives of those around me better. I choose challenges that create platforms for God to establish his rule and reign more fully on this earth. I choose the challenges that help me embrace and experience God's active presence in my life. I choose challenges that will threaten to take me off course from something important God wants to happen on this earth so I can see God dramatically keep his plans from getting derailed. I choose challenges that will require God to guard my body, mind, and spirit so that I come out the other side, protected and stronger to choose yet another challenge that will change the world for God.

It was amazing the fresh creative perspective this journaling gave me. I was able to tackle the day with a sense of joy and excitement that I got to choose this set of challenges and it built my faith and creativity in persisting with a new plan of action. God stepped in and added his super to my natural. Somehow all potential capital sources were able to change schedules to meet at the building site in Minneapolis on May 17. People from all over the country and from China changed schedules with very short notice to be there on that day. We started that day with only a small portion of the capital committed and in default on our contract to purchase the land. By the end of the day we had signed agreements for the full $50M and a signed extension agreement with the land seller. The impossible became possible!

Succeeding Through Suffering

The challenges and suffering we go through often purify and refine us so we are better after we come out of them than we were when we entered them. What is more, God will make certain we are not destroyed in the process. When you are facing challenges, God promises in the portion of Scripture that I referenced in my journal that he will do three things:

1. **God will be with you.** His presence is the primary most important thing in the middle of a challenge. At minimum, every challenge can create the value of increasing awareness of God's presence. There are no atheists in foxholes, as the saying goes. Most of us think about God a lot more during challenging times. So every challenge is at minimum the perfect environment to increase focus on God and your ability to seek and receive his wisdom and strength. The best preparation for challenges is the presence of God–the hand that never lets go even in the worst storms. You can

choose the pathway of peace by trying to perceive God's perpetual presence in problems.

1. **God will keep you on track.** The river of this challenge won't sweep you away. Even though the torrent of challenges seems overwhelming, this won't take you off the course you've chosen which took you into this challenge. These challenges won't take you out.

1. **God will protect you.** You will not be drowned or burned up. The challenges will make you better not bitter. The challenges may char you, make you sputter and gasp, and change you, but they won't destroy you. You can choose to believe the challenges that seem to overwhelm you with waves are washing you clean, purifying you. You can choose to believe the challenges that seem to burn you are actually a refining fire.

Not only will God be with you when you pass through waters and keep rivers from sweeping over you and flames from scorching you, if you keep your faith while suffering the stress of challenges, God will be the wind in your sails and propel you faster and farther than you ever thought you could go

As the great overcomer Helen Keller said, "Character cannot be developed in ease and quiet. Only through experience of trial and suffering can the soul be strengthened, ambition inspired, and success achieved." This challenging pathway for success is rarely fun, but it is a predictable process to creating a powerful future.

CHAPTER 26

CAPTURE THE POWER TO CHANGE THE WORLD

Business leader, what I'm talking about here is a lifestyle of faith. Again, this is not a religious thing. It's a lifestyle of success. It's a way of doing life that allows you to pursue world-changing visions and empowers you to see those become reality. It happens by living by faith in what can be and not by what you see.

One of my favorite verses in the Bible is where God is quoted as saying, "But My righteous one shall live by faith; And if he shrinks back, My soul has no pleasure in him. But we are not of those who shrink back to destruction, but of those who have faith to the preserving of the soul."[119]

In this verse God is saying that the person he considers righteous is the person who lives by faith. God then goes a step further and says he takes no pleasure in the one who shrinks back from doing big things that require faith. Then Paul adds that, as followers of Jesus, we aren't among those who shrink back and are destroyed; we are people who have faith that preserves the soul.

Just for a minute, take the religious connotations out of the words "faith" and "soul." When I had "faith" that we could find a way to fund and build this wonderful hospitality complex, it "preserved my soul". In fact, it "saved my bacon"! It saved the soul of our company. There is nothing religious about that; it was just a very practical business process. We could have shrunk back and hunkered down and taken our losses, but we didn't. We went forward in faith that somehow we were going to pull this off.

So many times in life and in business, when the odds seem completely against the vision, it is tempting to shrink back and settle for where you're at, for something less than the vision. Yet people of great faith don't shrink back.

The phrase "shrinks back" is a nautical term that would have been very familiar to all the fishermen, boat owners and sailors back in biblical times. It was the term that was used for furling a sail. If you've never sailed, to furl your sail basically means to take your sail down and wrap it up. The phrase translated into English as "shrink back," literally means "furl your sail". It was a phrase the sailors used when they called it quits for the day and wrapped up their sail or when they were in a storm and they needed to pull down the sail and wrap it up because they were moving too fast.

What God is saying here is, "I take no pleasure in people who furl their sails, in someone who shrinks back instead of moving forward even in rough winds. Rather I take pleasure in the person who has faith. You don't preserve your soul, you don't save the ship by furling your sail; you get where you want to go by keeping your faith sail fully up, capturing the wind."

There's something you need to know about the culture and words of that time to grasp what this probably meant to the original readers. When experienced sailors think of a sail, the next word that pops into their mind is wind. The purpose of a sail is to catch the energy of the wind to move the boat toward the desired destination. What's interesting here is that in the Greek language, the word for wind, soul, and spirit are all the same. It's "psyche" which is from the word from "psyxō", which means "to breathe or to blow". This is also the root of the English words "psyche" and "psychology". The psyche (or soul) is a person's distinct identity, our unique personhood. Genesis 1 says that human beings became a living "soul" as the direct result of God breathing (blowing) his gift of life into Adam. At one point, Jesus directly compared the Spirit of God to the wind, explaining that both are something that you can't see but you can sure feel and see their effect.

So, what we don't see here in English is a fascinating and highly informative play on words with double and triple meanings. Let me rephrase it with all three meanings and see what you can make of it.

"But My righteous one will live by faith; And if he shrinks back, My soul **(God's wind, God's Spirit–his person and presence)** has no pleasure in him. But we are not of those who shrink back (furl our sail) to destruction, but of those who have faith to the preserving (or capturing) of the soul **(the wind, the spirit, the soul/essence of God)**."

Faith is like a sail that we put up to capture the wind, the power, the presence of God in our lives. It is that power of God that our faith catches which moves and propels the boat of our life, the vessel of our vision forward. Faith is the sail we put up to capture the empowerment of God to move us toward our vision. When the storms come and the seas get rough, we don't shrink back in fear. We don't furl up our faith sail and just let the storms of circumstances or challenges push us around. No! That's when we need all the power we can get from God to move us through the storm. That's when we need to lean into the tipping boat and be propelled toward our goals.

Notice that we do have the choice to raise the sail of faith or shrink it down and play it safe. We have the choice to keep going for our vision despite the challenges and keep our lives wide open to the presence and power of God to move us forward through the storm. Or we can choose to furl up the sail of faith and not take advantage of the power that is outside of our own.

I know I have furled my sail of faith way too often, especially when it came to business. For much of my life, I have seen God as being available to empower me to do important things in church ministry or missions. Yet when it comes to business, I've too often pulled my faith sail in and tried to do it on my own. I have not unfurled the sail of faith constantly and consistently in every aspect of my business life. Yet more and more these days, I have been testing what it feels like to put up my faith sail to capture God's presence and empowerment in my business life. The results are night and day different.

Catch the Wind

You too have a choice right now, business leader. You can choose to furl up your sail and say, "I don't really need the power of God in my life." That's fine, you can go right ahead and plop your little old oars into the water and keep paddling on your own. If you've got a direction and a vision, you can get somewhere and that may even take some faith too.

If you knew, though, that there was a great wind up there and all this time you've been sweating away stroke after stroke on the oars, why wouldn't you at least try it? Just try it! Work smarter, not just harder. Put up this thing called faith and believe there is a power outside yourself that can supercharge your vision for success. Just try unfurling your faith sail and see what God does.

You still have the authority to put the sail up or down and to pull it in or let it out to determine how much wind you want to catch. You're not giving up control of your life or business by opening yourself up to God's presence and empowerment. You still have control over the rudder. You still control the sail—and you can still furl it up any time you want.

The one who is in the right relationship with God will live life trusting in him and believing in where they are going as if they were already there. That kind of faith is like a sail that catches the wind of the spirit to produce momentum. As a business leader, I need to have faith and not shrink back, not take my sail down. Faith is what captures the moving force of God, like the wind you cannot see that creates movement in the physical world.

Unfortunately, when many Christians go into the business environment, they look like a boat with a furled sail. Oh, they may ask God to be their copilot and give them some direction. They may occasionally ask him for assistance. They may even have their hand on the rudder moving it in the direction they think they get from God or from the Bible. But, their faith sail is furled in a puddle at the bottom of the boat. They are missing the power of faith and the active movement of God in and through their business. They think faith is more for church and "ministry" stuff. When they go into business, their boat is sitting still in the water or only being moved by the waves of circumstances or a slight movement effect from the wind on the boat itself. Then, because there's not enough movement, they try to move it on their own power. Some take a paddle and begin paddling. They work harder and harder. They sweat more and work longer hours to overcome. They just keep investing more time and money, hoping it will create momentum toward their vision. All the while they are missing the ability to capture the strong wind that is blowing just above them.

As business leaders who embrace the opportunity to rebuild our part of the world, we cannot be the kind of people who furl our sails. We are those who hoist our sails of faith to capture every bit of God's presence and power to move our life and our business forward to build a better society on this earth.

We are not "shrink back" people. We are not "sail furling" people. Instead we are those who have faith that preserves or captures the empowering wind of God. Put up your faith sail to capture the wind, the power of God to move you forward in life. Don't furl your sail. Keep yourself wide open to what he can do to move you toward your vision, more than you could ever do all on your own.

Turbo Charge Your Engine

If you are more of a car nut than a boater, maybe you'd rather think of your life as an automobile. If your life were a car, then faith is the fuel that propels you to your destination. Faith is the fuel that allows you to have great adventures in your vehicle. You don't produce the fuel. You just choose to put gas in the car or not. You don't produce faith. Faith itself is actually a gift from God. He is the source. You can choose, though, to inject it into your life.

The Bible says when you accept Jesus as your life leader, you become a new creation. You become like a new car. You have a new kind of engine that operates even more effectively on the high octane of God's presence and power in your life. You have greater capacity for living life to the fullest.

326

The hottest car in the world is only fun for a short time if it doesn't have any fuel.

There are a lot of people who say they are Christians and are filled with God. They go to church, read the Bible, and do all the right things. They have the right engine and they are probably going to heaven. Yet they never choose to put the fuel of faith in the engine to supercharge it on high octane gas, so they actually go somewhere in life. Maybe they put a little bit of fuel in and use low octane gas, and they putt along through life just getting by or getting from point a to b.

Faith is like high octane fuel you choose to put in your tank. You may not understand exactly how it works. You may not understand the specific chemical reactions that cause fuel to combust. You may not understand the specific mechanics of how combustion transfers energy to propel your vehicle forward. But you still choose to put the fuel in the tank. In the same way, faith is a choice you make. You may not understand exactly how it works, but you can make the choice to put faith into your life and into your business.

Again, in doing this, you aren't giving up control of your life. You still control the steering wheel. You still get to make a million choices. But you will find you have wisdom and empowerment you never had before you chose to fuel your life with faith.

Some may be thinking right now about that old country Christian song "Jesus, Take the Wheel". It's a nice thought. But near as I can tell, God has always given people free will to make their own choices. He doesn't take the wheel out of our hands. Even with great fuel in the car, we are still the ones making the choices that control the effectiveness of the drive. We can go in circles, take wrong roads, and detours. We can drive intentionally, skillfully, and effectively.

It's not enough to have a good car with good fuel. We still need to do smart things. A business with a good driver at the helm, using good business practices and God's presence will get farther faster than a business just with God's presence and a business leader/driver who is asleep at the wheel or using poor business practices. I see it happen all the time.

There are things we can do in the natural. Then there are things that require the supernatural.

Granted, the better your things in the natural world–the better your car, the better designed your business, the better designed your life, the more mileage and momentum you'll get from your "super" fuel. Do all you can with your natural capabilities. At the same time use faith to fill your life with God's super fuel. That will give you supernatural results in business and in life and you will have the power to build a better world for God.

Faith creates the power needed for all great success in business and life. Oh, you can choose to try to build your business and your life on your own power. You'll probably get somewhere that way. The next level of effectiveness happens when you choose to build your business and leave your mark on rebuilding this world based on your own power but with God's principles and values guiding you. You'll probably get even farther that way. But if you're ready for the next highest level of effectiveness, it happens when you build your business on God's principles *and* tap into the unlimited power and presence of God as your partner in everything you do.

If you want to really make a dent in rebuilding a better world, supercharge everything you do with faith and access the wisdom, resources, and guidance of the leader of the universe.

The bigger your vision, the bigger benefit you'll see in accessing the power of God. Start embracing your business as a vehicle to transform the world beginning with your employees, customers, suppliers, and stakeholders. Work on transforming your industry, your city, and then your nation. Embrace the vision of building God's purposes and his enduring systems for success into society. Pursue rebuilding the kingdom of evil and darkness into the kingdom of goodness and light. Chase this vision and capture God's power to change the world!

Conclusion

When you started this book, you may not have seen yourself as someone who was building God's kingdom. Maybe you aren't so sure about that even now. If you're at the stage where your primary focus is simply building a business that provides value and makes a profit, congratulations. You are already doing something good to build a better world. If you are at the level where you are starting to go the extra mile to build beyond business, congratulations. You are creating real value that is building a better world. If you are at the level where you are intentionally doing commerce in a way that transforms society to look more like God's vision for the world, congratulations. You are definitely building a better world.

Whatever level you are at, I challenge you to take your business beyond where it is now to become even more successful at building a better world. I challenge you to rebuild your definition of success to align with the eternal systems for success described in this book. I challenge you to deconstruct any paradigms and processes that are holding you back from having an abundant life with maximum impact on this world.

If you were to list the paradigms and practices you might change as a result of reading this book, what might those be? Write them down. Now look at the list. If you're honest, there's probably something on that list that puts butterflies or knots in your stomach when you think about actually doing it. It's never easy to let go of cherished notions and practices you've worked hard to put in place. But releasing and rebuilding something cherished is often the only way to create something brand new and more effective.

Let me share one more illustration to help you embrace the process of rebuilding some paradigms you may hold dear in order to build a better world for yourself and for others.

I still remember the thrill of designing and building our first dream home. We had found the perfect acreage on a mountain lake and couldn't wait to create our perfect home. Shelley and I dreamed about the best possible use of every inch of space to create our ideal living conditions. I stayed up many late nights dreaming and drawing out every detail. I'm not anything close to an architect or a contractor. But we wanted it to be just right. So, I played architect and general contractor to make sure it was designed and built exactly as we wanted. Tremendous thought, care, and work went into making it just like our family wanted it to be. When we finally finished building our new home, we couldn't imagine changing anything.

One day we came home after having been gone for three weeks to find our entire house destroyed by a massive flood. The main water supply pipe broke on the top floor of our beautiful three-story home. The break was behind the furnace where water sprayed into the HVAC duct system which conveniently distributed thousands of gallons through the ceiling vents into every room of the house. A chunk of ice had slid off our roof and broke the propane line, causing our furnace to quit working during a cold snap in the winter. The water froze in the pipes and burst apart. Then it warmed up enough to thaw and our well pumped water into nearly every room on every floor of the house for a couple of weeks. It completely soaked the sheetrock, and even the light fixtures fell off the ceilings and walls.

I got the best restoration construction companies to give us proposals, and they all essentially said, "Sorry to tell you this, but we basically can't salvage much of anything. This is a total rebuild. We may be able to save the basic structure and frame but that's it."

It was such a shock to hear we had to rebuild something we

had worked so hard to create and felt comfortable we would never need to change. We went through a phase of shock and grieving. We had invested so much in getting this to where it was, and now we couldn't bring our minds to think about rebuilding it. We couldn't imagine rebuilding something that was as good as what we already had.

Of course, you've probably guessed the rest of the story. We eventually wrapped our minds around the possibility that we could rebuild and maybe make something even better than what we'd had. We started to get a little excited as we thought of new and better uses of the same basic framework. There were now better and more natural materials available. We had new perspectives and new design ideas that were an even better fit for the current trends. We thought of ways to make it even more functional and effective for this next phase of our lives. We put in real granite were we previously had fake stuff. We added some real stone where we previously had wood. We included updated colors and designs.

Now we have an old house that people think is brand new. Of course, it really isn't brand new. It's the same house on the same foundation. But we got the rare opportunity to rebuild something in order to make it even more than it was.

What I have given you in this book is the rare opportunity to rebuild some paradigms and practices you may have invested a lot in to get them to where they are right now. It's a rare opportunity because it is a rare person who has the courage to deliberately deconstruct something to rebuild something even better. It's your choice whether you are willing to deconstruct some paradigms that are good but could be more. It's your choice whether you are willing to rebuild some practices that have worked to some degree but could be better. It's your choice whether you want to build something that may look and feel brand new and give you even greater freedom and functionality in your business and in your life. You will probably build on the same business, the same life and some of the same foundational principles. But you have an opportunity to build something with brand new meaning, greater purpose and impact.

I'm inviting you to choose to reconstruct some of your paradigms and practices in order to become more effective at rebuilding the world. Go to the next level and embrace the reality that:

- Your business can be your most powerful platform to build a better world.

- Your business can be a prime vehicle to follow Jesus, the highest impact business leader ever!

- Your business can be your your highest expression of ministry and missional service to the world.

- Your business can actually be building the church Jesus originally designed to transform this world.

- Your business can be the most effective tool to build God's kingdom–infiltrating the world with God's good leadership and values.

- Your business and your life can be supercharged by faith in a powerful God who has unlimited resources to help you accomplish world changing visions.

God is the consummate entrepreneur, designer and CEO of the universe. He is the intelligent designer of all universal systems for success. His ideal is to see all of society following his systems and his leadership so we all function at optimal levels of fulfillment and prosperity. Jesus was the perfect demonstration of what that looks like and he is now ready, willing and able to help you live that dream.

If you're ready to try the ultimate leadership adrenaline rush,

I challenge you to embrace Jesus as your life leader and accept his mission to use your business as your platform to rebuild the world to be more like his ideal for society.

Do something to declare your intent now. Get in some quiet place by yourself and speak a declaration of faith something like the following statement. Say it out loud with all the conviction you can muster up:

"My business is my platform to build a better world! I accept the challenge to build beyond business! I accept the challenge to rebuild the world to look more like God's ideal for society through doing transformational commerce! I seek wisdom, guidance, and resources beyond my own to accomplish such an important vision and I trust God to provide everything I need to succeed. I choose to follow Jesus as the leader of my business and my life. And I believe that with his leadership and empowerment, I can rebuild my part of the world!"

Now, decide what you will do next to act on this statement of faith which you just declared. What would it look like if you really believed this enough to actually pursue this vision? What would you do different in your business and in your life? Write down a few next steps that come to your mind. Put them on your calendar. Share your vision and action plans with a few others who can support you on this exciting journey. Don't let this just be another book you read. Do something that will begin transforming your business into a more effective platform to build a better world!

Thank You!

Any value you have received from reading this book is a direct result of the value that has been given to me from God and from my family, friends, and mentors over the years. We can only give what we have already received. So I can't help but say a heartfelt thank-you to the many people from whom I have received rich friendship, encouragement and wisdom, which are the basis for anything of value in this book.

To my life-leader Jesus: Thank you for being the ultimate example of doing life and business in a way that creates abundant life for individuals, societies, and the world. Your love, wisdom and empowerment are my secret sauce to success.

To my amazing wife Shelley: Thank you for making me the number-one recipient of your exceptional gift of encouragement, which has supported me through the tedious days of writing and editing. You respect me more than I deserve, and you always make me feel that I can change the world. Your passion for me and your commitment to God always light my fire!

To my daughter Lachelle and son-in-love Auren: Thank you for giving us our first grandbaby who provides yet another motivation to do whatever I can to make the world better for future generations. And Lachelle, thanks for helping me transcribe many hours of our recorded discussions on these topics.

To my daughter Chelann: Thank you for taking away my excuses about not having enough time to finish this book that I started years ago. You set the example and raised the bar (as you so often do) by writing your own book from concept to published in four months.

To my son Sky: Thank you for editing the audiobook so professionally … and deleting all the weird sounds my throat makes when I'm too close to the mic!

To my son Kylon and daughter-in-love Teliah: Thank you for inspiring me with your constant commitment to make the world a better place through your own businesses and in everything you do.

To my dad and mom Ed and Allegra Gienger: Thank you for giving me a solid foundation of unconditional love and for training me to live life guided by kingdom principles and connection with God. Your teaching and consistent example of putting God first in everything has inspired much of who I am today.

To my parents-in-love Mickey and Verdene Meyer: Thank you for raising the woman of my dreams! Your example of living God's values, leadership, and generous love in everyday life continually inspires me.

To my siblings Dean, Lynae, LoAnn, Skip, and Krissy: Thanks for never criticizing my crazy, out-of-the box ideas and for accepting me just as I am.

To Russ and Jim Wilkinson: Thank you for a lifetime of loyal friendship where I always know you are in my corner. I couldn't ask for better business partners who live Kingdom values regardless of the personal or corporate cost and give me the freedom to find ways to make our businesses better platforms to build people and build the world.

To Greg Gunn: Thank you for helping me learn to lead my family as intentionally as I lead my businesses through your personal mentoring over the last 16 years and through your high-impact ministry, www.family-id.com. Thank you for being my chief encouragement to write this book and for the many brainstorming sessions and the practical ideas you have shared from your own experience. The vision for this book would not have become a reality without you, buddy!

To Randy Alsbury: Thank you for the specific coaching on how to start writing this book by turning the years of journaling on this subject into a working outline.

To Paul and Teryl Monson: Thank you for partnering to research and develop the Systems for Success approach and content. Paul, even though you are no longer with me on this planet, your legacy lives on through what you poured into me and so many other leaders.

To Russ Olmon: Thank you for being my friend and confidant for over 20 years and for always being willing to think and act outside the box about how to systematically develop churches that change the world.

To Ed Silvoso: Thank you for your faithfulness to develop the Transform Our World Conference where for the first time, I realized there are many other business leaders who are thinking about using their business as a platform to build God's kingdom.

To Shaji and Shiney Daniel: Thank you for living such a compelling case study example of what it looks like when successful business leaders truly embrace business as ministry.

To Eric Bahme: Thank you for being a faithful friend for 38 years, always challenging me to expand my paradigms about God and the role business can play in building the church.

To the many family offices and purpose-driven, high-net-worth individuals I've connected with in recent years: Thank you for inspiring me with your passion to impact society and the planet through your businesses and investments.

To the twenty CEO's and Presidents who read and gave feedback on the early manuscript of this book: Thank you for convincing me that this is something the world needs to hear and for pushing me to actually publish the book.

To June Sanders and to the Useful Group: Thank you for helping me get my draft manuscript into publishable form that will benefit many business leaders.

To you, the reader of this book: Thank you for having an open mind to consider new paradigms and practices that could help you lead your company to build a better world.

To those of you who embrace the vision of this book and put it into practice: Thank you in advance for inspiring and instructing me and many others with more case study examples. I am eager to learn from you. Together we will create a movement of leaders who build better businesses that build a better world!

Appendix

Overview of the Nine Categories of Systems for Success in Business

Building a business that gives you the margin needed to build beyond business and do more to rebuild the world requires the disciplined planning and implementation of nine foundational categories of business systems. Each of these business operating systems are powerful tools that will help you organize key areas of your business for maximum effectiveness. Together they work to make your entire business run like a perfectly constructed machine that will give you the consistent results and margin you need to change the world through your business! I'll give a brief overview of these nine categories of systems, and also give a little insight into why each one is important to the success of your business.

Like the designer of anything great, you can't build a successful business that gives you the results you want and the margin you need to rebuild the world without first creating a blueprint; a vision of what you want your business to be. That's why the first and most important system you use is the strategic planning system.

1. Strategic Planning Systems

Do you have a clear vision for your company and a step-by-step plan to achieve it?

Success doesn't just happen; you have to plan for it. In fact, the biggest mistake business owners make is failing to come up with a blueprint for their success. When you get caught in a cycle of firefighting, it is difficult to do anything but react to the crisis of the moment. Strategic planning is the way to get proactive about your business. It starts with a clear understanding of your personal mission, vision, and values so that you can intentionally build a business that is an outgrowth of who you are called to be. Then you will develop a crystal clear mission, vision, and the core values that set the direction and DNA for everything you do in your business. Based on this, you will develop specific strategies, objectives, goals, and action plans where you decide in advance exactly what needs to be done, and how you'll do it. Your direction, strategies and goals will be in writing so it can be clearly communicated and consistently executed.

You and your employees will know the specific tasks needed to accomplish each goal. With each positive change you make, your business will become what you designed it to be. But your designing work doesn't end with the creation of an overall strategy for your future success; you also need to design each of the individual systems that have to work together to achieve your strategic plan.

Here's one powerful tool you can use to identify which systems you need to implement or improve in your business. It's called the Performance Gap Analysis. In strategic planning, the performance gap is the difference between where your business is today, and where you want it to be in the future. Once you define what lies between you and your goals, you'll be able to come up with a strategy to bridge the gap between the two. When you analyze where your business is today in terms of its strengths and weaknesses, you'll be able to create a specific plan to leverage your strengths, and overcome your weaknesses and take your business where you want it to be.

2. Marketing Strategy Systems

Every business needs customers, but where do you find them and how do you get their attention? The purpose of your marketing strategy system is to create and communicate your unique competitive advantage that will attract the most probable and profitable customers to your business.

Do you have a written marketing plan that clearly identifies your product, pricing, distribution and promotional strategies, and how they will be implemented?

When you understand the characteristics of your target market, the trends in your industry, the strategies of your competition, and your products' unique benefits, you're able to make sure you spend your marketing dollars where they will produce the best results. Your marketing strategy takes into consideration everything you do in your business that impacts your customer, like your products' features and benefits, hours of operation, customer service policies, and credit terms.

But it goes deeper than that. Did you know that something as simple as changing the color of the clothes you wear can increase or decrease your sales? So can the image your correspondence or invoices present, and the expression on your face or the tone of your voice. You can lose a customer just as easily over a little thing as you can over a big one.

Your strategic marketing system will give you the confidence to launch a successful marketing program based on research and planning rather than on a gut feeling. It's a powerful tool you can use to take the guesswork out of all of your marketing systems.

3. Workflow and Organization Systems

More effective marketing systems will attract more customers, but more customers can lead to more chaos. That is, unless you have work flow and organization systems to keep the inner workings of your business running smoothly.

Do you have systems in place that ensure time is spent on

the most important priorities for your business, and nothing is falling through the cracks?

Workflow and organization systems specifically address the issues of time and your efficiency. Where is your time going now? And how can you create more time to do what is most important? For example, when you use a *delegation system*, you create time for yourself by assigning responsibilities in a way that ensures the task will be done properly, and on time. A *project control* system helps you save time by giving you instant information about every activity and deadline in your business. That's so you don't have to chase people down to see what is getting done. If you have inventory, an *inventory control system* ensures you have the right amount of the right products in stock. It also makes certain your cash isn't tied up in a lot of slow-moving products.

With business operating systems in place, you don't have to spend time rethinking or explaining each and every task over and over again, hoping it gets done correctly. Organization systems create procedures for everything your business does on a repetitive basis, like opening and closing your business each day, maintaining equipment, handling customer complaints, or any other area of your business where you want consistent, predictable results.

There is no such thing as "good enough" when it comes to building as successful business. Your operating systems can't remain static. Your business environment is constantly changing. What works today may not be sufficient tomorrow. So you need a way to continually improve all of your business operating systems; a system to improve your systems! Here's how:

First, you have to decide which system to improve. Next, identify the specific goals and purpose of that particular system. Third, evaluate your current situation, and do a Performance

Gap Analysis to identify your desired outcome. Next, brainstorm new ideas to bridge the gap, to improve the existing system. Then evaluate your ideas and select the one that seems most likely to succeed.

That last step is where many business owners go wrong. They may have plenty of new ideas to work with, but most business owners don't have a system to help them choose and implement the right ideas. Your strategic plan and market strategy help you identify the right ideas. Then you can use a different system to test, measure, and implement each one.

This is called your "TMI Formula". The first portion of the TMI formula is to test your new Ideas. For example, you may want to test a new digital marketing campaign by limiting the duration or audience exposure for each concept before committing to an extensive campaign. New ideas can be expensive, especially if they don't accomplish what you hoped they would.

The second portion of the TMI Formula is what really separates the designer from the specialist. The designer doesn't just try something new; the designer measures the actual results of the change to determine its success.

So a designer who creates an online ad campaign will also set up a tracking system to monitor the new business that ad brings in. To measure the new business, you need to know where all of the new business comes from. Did the customer see the new ad? Or did they walk into your business off the street? Or did a friend recommend they come in? One simple way to gather information is to ask, "How did you hear about us?" whenever a person walks into your business or calls. With a good system for measuring results, a designer can tell how many responses the ad generated, how many sales resulted, and how profitable the sales were. Then you can determine with absolute accuracy whether or not the idea was a success.

That brings us to the third step of the TMI Formula: <u>Implementation</u>. This is more than saying "Let's do it". Implementation is taking what works and turning it into a system. It's taking the results of testing and measuring your ideas, and using that information to create procedures that will produce the same positive results over and over again. For instance, if you discover that greeting a customer with a question like "Have you ever been in our store before?" leads to a higher percentage of sales than greeting them with "May I help you?" you'll want to implement that greeting into your sales process. The procedure that gets the best results is then documented in writing; every employee is trained to follow it properly, and each person is accountable for using the system you've developed for a particular situation. The final result of the TMI Formula isn't simply the creation of positive changes; it's the systematic use of the changes to achieve consistent, predictably good results in your business.

4. Personnel Management Systems

Your employees are crucial to the success of your business, whether you already have people working for you, or you're thinking of bringing someone on. Personnel management systems will help you get the most productivity and profit from your employees and create a highly empowering work environment that fully engages the best of each person. This helps you manage the entire personnel process, and it goes far beyond hiring and firing. You know you need to hire someone when an employee quits. But your personnel management systems will also help you forecast your future work force needs and develop a step-by-step process that will attract the right people for the right jobs.

Your orientation systems will prepare your new employees to

become a dedicated part of your business and share your vision of what your company is all about. With effective personnel management systems in place, even disciplinary problems can be dealt with in a way that will reduce stress and miscommunication.

How would you feel if everyone in your company loved what they did and consistently went above and beyond the basics of their jobs?

When you take the time to develop your personnel management systems, you will reap the benefits of having employees, while you minimize the headaches. The right people, with the right qualifications bring valuable experience, needed skills, and renewed enthusiasm to the business. You will be creating a positive work environment where productivity is higher, communication and cooperation is better, and potential problems like low morale are likely to be avoided. It's an effect that will be felt by everyone; you, your employees, and even your customers.

5. Promotions and Advertising Systems

Good advertising is as much a result of good planning as creative talent; whether you are selling a product or a service. Your advertising and promotion systems will help you get the most out of your advertising dollars, regardless of your budget.

Do your advertising and promotional efforts generate the response you would like?

While the marketing strategy systems help you to position your product in your market, promotions is the job of presenting your product in a way that makes the consumer want to buy it. Advertising, personal selling, public relations, and online marketing are all considered promotional activities because their ultimate objective is to make sales. Advertising is one of the best ways to promote what you are selling. But unless you know what you are doing, it can be risky for a small business owner with a limited budget. The promotional and advertising systems you implement will help you understand the ad buying and pay per click process, so you can create advertising that gets noticed by the right people. Even if you have someone else create your advertising, it's important that you understand the elements of an effective ad, to give the direction needed to ensure success. Whether creating an ad for a print publication or for online presentation, your promotional systems will help you create an effective message that will reach the right people at the right time, and generate the sales you want.

6. Business Communication Systems

As a business owner, you probably spend most of your day writing, speaking or listening to someone. Business communication systems help you master the skills you need to document your other systems, and clearly communicate your ideas to form better relationships with everyone you come in contact with. If a breakdown in communication has ever caused problems with your employees, or your customers, you know resolving these problems will cost you valuable time; sometimes money. Business communication systems will help you get your message across in any situation: one on one, in a group or when you need to resolve conflicts or negotiate agreements. Most importantly, you will hone your listening ability and use it as a tool for better understanding.

Without good communication skills, your strategic plan will never get off the ground. Your promotional strategies won't reach their full potential, and you certainly won't be able to lead and motivate your employees, or build strong relationships with your customers. Since so much is riding on how you communicate, it is important you develop the systems to help you do it well.

7. Personal Selling Systems

While your marketing and promotion systems will attract prospects to your business, you still need effective personal selling systems to turn those prospects into customers and achieve consistent sales results.

Do your sales people have a systematic way to discover what the customer needs and wants? Do your sales depend on the talent of a particular person? Or do you have a sales system that enables all your people to produce consistent results?

You can reach a certain level of growth while your sales are still dependent on you or another sales person. But unless you have the right systems in place, you'll eventually hit a ceiling, where your sales will eventually drop off. Maybe you suffer from the "Peak and Valley" system. You can go out and sell as much as you can; then your business comes to a grinding halt while you switch hats and deal with the orders you just got. You may be waiting for a superstar sales person to show up and solve your problems, but there is no guarantee they will be able to work their magic in your particular business, and if they leave, your sales expertise goes with them. When results depend on your own selling skills, or those of someone else, your bottom line will constantly change, and so will the messages sent to your customers. Personal selling systems will give you predictable control over increasing sells from your existing customers and developing the new business you want.

8. Financial Management Systems

Financial management isn't just about keeping track of historical information or keeping the IRS happy. It's about systems to plan and create the future of your business. Your financial management systems will give you a complete and accurate picture of what you did in the past, where you are now, and what adjustments you need to meet your future financial goals.

Do you have a system in place to project your income and expenses so you can accurately predict your cash flow?

Do you know how to use the information on your financial statements to help you anticipate and prevent problems in your business? How your business is doing financially at any given time should never be a mystery to you, or an assumption you make based on appearances. When you have the right financial systems in place, you will always know where you stand. But you will also have the ability to forecast future sales and expenses, so you can prepare for the future. Once you understand the key components of financial management, and the systems you need to run your business properly and predictably, you can begin to solve problems before they get out of hand, and you can take advantage of new opportunities that come your way.

9. Leadership and Motivation Systems

This final system for success you need to have in your business may be the most important of all. Your leadership and motivation systems have the power to make all of your other systems exceed your expectations. No matter how good they are, systems by themselves can't create success; people do. When well led, highly motivated people turn on the systems you design, you will be able to expand your vision for your company to create whatever success you desire.

Do you have systems in place to lead, motivate, and inspire your employees to pursue your vision for your business as passionately as you do?

Do you have a system to assess the levels of ability and motivation of each employee? And a plan to lead each one to a new level, where they can operate independently and with confidence? You probably know you can't motivate anyone yourself. You can't control or reward your employees into consistently effective behavior. To go above and beyond the basic requirements of their job, employees need to be internally motivated. What you can do is put the right systems in place to create an environment that fosters self-motivation. The ultimate level of effectiveness you can reach with your leadership and motivational systems is to have systems in place that not only develop followers, but develop other leaders in your business. When your business grows with followers, you will be limited to growth by addition. You merely begin to develop and add new employees. But when you develop by leaders, you're able to grow by multiplication. You have other leaders in your company who can add and develop new employees, expanding in leadership effectiveness. Your leadership and motivation systems are the secret to creating a self-running and self-perpetuating business that provides a platform for you to change the world!

Imagine what it would be like for your business to take on a life of its own, apart from you, but according to your design. These nine systems are the crucial components of your ideal business. If each one is in place and working together, they become your systems for success.

This all starts with the mindset and practice of approaching your business from a designer's perspective, rather than the perspective of a specialist. The designer perspective helps you recognize and bridge the gap between where your business is today, and where you want it to be. From this basis you will then design and implement the specific systems that work together to get your business to the point where it is achieving consistent and predictable results, giving you the time and money margin you want to do even more to build beyond business and build a better world. You will have a business that works hard for you, rather than you working so hard for your business.

The goal of this appendix has been to stimulate your thinking and give you some proven concepts that will help you get even better results from your business. But just knowing what to do isn't enough, you also need to know how to go about it.

For more information on how to implement these systems, go to www.Systemsforsuccess.com and click on Courses. You'll find practical tools and processes that will help you become an effective designer of your business, and help you implement the specific operating systems you need to gain control over the chaos and stress of running a business—and start having fun again. I'd like to give you access to a proven system that takes you through the design process step-by-step, and helps you create and implement the unique systems your business needs to become a self-running, self-perpetuating organization that fulfills your goals and dreams. If you want to solve problems that stay solved, if you want to create that special kind of business where customers love doing business with you; if you want a place where you and your staff can't wait to come to work each day; if you want a business that gives you the time and money you need to build a better world, don't just read this. Take action now to develop the systems you need to take your business beyond where it is now.

Endnotes

[1] Mead, Margaret and Heyman, Ken, Family (New York: MacMillan, 1965) pp. 77-78.

[2] Ferguson, Niall, The Ascent of Money, (New York: Penguin, 2009) P. 342.

[3] 1 Timothy 6:10

[4] Acts 20:33

[5] Acts 20:34

[6] Acts 20:35

[7] Pinker, Steven, The Better Angels of Our Nature (New York: viking, 2011) pp. 286-287.

[8] Matthew 28:19-20

[9] Luke 10:27

[10] 1 Peter 2:9

[11] Ortberg, John. Who Is this Man?(Zondervan, 2012,) p. 95.

[12] Ibid., p. 70.

[13] Luke 10:38-42

[14] Ortberg, John. op. cit., p. 30.

[15] Matthew 19:13-14

[16] Romans 8:15-16

[17] Luke 12:32

[18] John 14:1-2

[19] Acts 11:26

[20] Acts 26:28

[21] 1 Peter 4:16

[22] Tacitus, Annals 15, 44

[23] Acts 9:2

[24] John 14:6

[25] 1 Samuel 24:6

[26] Isaiah 43:19

[27] Matthew 5:23

[28] Galatians 5:1

[29] Galatians 5:6

[30] John 13:34

[31] Matthew 5:27-28

[32] Matthew 5:21-22.

[33] Galatians 5:13-14

[34] Phil. 2:13

[35] Psalm 37:4

[36] John 2:3

[37] John 2:6-7

[38] John 2:6

[39] John 2:10

[40] John 21:1-15

[41] Matthew 4:19

[42] James 1:27

[43] Revelation 18:4

[44] Colossians 3:23

[45] Ephesians 4:13 ESV

[46] Matthew 28:19

[47] Matthew 13:55

[48] Mark 6:3

[49] Luke 20:17–18

[50] Matthew 16:18

[51] Acts 4:11

[52] Genesis 12:4

[53] Genesis 12:1

[54] Genesis 12:7

[55] Genesis 12:16

[56] Genesis 14:14

[57] Genesis 14:18

[58] Genesis 26: 3 -5

[59] Genesis 26: 12

[60] Genesis 27:43-44

[61] Genesis 30:43

[62] Genesis 32: 14-15

[63] Revelation 1:6

[64] Luke 4:18

[65] Matthew 16

[66] Pew Research Center. (November 3, 2015). U.S. Public Becoming Less Religious. Available at http://www.pewforum.org/2015/11/03/u-s-public-becoming-less-religious/.

[67] Acts 19:39

[68] Luke 19:46

[69] Isaiah 56:7

[70] John 4:23-24

[71] Acts 13: 44, 47, 49

[72] Acts 19:8-10

[73] 1 John 2:15

[74] John 17: 13-26

[75] 1 Corinthians 14:26

[76] Matthew 9:35

[77] Luke 4:43

[78] John 14:9

[79] Benjamin Wiker and Jonathan Witt. (2006). A Meaningful World. Intervarsity Press. Downers Grove, Illinois. Pp. 159-160.

[80] Matthew 20:25-28

[81] Deborah Rhode, PROFITS AND PROFESSIONALISM, 33 FORDHAM URB. L.J. 49 (2005). Available at: https://ir.lawnet.fordham.edu/ulj/vol33/iss1/11.

[82] Greg Smith. (March 14, 2012.) "Why I Am Leaving Goldman Sachs." The New York Times. Available at https://www.nytimes.com/2012/03/14/opinion/why-i-am-leaving-goldman-sachs html.

[83] Ibid.

[84] Matthew 22:34-40

[85] 1 John 5:3

[86] John 10:10

[87] James 2:8

[88] Galatians 5:22-23

[89] Witvliet, Charlotte van Oyen, Thomas E. Ludwig, and Kelly L. Vander Laan. "Granting Forgiveness or Harboring Grudges: Implications for Emotion, Physiology, and

Health." Psychological Science 12, no. 2 (March 1, 2001): 117–23. doi:10.1111/ 1467-9280.00320. American Psychological Association. Available online at https:// digitalcommons.hope.edu/cgi/viewcontent.cgi?referer=https://scholar.google. com/&httpsredir=1&article=2300&context=faculty_publications.

[90] Steptoe, Andrew, Shankar, Aparna, Demakakos, Panayotes, & Wardle, Jane. (2009). Social isolation, loneliness, and all-cause mortality in older men and women. Proceedings of the National Academy of the Sciences of the United States of America, 110(15): 5797-5801. Doi: 10.1073/pnas.1219686110. Available online at http://www.pnas.org/content/110/15/5797.full.

[91] Matthew 6:33

[92] James 1:25

[93] Mark 1:15

[94] Matthew 21:43

[95] Matthew 7:21

[96] Matthew 6:10 KJV

[97] Matthew 13:24

[98] Matthew 13:31

[99] Matthew 13:44

[100] Matthew 13:45-46

[101] Matthew 13:47-48

[102] Matthew 13:52

[103] Matthew 20: 1

[104] Matthew 18:23

[105] Matthew 22:2

[106] Matthew 13: 33

[107] Luke 19:11-26

[108] Revelation 21:24-27

[109] Luke 19:10 NASB

[110] Luke 1:32-33

[111] Revelation 11:15

[112] Revelation 15:3

[113] Hebrews 11:1

[114] James 2:26

[115] Vale, M. G. A., Laners, Y. Saint Joan of Arc. Encylcopedia Brittanica. Available online at https://www.britannica.com/biography/Saint-Joan-of-Arc. Accessed June 16, 2017.

[116] Richey, Stephen W. (2000) Joan of Arc: A Military Appreciation. St. Joan Center. Available online at http://www.stjoan-center.com/military/stephenr.html. Accessed June 19, 2017. Richey's sources include Regine Pernoud's The Retrial of Joan of Arc (Ignatius Press, 2007) and Joan of Arc By Herself and Her Witnesses (New York: Scarborough Press, 1990).

[117] Hebrews 11:6

[118] James 1:2-4

[119] Hebrews 10:38-39 NASB